Labour Law in Belgium

Labour Law in Belgium

Frank Hendrickx

This book was originally published as a monograph in the International Encyclopaedia of Laws/Labour Law and Industrial Relations.

Founding Editor: Roger Blanpain
General Editor: Frank Hendrickx
Volume Editor: Frank Hendrickx

Wolters Kluwer

Published by:
Kluwer Law International B.V.
PO Box 316
2400 AH Alphen aan den Rijn
The Netherlands
E-mail: lrs-sales@wolterskluwer.com
Website: www.wolterskluwer.com/en/solutions/kluwerlawinternational

Sold and distributed by:
Wolters Kluwer Legal & Regulatory U.S.
7201 McKinney Circle
Frederick, MD 21704
United States of America
Email: customer.service@wolterskluwer.com

ISBN 978-94-035-4851-7

e-Book: ISBN 978-94-035-4612-4
web-PDF: ISBN 978-94-035-4373-4

The Author

Prof. Dr Frank Hendrickx obtained his law degree (1992) as well as a baccalaureate in philosophy at KU Leuven (Belgium). In 1997, he obtained an LLM from the London School of Economics (United Kingdom). He obtained his doctorate degree at KU Leuven in 1999. Between 1994 and 2000, he worked as an attorney at the Antwerp and Brussels Bar. He is Full Professor of Labour Law at the Law Faculty of KU Leuven (Belgium). He has been a visiting scholar at the Wharton School of the University of Pennsylvania (2008) and has held a part-time chair in European labour law at Tilburg University (the Netherlands) between 2001 and 2018.

Frank Hendrickx specialises in Belgian, European and comparative labour law, employment privacy law and sports law. He is the General Editor of the *International Encyclopaedia of Laws*, Editor of the *International Encyclopaedia of Labour Law and Industrial Relations*, Editor of the *Bulletin of Comparative Labour Relations* and Editor-in-Chief of the *European Labour Law Journal*. Frank Hendrickx is also involved in key Belgian labour law journals, founding editor and editor-in-chief of the '*Arbeidsrecht Journaal*' and member of the editorial board of the '*Tijdschrift voor Sociaal recht/Revue de droit social*'. He is past President of the Belgian Association for Labour and Social Security Law (2016–2018) and Board Member of the Belgian Association for Labour Relations. He has published numerous articles and books and regularly advises national and international governmental institutions as well as private organisations in the areas of labour law and sports law.

The Author

Table of Contents

List of Abbreviations

ADA	Anti-Discrimination Act
CA	Collective Agreement
CPPW	Committee for Prevention and Protection at Work
ECHR	European Convention on Human Rights
ESC	European Social Charter
EU	European Union
GDA	Gender Discrimination Act
GDP	Gross Domestic Product
GDPR	European General Data Protection Regulation
ILO	International Labour Organisation
NLC	National Labour Council
RD	Royal Decree
RDA	Racism Discrimination Act
TBU	Technical Business Unit
TFEU	Treaty on the Functioning of the European Union

List of Abbreviations

Preface

This monograph is part of the *International Encylopaedia of Labour Law and Industrial Relations*. Within the *International Encyclopaedia of Laws* (IEL), the volumes on labour law have been central since the start of the 1970s. The concept of the IEL monographs is to deliver a qualitative insight, with sufficient depth, into the different legal systems around the world in various important branches of the law. At the moment, the IEL covers twenty-five subjects of the legal discipline, each containing a wide series of distinct country monographs.

This monograph deals with labour law in Belgium. Until 2016, the Belgian labour law monograph was drafted by Professor Roger Blanpain (1932–2016), a widely recognised pioneer in the field and founder of the IEL. With respect to the purposes and standards of the IEL and taking into account the evolving demands of our readers, the monograph has now been given a complete reset and makeover. From this new take, the labour law monograph keeps the approach of the IEL. This means that it follows the structure and outline shared by the labour law monographs within the IEL series, allowing for comparative insights and accessible use. Within this context, this monograph aims to combine inside perspectives of labour law with the needs of readers from outside the legal system. At the same time, it offers itself to be relevant within the Belgian system to the extent that a growing usefulness arises with the coverage of national legal subjects in the English language. In this manner, this monograph aims to be available and valuable for academics, practitioners and policymakers, or for all those interested in labour law in Belgium.

The text is up-to-date, until and including the year 2021.

Leuven, 21 January 2022

General Introduction

§1. General Background

I. Geography, Location, Size

1. Belgium started as a country in 1830. At that time, the different regions of Belgium already had a very long history. The territory and culture in the country received different influences from the past, from both Latin and Germanic origins. Belgium has three official languages: Dutch, French and German.

2. Belgium has a territory of about 30,500 square kilometres. The immediate neighbouring countries are France, Germany, the Netherlands and Luxembourg. The west side of the country has the North Sea as its border.

3. Brussels is the capital city of Belgium. The country has over 11.5 million inhabitants. The official currency is the Euro. Brussels is also the capital of the European Union. Belgium is one of the six founding Member States of the European Union.

II. The Political System

4. In order to recognise the existence of different communities, Belgium has been organised as a federal state. While Belgium started as a unitary state, the federal structure gradually took form in the twentieth century, with a process of institutional reforms that started to take place since the 1970s. The reforms were further elaborated and modified over the years and, even today, have not yet come to a full closure.

5. Within the federal structure, there is thus not only the federal (Belgian) government. There is also the governmental level of the communities (more culturally and language driven) and the regions (more economically driven). As a result, Belgium is divided into three regions: the Brussels-Capital Region, the Flemish Region and the Walloon Region (Wallonia). Belgium also has three communities: the Flemish Community, the French Community and the German-speaking Community. The Brussels Capital has two languages, French and Dutch.

III. The Legal System

6. The Belgian legal system is a civil law system. It has a constitutionally and parliamentary based system with a monarchy. All powers, with a separation of powers, are based on the Constitution, the highest legal norm in the Belgian legal order. The original Belgian Constitution dates from 7 February 1831. The Constitution was revised on 17 February 1994.

Since the beginning, Belgium has always had a bicameral parliamentary system, with two assemblies: the House of Representatives and the Senate. These two assemblies now still exist and form together the Federal Parliament. For each of the regions and communities, there are, however, also separate parliaments. The federal parliament enacts through 'laws' or Acts,[1] while the regional parliaments enact via decrees[2] or ordinances[3] (this latter is the case for the Brussels-Capital Region). The official publication of all legislation is the *Belgian Official Gazette*.[4]

7. In the federal structure of Belgium, the powers of the government are divided over the federal government and the regional governments of the regions and communities. The division of competences in the federal structure is based on the Constitution and on special Acts regulating the state reform. The federal government acts through Royal Decrees (since the King signs on behalf of the government) or Ministerial Decrees. The regional governments act through Government Decision or Ministerial Decision.

8. The judiciary is independent. It is structured according to constitutional principles and specific legislative provisions, such as the Judicial Code, the Criminal Procedural Code, or specific legislation regarding, for example, the Council of State (administrative court) or the Constitutional Court. The Constitutional Court was founded in 1984 in order to decide over questions about constitutionality of legislative acts. This constitutional review can be related to the principle of equality before the law, to the fundamental rights under the Constitution, or to the division of responsibility of legislative powers in the federal structure. The Council of State is the highest court that deals with questions in administrative matters, including decisions made by government or organs of the government(s). The Cour de Cassation is the Supreme Court in the Belgian judicial system. As a highest court, it can nullify court decisions by 'lower' instances, such as appeal courts. It does not rule on the facts of a case, but on the law and the lawfulness of judicial decisions.

9. Various sources of Belgian law can be accessed online through the website of the government, which links to the *Belgian Official Gazette* and case law.[5]

---

1. 'Loi' / 'Wet'.
2. 'Décret' / 'Decreet'.
3. 'Ordonnance' / 'Ordonnantie'.
4. 'Moniteur Belge' / 'Belgisch Staatsblad'.
5. Cf.: www.belgiumlex.be.

10. As a member of the European Union (EU) and the Council of Europe, the Belgian legal order is strongly influenced by European law. Due to the primacy of European Union law, EU law has precedence over national law.

IV. Vital Statistics and Data

11. Belgium[6] is a country with a developed economy and a highly skilled workforce. It has an advanced education system, a stable financial infrastructure and important transport systems, including a network of roads, railways and waterways, international airports (Brussels, Liege, Charleroi, Ostend, Antwerp) and seaports (Antwerp, Seabruges, Ghent, Ostend).

12. Belgium is called an 'open economy'. As a small but centrally located country, it strongly rests on export processing, with its neighbouring countries as key trade partners (Germany, France and the Netherlands count for over 60% of foreign trade).

13. The gross domestic product (GDP) is about EUR 450 billion (in 2020), accounting for 3.4% of the GDP of the European Union.

14. Services constitute the main driver in the Belgian economy. However, there is still a strong traditional industry in the country, including chemicals, vehicles and transport, machinery and electric equipment. Typical other strong sectors are food and beverages, pharmaceutics, information technology and textile. In general, market services (including wholesale and retail, financial activities and insurance) take a share of about 56% in the total gross value added in the country, compared to 13.8% for industry and 5.3% for construction. Other important sectors are energy, healthcare and agriculture.

15. The supply of labour consists of the 'active population',[7] which includes both the active workers and the workers looking for a job, in other words the unemployed. The employment rate[8] corresponds to the share of the population that is working within the part of the proportion of the population that is of working age. The total employment rate is the share of people working, full- or part-time, within the total population aged 15–64. It is therefore different from the activity rate,[9] which represents the ratio of the working-age population (the total number of people employed and unemployed) to the total population.

6. Information based on: FPS Economy, Belgium's economy in a nutshell Economic outlook July 2021, https://economie.fgov.be/en/publication/belgiums-economy-nutshell-4.
7. 'La population active' / 'Beroepsbevolking'.
8. 'Le taux d'emploi' / 'Werkzaamheidsgraad' or also 'Werkgelegenheidsgraad'.
9. 'Le taux d'activité' / 'Activiteitsgraad'.

16. The Belgian employment rate is about 70%.[10] An overview of the evolution according to the statistics published by the government shows the following data:[11]

		20–64 Years				
		2016	*2017*	*2018*	*2019*	*2020*
Flemish Region	M	76.3	77.7	78.5	79.3	78.5
	V	67.7	68.2	70.7	71.5	70.9
	T	72.0	73.0	74.6	75.5	74.7
Walloon Region	M	67.3	67.7	68.2	68.2	68.5
	V	57.9	58.7	59.3	61.1	60.7
	T	62.6	63.2	63.7	64.6	64.6
of which German Community	M	76.8	78.1	79.8	79.2	80.7
	V	63.8	67.9	69.6	71.6	73.2
	T	70.4	73.1	74.8	75.5	77.0
Brussels Capital Region	M	65.3	67.0	66.3	67.4	67.3
	V	54.3	54.6	56.6	56.0	55.3
	T	59,8	60.8	61.4	61.7	61.3
Belgium	M	72.3	73.4	73.9	74.5	74.1
	V	63.0	63.6	65.5	66.5	65.9
	T	67.7	68.5	69.7	70.5	70.0

10. Ending 2020 with 69.9% according to https://ec.europa.eu/eures/public/living-and-working/labour-market-information/labour-market-information-belgium_en; 71.4% in the third quarter of 201 according to https://statbel.fgov.be/en/themes/work-training/labour-market/employment-and-unemployment#figures.
11. INB01, https://werk.belgie.be/nl/statistieken.

17. The evolution of the activity rate in Belgium, covering the active population (including working and jobseeking persons) in relation to the total number of the population, is displayed as follows in the statistics of the government:[12]

			2016	*2017*	*2018*	*2019*	*2020*
Activity rate BELGIUM	20–29 years	M	70.2	70.0	69.3	70.7	67.2
		F	63.2	62.2	61.9	63.6	61.9
		T	66.7	66.1	65.7	67.2	64.6
	30–54 years	M	90.9	90.5	90.3	89.5	89.5
		F	79.7	79.6	80.7	80.6	80.4
		T	85.4	85.1	85.5	85.1	85.0
	55–64 years	M	53.6	56.9	57.9	59.8	61.5
		F	42.8	45.8	47.4	48.9	49.8
		T	48.1	51.3	52.6	54.3	55.6
	65–69 years	M	6.8	7.4	7.4	7.7	7.7
		F	2.9	3.0	3.4	4.1	4.2
		T	4.8	5.1	5.3	5.8	5.9

These indicators were compiled by the Directorate for Studies and Statistics of the Federal Public Service Employment, Labour and Social Dialogue with the assistance of Statbel and the competent departments of the Federal State, the regions and the communities.

18. The unemployment rate fluctuated around 6.5% in 2021.[13] The evolution according to the statistics of the government shows the following data:[14]

12. INA10, https://werk.belgie.be/nl/statistieken.

13. https://statbel.fgov.be/en/themes/work-training/labour-market/employment-and-unemployment#figures.

14. INC01, https://werk.belgie.be/nl/statistieken.

		20–64 Years				
		2016	*2017*	*2018*	*2019*	*2020*
Flemish Region	M	4.8	3.8	3.3	3.1	3.3
	V	4.5	4.7	3.2	2.9	3.4
	T	4.7	4.2	3.2	3.0	3.3
Walloon Region	M	10.6	10.3	8.9	8.1	8.0
	V	10.2	8.9	7.8	5.9	6.3
	T	10.4	9.6	8.4	7.1	7.2
Brussels Capital Region	M	17.5	15.0	14.3	12.6	11.8
	V	15.9	14.8	11.6	12.5	12.7
	T	16.8	14.9	13.1	12.5	12.2
Belgium	M	7.9	7.0	6.2	5.6	5.6
	V	7.4	7.0	5.4	4.8	5.2
	T	7.7	7.0	5.8	5.2	5.4

19. Some data on the Belgian labour market give the following table:[15]

Numbers[16]		**Status**			
Main sector	*Age*	*Employed*	*Self-employed*	*Helping*	*Grand Total*
Primary sector	15–24	2,403	2,363	665	5,431
	25–49	10,274	27,095	3,961	41,330
	50–64	4,551	21,425	6,012	31,988
Primary sector total		**17,228**	**50,884**	**10,638**	**78,750**
Secondary sector	15–24	47,609	4,472	892	52,973
	25–49	436,798	69,882	6,294	512,975

15. https://www.steunpuntwerk.be/cijfers.
16. Table 'Werkenden' https://www.steunpuntwerk.be/cijfers?page=1.

Numbers[16]		Status			
Main sector	*Age*	*Employed*	*Self-employed*	*Helping*	*Grand Total*
	50–64	219,003	39,216	3,036	261,255
Secondary sector total		**703,410**	**113,571**	**10,222**	**827,203**
Tertiary sector	15–24	188,335	14,116	894	203,345
	25–49	1,105,665	266,113	12,160	1,383,938
	50–64	439,485	178,288	11,509	629,282
Tertiary sector total		**1,733,486**	**458,517**	**24,562**	**2,216,565**
Quaternary sector	15–24	79,362	2,757	63	82,182
	25–49	962,748	36,495	802	1,000,044
	50–64	514,635	29,517	961	545,113
Quaternary sector total		**1,556,745**	**68,768**	**1,826**	**1,627,339**
Unknown	15–24		3,099	158	3,258
	25–49		15,988	735	16,723
	50–64		3,992	267	4,259
Unknown total			**23,079**	**1,161**	**24,240**
Grand total		**4,010,868**	**714,818**	**48,410**	**4,774,096**

20. 'Helping' workers (mentioned in the table) are workers that help self-employed persons. As a rule, 'helping' workers are also registered as self-employed persons. According to the data of the Belgian government, there were 1,182,747 registered self-employed persons and entrepreneurs (as defined by the social security administration for the self-employed).[17]

21. Most workers work on a full-time basis in Belgium. Part-time work is, however, taking up an increasingly significant part of the labour market. To illustrate this, the following data on part-time work can be given:[18]

17. https://economie.fgov.be/nl/themas/ondernemingen/kmos-en-zelfstandigen-cijfers/zelfstandigen-belgie.
18. https://www.steunpuntwerk.be/cijfers.

Part-time work						
Region	*2015*	*2016*	*2017*	*2018*	*2019*	*2020*
Flemish Region	25,03	25,404	25,326	25,734	26,068	25,651
Walloon Region	24,076	24,43	24,325	23,392	23,493	23,026
Brussels-Capital Region	20,239	20,816	20,214	20,474	21,224	20,41
Belgium	24,295	24,674	24,536	24,547	24,857	24,377

22. Belgium has a legally established weekly working time limit of thirty-eight hours. This is not only an average, it is also deviated from in collective agreements. More information on the legal regime of working time in Belgium will be given below in this monograph. The following data on working time can be shared hereinafter:[19]

Average weekly working time					
Region	*2015*	*2016*	*2017*	*2018*	*2019*
Flemish Region	37,23	37,2	37,83	37,4	37,44
Walloon Region	36,24	36,2	36,35	36,44	36,35
Brussels-Capital Region	37,28	37,02	37,15	37,07	36,74
Belgium	36,94	36,88	37,33	37,09	37,05

23. Belgium has a highly developed social security system, largely based on contributions from employers and workers, although significant parts are also financed through the broader available public budget of the country. As an example, on a yearly basis, the Belgian social security system spends about EUR 47.5 billion in order to pay the pension benefits to 2.37 million retired persons.[20]

§2. Definitions and Notions

I. Distinction Between Labour Law (and Industrial Relations) and Other Branches of Law, Especially Social Security Law

24. In a number of countries, labour law is embedded in a broader legal area that is called ‘social law’. It is then said that social law consists of two major parts, namely labour law on the one hand and social security law on the other hand. This is a conceptualisation which is also broadly used in Belgium.

The term ‘social’ in the notion of ‘social law’ can partly be explained historically. By this, we mean to describe the law that, historically speaking, came into being as a result of the ‘social question’ in the nineteenth century, with poverty, exploitation

19. https://www.steunpuntwerk.be/cijfers.
20. https://www.sfpd.fgov.be/nl/over-ons/jaarverslag-2018/fpd-in-cijfers#WNenZelfstandigen.

and social injustice to the working population. Today, the term 'social' in the notion of social law could be explained by the connection of labour law and social security law with sociopolitical choices, or social policy, of which they are usually a result, or by referring to social relations (relations between employers and workers or relations between the government or institutions and socially weaker parties or other parties worth of protection) which they are the object of in their regulations.

25. There is, however, a separate approach to labour law and social security law. This has logical reasons. They are distinct and fully fledged areas of law, with their own structures, principles, context and dynamics. They share historical roots and have overlaps in their arrangements and protections. Their scope of application also strongly overlaps. A person who performs work as an employee will, in principle, be involved in both labour law and social security law, if only because of the way in which social security is financed and set up or how benefits are distributed (often based on wage-income and related to the kind of employment status). At the same time, the mechanisms and substantial rules of labour law and social security law differ significantly and cover basically different branches of the law.

26. The concept of labour law is traditionally defined as the law that applies to work performances delivered in subordination. With the subordinate employment relationship as the key element, this allows labour law to be distinguished or receive autonomy from other fields of law (such as general contract law). However, given the fundamental objectives and foundations of labour law, an alternative conceptualisation is possible. In this broader perspective, labour law can be defined as the body of legal rules that govern the performance of work on the labour market and that aim to promote human dignity and social justice.

27. Labour law in Belgium includes both individual employment law and collective labour law. Individual employment law interacts with the rules and premises of civil law. To a certain extent, this also counts for collective labour law, certainly when collective bargaining is concerned. The civil law angle of labour law is rather indispensable. Throughout the centuries, labour law has developed into more 'modern labour law' that is ultimately built and conceived through a contractual relationship. However, labour law is also an answer to inequality, within the employment relationship or on the labour market. One can derive a function of labour law from this, namely to form a counterbalance to the superior position of the employer. In that sense, Belgian labour law can be understood not only as protective law but also as organising law. It not only protects the position of the employee but also regulates and channels the relations between the parties involved. Labour law 're-orders' employment relationships that would otherwise originate with only the parties themselves. The ordering or organising dimension of Belgian labour law may also come through in collective labour law and industrial relations, where the legislator strongly interfered with institutional and procedural rules governing social dialogue, collective bargaining and different forms of workers' representation and workplace involvement.

II. Scope of Labour Law and Employee Concept

A. *Employment Contract*

28. The employment contract is defined as the agreement whereby an employee undertakes, in return for remuneration, to perform work under the authority of an employer.[21] These elements are essential in order to be able to speak of an employment contract.

It is assumed that only natural persons can be employees. On the employer's side, it can be either a natural or a legal person.

29. The employment contract is a contract which, in principle, is subject to the rules of civil law. This is important, among other things, with respect to the binding force of the contract (Article 1134 Old Civil Code) and the conditions of validity of the employment contract (Article 1108 Old Civil Code).

30. This also means that, in principle, statutory employment (employment of civil servants) is not possible under an employment contract. As a general rule, an employment contract only concerns the relationship between an employee and an employer in the private sector. Workers employed by public-law institutions (the state, the communities, the regions, the provinces, the municipalities, the public institutions falling under them, the institutions of public utility, the community education system) are generally not bound by an employment contract, but are employed under a civil servant status. It implies that their situation is regulated by specific statutes. However, this does not mean that public sector workers cannot be employees. Some workers may be employed on the basis of an employment contract. Increasingly use is made of the employment contract as a legal basis of employing workers in the public sector.

31. In principle, any work can be considered to be performed within the framework of an employment contract. Agreeing on remuneration (wages) is constitutive for the existence of an employment contract. It is irrelevant what or how the remuneration is called.

B. *Volunteer Work*

32. If one provides work for free, he/she will generally be considered to be a volunteer. Since the Act of 3 July 2005 on the rights of volunteers,[22] Belgium has a legal framework for volunteer work. Article 10 of this Act states that the essentially unpaid nature of volunteer work does not prevent certain expenses from being reimbursed, subject to certain limits.

---

21. Cf. Arts 2 and 3 of the Employment Contracts Act of 3 July 1978.
22. *Belgian Official Gazette (Moniteur Belge / Belgisch Staatsblad),* 29 Aug. 2005. In the meantime repeatedly amended.

33. Being a volunteer does not mean that one is completely exempt from labour law. Some labour law provisions (e.g., the Labour Code of 16 March 1971, the Well-being Code of 4 August 1996, etc.) may also apply to work carried out under someone's authority but without an employment contract.

34. Moreover, the question of whether or not one is a volunteer can be subject to debate. For example, the Court of Cassation had to rule on whether or not work performed by 'volunteers' whose cooperation was not aimed at earning an income through work, but who essentially performed an activity in their free time, for limited remuneration, should be considered as work within the meaning of the Employment Contracts Act of 3 July 1978. The Court of Cassation stated that work performed by an employee who has agreed to do so, in return for remuneration and under the authority of an employer, must be considered as work within the meaning of the Employment Contracts Act, regardless of whether the agreed remuneration is limited or not and regardless of whether this work is performed as a leisure activity without the intention of obtaining an income.[23]

C. *Untaxed Additional Income*

35. The federal government introduced some legislation with the aim of exonerating some forms of work from labour and social laws. It did so with legislation on the 'untaxed additional income' in 2018.[24] It meant that one could perform work for remuneration without having to pay taxes on it, or even apply labour law or social security law. The idea was that anyone who already has a main status (employee, self-employed, pensioner) could additionally earn EUR 6,000 on an annual basis by way of 'occasional work' or 'work in one's free time', untaxed. The legislator thus assumed that this form of work did not fall under social legislation.[25] While it had to involve certain activities (association work, occasional services between citizens, or services in the sharing economy) and a maximum annual amount applied, the legislation was very controversial.[26] This legislation was nullified in 2020 by the Constitutional Court for being unconstitutional.[27]

---

23. Cass. 10 Mar. 2014, AR S.12.0103.N.
24. Act of 18 Jul. 2018 on economic regeneration and the strengthening of social cohesion, *Belgian Official Gazette* 26 Jul. 2018.
25. Bill of 11 Dec. 2017 on economic relaunch and strengthening social cohesion, *Parl.* Chamber, 2017–2018, no. 54-2839/001, p. 149 (association work) and p. 158 (occasional services between citizens).
26. The income may not exceed EUR 500 per month (to be indexed). For income in the sharing economy, only the annual ceiling of EUR 6,000 (will be indexed) applies. In sports clubs, a maximum of EUR 1,000 per month applies with the annual ceiling of EUR 6,000 (to be indexed).
27. Constitutional Court 23 Apr. 2020, no. 53/2020.

D. Authority

36. In order to speak of an employment contract, authority (or subordination) must be present in the employment or work relationship. It relates to the exercise of authority by the employer. One also speaks of the 'subordinate relationship' in which the employee works.

37. The authority of the employer does not necessarily mean that the employer must exercise that authority in person. Authority can also be exercised by an agent or an employee of the employer. However, authority remains a necessary component of the employment relationship. Without authority, there is no employment contract. This element distinguishes a contract of employment from other contracts in which it is agreed to perform work in return for payment (e.g., a contract for services). Whether a shop assistant, a sales representative, a doctor, a legal adviser, etc., are linked by an employment contract or rather by a contract for services will be determined by the existence or absence of authority.

38. It also implies that this leads to a *summa divisio*: employment contract versus contract for services. If an agreement is entered into for the performance of work in which no relationship of authority is present, then in a legal sense, this is called contracting for services, under the Old Civil Code. This situation is regulated by Articles 1787 ff. of the Old Civil Code. In practice, other terms such as 'contract labour' or 'self-employed work' are also used.

39. The existence or non-existence of an employer-employee relationship may lead to discussion. It is a *question of fact* to be decided by the courts, on the basis of an assessment.[28]

40. We will explain more about the scope of labour law and the relevance of the employee concept further below in this monograph.

§3. Historical Background

I. Early Origins

41. Labour law, as we know and understand it in Belgium, has its origins in the late eighteenth and early nineteenth centuries. The French Revolution (1789) can be seen as a point of reference (at a time when the country Belgium did not yet exist). Based on the ideal of individual freedom and equality, the freedom of industry and labour was propagated. This led in 1791 to the prohibition of guilds by the

28. Cass. 7 Sep. 1992, *Arr.Cass.* 1991–1992, 1077; Labour Court Ghent 9 Oct. 1996, *TGR* 1997, 47; Labour Court Antwerp 15 Oct. 1993, *Soc.Kron.* 1996, 285; Labour Court Gent 15 Nov. 1996, *TGR 1997*, 94; Labour Tribunal Gent 22 Nov. 1991, *De Verz.* 1992, 242; *see also* Cass. 6 Feb. 1995, Soc.*Kron.* 1995, 218.

'Decree d'Allarde'[29] and to a prohibition of free trade unions by the 'Act Le Chapelier'.[30] The employment relationship itself was mainly based on civil law principles.

42. In 1804, the French *Code Civil* was also in force in the Belgian region. As is known, the French Civil Code remained in force in Belgium after the declaration of independence in 1830. It still exists in the current legal system as the Old Civil Code. In the original 'Code civil', the employment relationship was seen as 'rent of work'. Relying on the fundamental equality of the parties and on their autonomy of will, the drafters of the Civil Code devoted only a few articles to the employment relationship. Articles 1780 and 1781 of the Civil Code were the only two articles under the section '*Du louage des domestiques et ouvriers*'. They contained the substantive rules that specifically dealt with the employment relationship.

II. First Labour Legislation

43. The idea of free and equal contracting parties did not correspond to the nineteenth-century reality. The emergence of the first labour legislation at the end of the nineteenth century is in fact a direct consequence of social abuses. The year 1886 is a pivotal one. As one of the most industrialised countries in Europe, Belgium, like its neighbouring countries, had been hit for a long time by a deep and comprehensive economic crisis. This was followed by a period of social unrest and strikes, which came to a head particularly in 1886. In response, a whole series of laws were enacted. In 1887 the first Wage Protection Act came into being.[31] In 1889 this was followed by a law on child and female labour.[32] In 1896 followed the first Work Regulations Act[33] and in 1899 a legal framework for health and safety at work was introduced.[34]

44. However, it was not until the twentieth century that more comprehensive regulations of the employment contract emerged. The beginning of the twentieth century marked a growing intervention of the legislature in various areas of labour law. In 1903 an Occupational Accidents Act saw the light.[35] In 1905 a law on Sunday rest was born.[36] At the international scene, in 1919, the International Labour Organisation (ILO) came into being. In the Treaty of Versailles (1919), which sealed the peace after the First World War, the ILO was established as part of the larger

29. Loi 2–17 mars 1791 portant suppression de tous les droits d'aides, suppression de toutes les maîtrises et jurandes et établissement de patentes.
30. Décret 14–17 juin 1791 relatif aux assemblées de citoyens d'un même état ou profession.
31. Act of 16 Aug. 1887 regulating the payment of wages to workmen, *Belgian Official Gazette* 21 Oct. 1887.
32. Act of 13 Dec. 1889 on child and women labour, *Belgian Official Gazette* 22 Dec. 1889.
33. Act of 15 Jun. 1896 concerning workshop regulations, *Belgian Official Gazette* 25 Jun. 1896.
34. Act of 2 Jul. 1899 on the health and safety of workers employed in industrial and commercial enterprises, *Belgian Official Gazette* 12 Jul. 1899.
35. Act of 24 Dec. 1903 concerning compensation for damage resulting from accidents, *Belgian Official Gazette* 28–29 Dec. 1903.
36. Act of 17 Jul. 1905 concerning Sunday rest in industrial and commercial enterprises, *Belgian Official Gazette* 26 Jul. 1905.

peace project. Soon after this, in 1921, Belgian legislation formally introduced the eight-hour working day and the forty-eight-hour working week.[37]

45. The Act of 10 March 1900[38] is the first real law on employment contracts. With this Act, the legislator continued to attach importance to the freedom of the individual, which was expressed in the priority of the will of the parties over the protection provided by the law. Moreover, the Act only applied to blue-collar workers. White-collar employees were considered as collaborators of the head of the company, and it was not considered opportune to regulate their situation. However, this view was soon changed. A regulation of the employment contract for white-collar workers was introduced with the Act of 7 August 1922 on the employment contract for white-collar workers.[39] The main purpose of this Act was to fill in the gaps left by civil law. However, it was by no means the intention of the legislator to create a coherent and exhaustive regulation. That only came later. The distinction between blue-collar and white-collar workers later also led to some major problems in the legal system, as will be discussed below.

46. With the Act of 24 May 1921 on the freedom of association and the lifting of the ban on coalitions,[40] the trade union movement received a major boost. The freedom of the trade unions eventually led to a major (and historically famous) national strike in 1936. With the help and mediation of the government, this strike gave rise to a national agreement between trade unions, employers and the government. The joint committees, established per sector, were gradually put into use. In this context, collective bargaining took more and more shape. Because of the relative absence of the government in labour matters, various initiatives to improve the position of needy employees and the unemployed started to develop in the course of the nineteenth century. The best known initiatives were the mutual health organisations and the unemployment funds. It is in this context that the 'Ghent system' characterised the idea of social protection. In this Ghent system, unemployment funds were run by trade unions.[41] Nowadays, trade unions are still involved in the administration of public unemployment insurance.

III. Development of Labour Law

47. The period after the Second World War was characterised by the development of collective labour relations, social security and the further expansion of

37. Act of 14 Jun. 1921 to introduce the eight-hour day and the forty-eight-hour week, *Belgian Official Gazette* 21 Jun. 1921.
38. Act of 10 Mar. 1900 on employment contracts, *Belgian Official Gazette* 14 Mar. 1900.
39. Act of 7 Aug. 1922 on the servants' labour agreement, *Belgian Official Gazette* 16–17 Aug. 1922.
40. Act of 24 May 1921 to guarantee the freedom of association, *Belgian Official Gazette* 28 May 1921; Act of 24 May 1921 to abolish Art. 310 of the Criminal Code, *Belgian Official Gazette* 28 May 1921.
41. K. Vandaele, *A Report from the Homeland of the Ghent System: The Relationship Between Unemployment and Trade Union Membership in Belgium, Transfer* 4/0206, 647–657.

employment protection. A Social Pact of 1944, concluded[42] during the final phase of the Second World War between a number of leading figures from employers' and employees' organisations,[43] expressed the demand for far-reaching state intervention to meet the growing demand for stability and security. The central objectives were solidarity and stability, an increase in purchasing power and full employment, and a system of social security. To this end, the 'Social Pact' initiated a clear wage policy, set out the main principles on which the system of social security for workers should be based, and provided for a new, joint structure for social consultation. It laid the foundations for collective labour relations as we know them today. This was followed by the Decree Law of 9 June 1945 establishing the status of joint committees,[44] the Act of 20 September 1948 establishing works councils, which is still in force, and the Act of 29 May 1952 establishing the National Labour Council (NLC). The Decree Law on the Social Security of Workers, the basis for social security for employees, dates from 28 December 1944.[45]

48. In the sixties and seventies, a series of other important laws followed, including the Closure Act (1966),[46] the Labour Regulations Act (1965),[47] the Wage Protection Act (1965),[48] the Collective Labour Agreement Act (1968),[49] the Labour Act (1971),[50] the Workplace Accidents Act,[51] the Co-ordinated Acts on Annual Vacation (1971),[52] and the Labour Inspection Act (1972).[53] In this way, a wide range of binding legislative measures came into being. In the 1970s, the first national collective agreements also came into existence, concluded within the framework of the NLC. Collective Agreement (CA) no. 5 of 24 May 1971 concerning the status of trade union delegations of the staff of undertakings as well as CA no. 9 of 9 March 1972 organising the national agreements and collective labour conventions concluded in the NLC concerning works councils and CA no. 10 of 8 May 1973 concerning collective redundancies are all important early examples.

49. One of the central pieces of legislation for the employment relationship concerns the Act of 3 July 1978 on employment contracts (hereinafter 'the Employment Contracts Act').[54] Today, this act is still the reference for individual employment contract law. The Employment Contracts Act is actually a product of

42. Draft agreement on social solidarity, *Arbbl.* January–March 1945, 9–19.
43. *See* comments to the draft agreement in *Arbbl.* January–March 1945, 4.
44. *Belgian Official Gazette* 5 Jul. 1945; *see also* Regent's Decree 15 Oct. 1945 determining the general modalities of the functioning of the joint committees, *Belgian Official Gazette* 22 Oct. 1945.
45. *Belgian Official Gazette* 30 Dec. 1944.
46. Act of 28 Jun. 1966 concerning the indemnification of employees who are dismissed when companies are closed down, *Belgian Official Gazette* 2 Jul. 1966.
47. Act of 8 Apr. 1965 establishing labour regulations, *Belgian Official Gazette* 5 May 1965.
48. Act of 12 Apr. 1965 concerning the protection of workers' wages, *Belgian Official Gazette* 30 Apr. 1965.
49. Act of 5 Dec. 1968, *Belgian Official Gazette* 15 Jan. 1969.
50. Labour Act 16 Mar. 1971, *Belgian Official Gazette* 30 Mar. 1971.
51. Act of 10 Apr. 1971, *Belgian Official Gazette* 24 Apr. 1971.
52. Laws concerning the annual leave of the employees coordinated on 28 Jun. 1971, *Belgian Official Gazette* 30 Sep. 1971.
53. Act of 16 Nov. 1971 on labour inspection, *Belgian Official Gazette* 8 Dec. 1972.
54. *Belgian Official Gazette* 22 Aug. 1978.

several legislative steps, starting with the Act of 10 March 1900 on the employment contract[55] and the Act of 7 August 1922 on the contract for white-collar workers.[56] The distinction between blue- and white-collar workers remained throughout the twentieth century. Nevertheless, there was a desire to unify the legal status of these different categories of workers. However, insurmountable differences of opinion between employers' and employees' organisations were encountered. The call for unified legislation gradually became louder. On 4 September 1974, the then Minister of Employment and Labour submitted a bill coordinating the various laws. This eventually led to the Law on Employment Contracts of 3 July 1978. As will be discussed further, following some rulings of the Constitutional Court, the legislator sought to eliminate the distinction between blue- and white-collar workers with regard to notice periods and the 'carenz day' (the carenz day is a day without pay for sickness leave) with the Act of 26 December 2013.

IV. Various Influences

50. The 1980s showed a specific dynamic. New legislation was being drafted. But under the pressure of the crisis years, the growing unemployment problem and changing economic circumstances, including tertiarisation of the economy and emerging globalisation, a desire arose to deregulate labour law or to make it more flexible. Emphasis was now being placed on the flexibility of labour law arrangements and their relevance to the functioning of the labour market. The trend towards flexibilisation continued into the twenty-first century. However, new labour laws and national collective agreements, thus more regulation, continued to emerge.

51. Since the 1990s, the role of the European Union has increased in the field of labour law. The starting point of the initial Treaty of Rome (1957) was mainly to work towards economic integration. However, discussions on labour law at a European level soon began at a political level. Following the declaration by the Heads of State and Government in Paris in October 1972, in which it was stated that social policy in Europe was just as important as economic and monetary union, a whole series of plans and proposals arose concerning European labour law.[57] However, the call for flexibility and the enlargement of Europe held much back. Nevertheless, the social dimension took shape, under the impetus of Commission President Jacques Delors, and the Community Charter of the Fundamental Social Rights of Workers was finally adopted as a declaration of 11 Member States (the United Kingdom did not participate) at the Strasbourg summit on 9 December 1989. The 1989 Charter was an important step in establishing the political will to create social powers, as was shown during the negotiations of the Maastricht Treaty. This led to the conclusion of the Agreement of 31 October 1991 on social policy, the later (and current)

55. Act of 4 Mar. 1954, amending and supplementing the Act of 10 Mar. 1900 on the contract of employment, *Belgian Official Gazette* 12 Mar. 1954.
56. Act of 11 Mar. 1954 amending the Act of 7 Aug. 1954 on the contract for white-collar workers, *Belgian Official Gazette* 20 Mar. 1954.
57. 5 *Social Action Programme. Resolution of the Council of 21 January 1974*, 135–187 (BCLR 1974).

'social chapter' of the Treaty on the Functioning of the European Union (Articles 151 ff. TFEU). With the extension of these powers, the EU has been able to take legislative measures, among others, in the areas of employee participation, collective dismissal, transfer of undertaking, fixed-term employment, part-time employment, temporary employment, equal treatment. Nevertheless, a difficult tension persists between the social dimension of the European Union (and the role of labour law) on the one hand and the internal market and the economic dimension on the other.

52. Belgian labour law is always in development. This is not only due to the legislator but also due to the social partners, who have a large degree of initiative to conclude collective agreements, also at the national level. There are different major factors, such as economic governance of the European Union, globalisation and ever-increasing international competition, demographic change and new technologies, which lead to various discussions on the reform of labour law in Belgium. Within the Belgian system, consensus building is found important, and a compromise for employers and workers is part of that. At the Belgian level, the Act of 5 March 2017 on Workable and Agile Work is a good example of how a modern labour law not only pays attention to flexibility on the part of the employer but also provides incentives for flexibility for the employee, workable careers and a good work-life balance.[58]

§4. Sources of Labour Law

I. General

53. Rights and obligations in employment law can be found in a wide variety of legal sources. Legislation is obviously a very important source of rights and obligations in labour law. Nevertheless, the employment relationship still presupposes the existence of an agreement. The individual employment contract thus stands central. It can be concluded verbally as well as in writing. In the individual contract, the parties have the possibility to make all kinds of agreements. However, they must take into account the hierarchy of legal sources which largely consist in mandatory legislative provisions and binding collective agreements. Specifically for labour law, there are a number of other special sources of law: the collective labour agreement, the labour regulations and custom.

II. Hierarchy of Legal Norms

54. The Belgian legislator has explicitly provided for a hierarchy of labour law norms. This hierarchy is contained in Article 51 of the Act of 5 December 1968 on collective agreements and joint committees (known as the 'Collective Agreements Act').

58. *Belgian Official Gazette* 15 Mar. 2017.

The hierarchy of the sources of obligations in the employment relationship between employers and employees, in accordance with Article 51 of the Collective Agreements Act, is established as follows:

(1) the mandatory provisions of statutory law;
(2) the collective agreements declared universally applicable in the following order:
   (a) agreements concluded in the NLC;
   (b) agreements concluded within a joint committee;
   (c) agreements concluded within a joint subcommittee;
(3) the collective agreements not declared universally binding, when the employer has signed the agreement or is affiliated to an organisation that has signed this agreement, in the following order:
   (a) agreements concluded in the NLC;
   (b) agreements concluded within a joint committee;
   (c) agreements concluded within a joint subcommittee;
   (d) contracts concluded outside a joint body;
(4) the written individual agreement;
(5) a collective agreement which has not been declared universally applicable, concluded within a joint body, when the employer, although not a signatory to the agreement or not a member of an organisation which has signed it, falls within the area of jurisdiction of the joint body within which the agreement was concluded;
(6) the work regulations;
(7) the supplementary provisions of statutory law;
(8) the oral individual agreement;
(9) usage.

55. The hierarchy determines the precedence of the various sources of law when they are in conflict with each other. Provisions may not conflict with provisions of a source of law that is higher in the hierarchy. In the event of conflicting provisions, the conflicting provisions of the lower source of law are null and void. However, the invalidity of a conflicting provision does not imply the invalidity of the source of law as a whole.[59]

56. The top tier of the hierarchy is legislation, which is mainly mandatory or even, in some cases, of a public policy nature. The concern for the protection of the employee leads the legislator to limit the parties' freedom of contract. It is obvious that this reduces the role of the individual employment contract in formulating rights and obligations. The abandonment of party autonomy serves the logic of employment law, although it is not full. There is still room for the parties. The written individual employment contract is, however, ranked fourth in the hierarchy and the oral individual employment contract only eighth.[60]

---

59. Cass. 12 Oct. 1992, *JTT* 1992, 478 and *RW* 1992–93, 880.
60. Cf. Art. 51, 4° and 8° of the Act of 5 Dec. 1968.

57. Belgian employment law does not have a "principle of favouritism", which would always give priority to a provision which is more favourable to the employee over another provision. A provision in a lower source of law is therefore null and void when it conflicts with a higher source of law, even if the provision in question is more favourable for the employee.

58. In practice, however, both labour laws and collective agreements contain minimum provisions (e.g., a minimum wage in a collective agreement). This implies that they can be increased or improved by a lower source of law (e.g., a higher wage in the individual employment contract). For example, the Labour Code of 16 March 1971 refers to maximum limits on working time. Lower sources of law, e.g., collective agreements, can thus reduce working time.

59. Case law has set an important nuance to the hierarchy of norms. Article 51 of the Act of 5 December 1968 does not prohibit the parties from replacing or modifying a written individual employment contract by an oral agreement.[61]

III. Multilayered

60. In the context of the sources, one should take into account the 'multilayeredness' of the Belgian legal order. On the one hand, it is influenced by international and European law, but on the other hand, it is also embedded in a federal state structure, whereby communities and regions have powers in the field of labour law.

61. As far as the regional competences are concerned, there are 'Communities' and 'Regions' in Belgian's federal structure. The communities are responsible for, among other things, professional education and training and the use of languages in social relations between employers and their staff. The regions are responsible for employment policy, employment mediation, employment programmes, target group policy and the application of the regulations on the employment of foreign workers.

62. The international sources are mainly those of the International Labour Organisation and the Council of Europe. However, a number of UN conventions are also relevant to fundamental social rights, such as the Universal Declaration of Human Rights and the International Covenant on Economic, Social and Cultural Rights (ICESCR), adopted in New York on 16–19 December 1966.

Yet more importance is attached to the International Labour Organisation (ILO), established under the Versailles Peace Treaty in 1919 as part of the larger peace project. The principle that 'labour is not a commodity' is found in Article 427 of this Peace Treaty. Later, the ILO was incorporated as a specialised body into the United Nations system. Within the framework of the ILO, some two hundred conventions and about one hundred recommendations have been adopted.

---

61. Cass. 10 Sep. 1984, AR 102441, *Soc.Kron.* 1984, 582.

63. As far as the Council of Europe is concerned, both the European Convention on Human Rights (ECHR, 1950) and the European Social Charter (ESC, 1961, revised 1996) are important instruments for Belgian labour law.

64. The influence of the European Union has increased over the years. The impact on labour law is also quite special and must be considered from different policy areas within the legal framework of the European Union, such as social policy, the internal market and employment policy.

65. In a famous judgment of 27 May 1971 in the case of the *Belgian State v NV Fromagerie Franco-Suisse Le Ski*, the Court of Cassation ruled that international law must take precedence over internal law. It may be deduced from this that when a conflict exists between a norm of internal law and a norm of international law with 'direct effect' in the internal legal order, it is the rule laid down by international law that must prevail.[62]

IV. Work Regulations

66. The work regulations are one of the typical labour law sources of rights and obligations of employees and employers. It is mentioned in the legal hierarchy of sources of law (Article 51, Collective Agreements Act).

67. The work regulations are regulated by the Law of 8 April 1965 on work regulations (the Work Regulations Act).

68. A work regulation is a document prescribed by law in which a number of employment and working conditions are included that apply in the company. Every employer is required to have work regulations (Article 4, paragraph 1, Work Regulations Act). However, an employer may have several work regulations. Thus, separate work regulations may be drawn up for different categories of employees and for different departments of the company (Article 5, Work Regulations Act).

69. Work regulations can be distinguished from other documents drawn up within the company. In these cases, one can speak of 'company regulations'. Such documents exist under a multitude of names, such as: internal memoranda, company policies, memos, service instructions, and personnel handbook. They are often drawn up unilaterally by the employer with a view to clarifying his authority in the company. The basis of these documents can therefore be found in the employer's right to exercise authority. Pursuant to Article 17, 2° of the Law on Employment Contracts, the employee must act in accordance with the orders and instructions given by the employer with a view to executing the contract. Instead of continuously giving orders and instructions verbally or incidentally, the employer can also express the orders and instructions by issuing regulations.

62. Cass. 27 May 1971, A.C. 1971, 959.

70. There are therefore some differences between employment regulations and company regulations: Work rules find their origin in statutory law and must contain a number of obligatory provisions, including references to disciplinary sanctions. There is also a statutory procedure in order to establish work rules, with worker participation, including drawing and amending of the work regulations.

71. Work regulations are binding in the company. The employer and the employees are bound by the provisions contained herein (Article 4, paragraph 2, Work Regulations Act). The employer must provide each employee with a copy of the work regulations (Article 15, paragraph 5, Work Regulations Act). The work regulations of which the employee has not been given a copy are not binding on him, even if he was aware of them. The burden of proof lies with the employer.[63,64] In principle, however, a written document as proof of delivery is not necessary.[65] The work regulations must, furthermore, be available for inspection by every employee at any time and in an easily accessible place (Article 15(4), Employment Regulations Act).

72. As far as the content of the work regulations is concerned, a distinction must be made between the statements required by law and the optional statements.

73. What the labour regulations must state in a mandatory way is set out in Article 6, §1 of the Work Regulations Act. These include, among others:

(1) the beginning and end of the normal working day, the time and duration of rest periods, the days when work is regularly interrupted;
(2) the methods of measuring and monitoring work in order to determine remuneration;
(3) the method, time and place of payment of wages;
(4) (a) the duration of the periods of notice or the arrangements for determining the periods of notice or reference to the relevant statutory and regulatory provisions; (b) the urgent reasons which justify the termination of the contract by one or other party without notice, subject to the discretion of the courts;
(5) the rights and obligations of supervisory staff;
(6) the penalties, the amount and the purpose of the fines, and the shortcomings they punish;
(7) the appeal available to employees who wish to lodge a complaint or make a comment with regard to the penalties imposed on them or who contest these penalties.

In addition, there are other legal provisions, as well as collective agreement provisions, which prescribe mandatory entries in the work regulations (Articles 7–8, Work Regulations Act).

63. Cass. 3 Sep. 1970, *Arr.Cass.* 1971, 5 and *TSR* 1970, 263; Cass. 9 Jun. 1980, *RW* 1980–81, 1489 and *TSR* 1981, 12.
64. Cass. 9 Jun. 1980, *RW* 1980–81, 1489 and *TSR* 1981, 12.
65. Cass. 3 Sep. 1970, *Arr.Cass.* 1971, 5 and *TSR* 1970, 263.

The law expressly provides that the labour regulations may contain any other provisions on which the employer and the employees agree (Article 10, §1, paragraph 1, Work Regulations Act).

74. The Work Regulations Act refers to disciplinary sanctions. The right to exercise authority includes the disciplinary power of the employer. Disciplinary law is one of the ways in which the employer can ensure compliance with his orders and instructions. It should be noted that employment law itself does not contain any disciplinary standards. This is left to the level of the company. However, as a general rule, no disciplinary measure can be imposed unless both the disciplinary sanction and the shortcoming are provided for in the work regulations. Indeed, the work regulations must contain both the penalties and the shortcomings they punish (Article 6, §1, 6°, Work Regulations Act). Only the penalties provided for in the work regulations may be imposed (Article 16, Work Regulations Act). If the disciplinary measure consists of a fine, the amount and purpose of the fine must be specified (Article 6, §1, 6°, Work Regulations Act). Furthermore, the total of the fines imposed per day may not exceed one-fifth of the daily wage (Article 18, Work Regulations Act). The proceeds of the fines must be used for the benefit of the employees (Article 19, Work Regulations Act). The employer or his representative must, on pain of nullity, inform the persons who have incurred the penalties, at the latest on the first working day after the day on which the shortcoming was observed (Article 17, paragraph 1, Work Regulations Act).

75. The law provides for a procedure for drawing up and amending work regulations. There is an important difference depending on whether or not there is a works council in the company. If there is a works council, it drafts the regulations and makes amendments to existing regulations (Article 11, paragraph 1, Work Rules Act). This means that the employee representatives in the Works Council must also approve the work regulations, and any amendments. If there is no agreement in the Works Council about the provisions of the work regulations, the dispute will be submitted, at the latest fifteen days after the day of the Works Council meeting at which the lack of agreement has been definitively established, by the chairman of the Works Council to the competent official of the Labour Inspectorate, who will try to reconcile the positions (Article 11, paragraph 6, Work Regulations Act). If he does not succeed in doing so, the chairman of the Works Council shall bring the dispute before the competent joint committee (Article 11, paragraph 7, Work Rules Act) or, if that does not exist, before the NLC (Article 11, paragraph 10, Work Rules Act).

76. If there is no works council, any draft regulation or amendment to an existing one is drawn up by the employer, who must bring it to the attention of the employees by displaying it (Article 12, paragraph 1, Work Regulations Act). For a period of fifteen days from the day of posting, the employer shall keep a register at the disposal of the employees in which they, individually or through a staff delegation or union delegation, may record their comments (Article 12, paragraph 3, Work Regulations Act). As soon as this period has expired, the employer shall send the register for inspection to the competent official of the Labour Inspectorate (Article 15, paragraph 5, Work Regulations Act). If no comment has been communicated to that official and if no comment appears in the register, the new regulations or the amendment to the existing regulations shall enter into force on the fifteenth day after the date of posting (Article 15, paragraph 6, Work Regulations Act). If not, the competent official shall try to reconcile the positions (Article 15, paragraph 7, Work Regulations Act). If he does not succeed, the matter is referred to the competent joint committee (Article 15(9)) or, failing that, to the NLC (Article 15(12)).

Part I. The Individual Employment Relationship

Chapter 1. Definitions and Concepts

§1. The Employment Relationship

I. General

77. The employment contract is defined as the agreement whereby an employee undertakes, in return for remuneration, to perform work under the authority of an employer.[66] These elements are essential to be able to speak of an employment contract.

78. In practice, there is a lot of discussion about the distinction between an employment contract and a contract for self-employed services (a contract for services). It is clear that authority (subordination) is the determining element in this respect.

79. In Belgian labour law, the actual assessment of the presence of a relationship of authority (and subordination) has traditionally been made on the basis of indications or indicia, such as: the presence of orders and instructions, control of the work, control over the organisation of the activity, the place of employment, the work schedule, the method of remuneration, exclusive employment, the presence of a competition clause.

80. Economic dependence is generally not considered a relevant factor. Authority means that the employer has the right to give orders and exercise control. It is therefore a legal dependence of the employee on the employer. One who is economically dependent on someone else is not yet legally dependent.

81. Authority does not necessarily mean that the worker gives up all autonomy in relation to his work. A subordinate relationship may exist even if the employee 'retains full independence of the work and responsibility for the work'.[67] Thus, an

66. Cf. Arts 2 and 3 of the Employment Contracts Act of 3 Jul. 1978.
67. Cass. 27 Mar. 1968, *TSR* 1968, 110.

artist,[68] a pharmacist,[69] a teacher[70] or a doctor[71] may be linked by an employment contract, even though these persons retain a very large degree of autonomy in the performance of their duties. It is then important that authority exists in the organisation of the independent work performance. If, on the other hand, one can organise one's work oneself, one will normally not be considered as an employee but a self-employed person.[72] A nuance has to be made, however, since in many cases employees also enjoy a large degree of autonomy (e.g., in the case of telework), and 'grey zones' will exist.

82. According to the case law, the employer's authority does not necessarily have to be exercised in an actual, permanent manner. It is sufficient that the employer has the legal possibility to exercise authority.[73] This can be done, for example, by a series of checks on documents or accounts a posteriori.[74]

83. The presence or absence of authority is first of all a matter of principle. The mandatory nature of labour law means that the parties cannot decide on its application themselves. As soon as there is authority in a work relationship, labour law is applied (and the according social security regime). There is also a practical interest. In contrast to the employment contract, one considers a self-employed service (contracting for services) to be a more flexible form of collaboration with lower (remuneration) cost. Self-employment is not, or in a limited manner, covered by restrictive labour law regulations. In addition, there is a significant difference in treatment with regard to the social security regime (including contributions with a view to financing social security) depending on whether it concerns a self-employed service provider and his client or an employee and his employer. These 'costs' are much higher for employees and employers than for self-employed persons and their principal.

84. In practice, therefore, 'grey zones' or abuses may appear. There are many cases in which people work as a self-employed person, while in reality they work under the authority of their client, so that they are in reality an employee (and their client is therefore their employer). This sometimes happens deliberately in order to avoid social security contributions. In this case, we speak of false or bogus self-employed persons: 'workers who knowingly accept the social status of the self-employed when in reality they exercise their professional activity under the authority of their co-contractor, and therefore in the capacity of salaried employee'.[75]

68. Cass. 4 Apr. 1963, *TSR* 1963, 193.
69. Cass. 7 Mar. 1961, *TSR* 1961, 135.
70. Cass. 8 Oct. 1975, *TSR* 1976, 27.
71. Cass. 22 Feb. 1968, *TSR* 1968, 22.
72. Cass. 9 May 1988, *RW* 1988–89, 677.
73. Cass. 15 Feb. 1967, *TSR* 1962, 357; Cass. 6 Jun. 1968, *Pas.* 1968, I, 1142; Cass. 13 Jun. 1968, *Pas.* 1968, I, 1169.
74. Cass. 30 Jun. 1966, *Pas.* 1966, I, 1399.
75. *Parl.* Chamber 2006–07, no. 2773/001, 202.

II. Qualification in Case Law

85. Because of the mandatory protection, one cannot, in principle, freely choose whether or not labour law applies. In principle, the existence of a relationship of authority (and subordination) – and thus the qualification of the contract as an employment contract – depends on concrete elements or indications pointing to authority. Nevertheless, the role of the qualification given by the parties themselves to their agreement has long been a point of discussion. The question has been whether, and to what extent, the parties themselves are able to influence the qualification of the contract.

86. The role of the parties has been characterised in different ways. In the past, based on some important judgments of the Court of Cassation[76] – but also based on lower case law – a number of approaches were established.

According to a first approach, the reality of the performance of the employment relationship has to take precedence over the qualification given by the parties. In this view, therefore, the influence of the parties on the ultimate qualification of the employment relationship is limited or virtually non-existent. A court of fact is, in this approach, not bound by the qualification given by the parties to their contract, and a recharacterisation is possible on the basis of elements that appeared from the actual performance of the contract.

A second approach leaves less discretion to a court and states that when the parties have given a precise name to their contract pointing at a qualification (e.g., as a self-employed contract), the qualification given by them must prevail, so that the Court may only change the qualification in the event of fraud, error or clauses incompatible with the contract.

However, a third approach came up with the more recent case law of the Court of Cassation. Since a judgment of 23 December 2002,[77] the Court of Cassation became much stricter with respect to the possibility for a court to recharacterise (or requalify) an agreement. In this judgment, the Court stated that when the parties have given a name to their agreement, a court of fact cannot substitute another name for it if the information presented to it does not allow it to exclude the name given by the parties to the agreement.[78] Almost identical wording is found in a judgment of 28 April 2003[79] and in a judgment of 8 December 2003.[80] It has been the tendency ever since.

87. The importance of the qualification given by the parties increases even more when one accepts similar elements in a contract for independent services as in an employment contract. Thus, in its judgment of 23 December 2002, the Court of Cassation stated that it is possible for a contractor to work in the premises of the other contracting party, receive an hourly wage, use the tools and materials provided by

76. Cass. 16 Jan. 1978, *RW* 1977–78, 2596; Cass. 11 Sep. 1978, *RW* 1978–79, 1605; Cass. 16 Mar. 1981, *RW* 1981–82, 1847; Cass. 10 Dec. 1984, *JTT* 1985, 244.
77. Cass. 23 Dec. 2002, *JTT* 2003, 271 and *Or.* 2003, para. 4, 2.
78. Cass. 23 Dec. 2002, AR S.01.0169.F/1.
79. Cass. 28 Apr. 2003, *JTT* 2003, 261 and *NJW* 2003, 886, note M. De Vos.
80. Cass. 8 Dec. 2003, *JTT* 2004, 122.

the principal and not assume the economic and financial risk of the contract. The Court stated that the hiring of work does not exclude the possibility that general guidelines must be observed and that the performance of the tasks must be supervised.

III. The Employment Relations Act

88. Against the horizon of the evolving case law and the need for more legal certainty in practice, the legislator intervened. The government introduced the Programme Act of 27 December 2006,[81] with a number of provisions to determine the nature of the work relationship. The 'nature of the work relationship' actually refers to the qualification of the work relationship, i.e., that of an employment contract (in which authority is present) or a contract for independent work (a contract for services). The provisions of Title XIII of the Programme Law of 27 December 2006 are generally referred to as the Employment Relations Act.

89. It is important to note that the Act aims to regulate a legal qualification of the employment relationship and focuses on both labour law and social security law. Thus, not only the evasion of social security contributions but also the evasion of otherwise applicable labour law is identified as a problem.

90. Concretely, the Act aims at confirming certain general principles developed by the courts, by defining general criteria for assessing the nature of an employment relationship, by providing the possibility to elaborate a list of specific criteria adapted to the specific reality of a sector or a profession and by introducing a social ruling.[82] The Act of 25 August 2012[83] made a number of important changes to the Employment Relations Act, including the establishment of a statutory presumption.

A. *Principle of the Autonomy of Will*

91. The basic principle is that the parties are free to choose their form of cooperation. Article 331 of the Programme Act states: 'Without being able to violate public order, morality and mandatory laws, the parties freely choose the nature of their employment relationship where the effective performance of the contract must correspond to the nature of the employment relationship.'

B. *Requalification*

92. The choice of the parties and the qualification given by them to their employment relationship is valid in principle, but not unconditionally so. The actual

---

81. *Belgian Official Gazette* 28 Dec. 2006.
82. *Parl.* Chamber 2006–07, no. 2773/001, 204–205.
83. *Belgian Official Gazette* 11 Sep. 2012.

performance of the contract must be in line with the given qualification. A requalification is therefore always possible. The Employment Relations Act describes in two different ways the situation in which a requalification is possible on the basis of the actual performance of the contract:

(1) Article 331 states that 'precedence must be given to the qualification evidenced by actual performance if it excludes the legal qualification chosen by the parties'.
(2) Article 332 provides for the requalification of the employment relationship and the application of a corresponding social security system:
   - when the exercise of the work relationship gives rise to sufficient elements which, assessed in accordance with the provisions of the Act and its implementing decrees, are incompatible with the qualification given to the employment relationship by the parties;
   - or when the qualification given by the parties to the working relationship does not correspond to the nature of the work relationship as it is presumed in accordance with the provisions of Chapter V/1 and this presumption is not rebutted (Article 332, paragraph 1, Employment Relations Act).

93. The possibility of requalifying (and thus substituting the qualification initially given by the parties) is therefore only existing to a limited extent. The legislator clearly wants to follow the case law of the Court of Cassation. Furthermore, the legal presumptions (introduced by the 2012 amendment of the law[84]) are taken into account.

C. General Criteria

94. The elements which emerge from the actual performance of the contract and which may lead to its reclassification are assessed on the basis of a number of general criteria and, where appropriate, specific criteria of a legal or socio-economic nature (Article 332, Employment Relations Act).

95. The general criteria allowing to assess the existence or absence of a relationship of authority are (Article 333, §1, Employment Relations Act):

- the will of the parties as expressed in their agreement;
- the freedom to organise working time;
- the freedom to organise work;
- the possibility of exercising hierarchical control.

96. The obligations inherent in the exercise of a profession and imposed by or pursuant to a law cannot be taken into consideration to assess the nature of an employment relationship (Article 333, §2, Employment Relations Act).

---

84. Act of 25 Aug. 2012, *Belgian Official Gazette* 11 Sep. 2012.

97. Furthermore, the following elements are, in themselves, not capable of adequately qualifying the working relationship: the title of the contract; the registration with a social security institution; registration as a company; the registration with the VAT administration; the way in which the income is declared to the tax administration (Article 333, §3, Employment Relations Act).

98. The case law from the Court of Cassation provides some indications as to when authority may exist. In a judgment dated 4 February 2013, the Court of Cassation confirmed the reasoning of the Labour Court that a limited freedom to arrange leave can be an indication of a relationship of subordination.[85] The Court of Cassation also stated that the Labour Court had lawfully decided on a relationship of authority, *inter alia* by referring to the absence of choice as to whether or not to perform the work activity and the fact that there could be direct control and supervision of the performance by those concerned who had exclusively a function of executor by merely making their labour force available.[86]

The Court of Cassation has already ruled on whether the possibility of imposing disciplinary sanctions is sufficient to exclude the possibility of independent cooperation. The Court considers that the finding that disciplinary sanctions can be imposed excludes the possibility of independent cooperation, provided that such sanctions are not inherent in the exercise of the profession and are imposed by or pursuant to a law.[87]

D. Special Criteria

99. In addition to general criteria, the Employment Relations Act also establishes special criteria. The King (executive power) may draw up a list of criteria specific to one or more sectors, one or more professions, or one or more professional activities which he shall determine (Article 334, §1, Employment Relations Act).

100. The legislator thus finds that a given profession or a given sector may be faced with specific problems regarding the nature of the work relationship. In order to solve these cases, the government may thus draw up a list of specific criteria, which will only be valid for this profession or sector. However, these specific criteria will have to be established in accordance with the procedure described in the Employment Relations Act, which can only be started after an objective uncertainty about the nature of the employment relationships concerned has been demonstrated.[88]

101. The special criteria supplement the general criteria (Article 334, §1, Employment Relations Act), and can only consist of elements which may or may

85. Cass. 4 Feb. 2013, AR S.11.0051.F.
86. Cass. 26 Mar. 2013, AR P.12.0387.N.
87. Cass. 10 Oct. 2016, AR S.14.0074.N.
88. *Parl.St.* Chamber 2006–07, no. 2773/001, 219.

not point to the existence of authority, cannot deviate from the general criteria (Article 334, §2, Employment Relations Act).

E. Legal Presumption

102. In 2012, a legislative amendment[89] added a new chapter to the Employment Relations Act regarding a legal presumption of the presence or absence of a relationship of authority between the parties to the employment relationship (Chapter V/1: 'Presumption regarding the nature of the employment relationship').

103. The chapter consists of two articles, 337/1 and 337/2. Article 337/1 sets out the scope of the presumption. The presumption does not apply to all working relationships, but only to working relationships that fall within the scope of certain sectors, professions, categories of professions or professional activities.[90] The law already specifies three sectors where the presumption applies, namely the construction sector, the sector of security services and the sector of transportation of persons and goods (cf. Article 337/1, §1, Employment Relations Act). In addition, the scope of the presumption can be extended to other sectors by Royal Decree (Article 337/1, §2, Employment Relations Act).

Article 337/2 sets out the operation of the presumption. It introduces a number of socio-economic criteria. In relation to this, it provides that there is a presumption of the presence or absence of a relationship of subordination when more than half of the socio-economic criteria set out in this article are met. If more than half of the criteria are met, the employment relationship is presumed to be an employment contract (Article 337/2, §1, Employment Relations Act). If this is not the case, the working relationship is presumed not to be an employment contract, but a self-employment contract (Article 337/2, §2, Employment Relations Act).

104. It is expressly provided that the presumption is rebuttable (cf. Article 337/2, §1 and §2, Employment Relations Act). The law states that the presumption can be rebutted by all means of law, including by reference to the general criteria set forth in this law (Article 337/2, §2, paragraph 2, Employment Relations Act).

105. The presumption has limitations. It is (at the time of writing) only applicable in the following sectors:

- Construction
- Security
- Transport
- Cleaning
- Agriculture
- Horticulture.

89. Act of 25 Aug. 2012, *Belgian Official Gazette* 11 Sep. 2012.
90. *Cf. Parl.St.* Chamber 2011–12, Bill no. 2319/001, 8.

106. The (socio-economic) criteria which play a role in the presumption are the following (Article 337/2, §1, Employment Relations Act):

(a) the absence of any financial or economic risk on the part of the person carrying out the work, like this is the case in the absence of a personal and substantial investment in the company from its own resources, or in the absence of a personal and substantial participation in the profits and losses of the company;
(b) the absence of responsibility and decision-making power for the undertaking's financial resources on the part of the person who carries out the work;
(c) the absence of decision-making power on the purchasing policy of the undertaking on the part of the person carrying out the work;
(d) the absence of any control over the pricing policy of the undertaking by the person carrying out the work, except where prices are established by law;
(e) the absence of an obligation to produce results in relation to the agreed work;
(f) a guarantee of payment of a fixed fee, irrespective of the operating results or the extent of the services provided by the person carrying out the work;
(g) not being an employer of personally and freely recruited personnel or not having the possibility of recruiting personnel or having them replaced for the performance of the agreed work;
(h) not acting as an undertaking vis-à-vis other persons, or working principally or habitually for a single co-contractor;
(i) work in premises of which one is not the owner or tenant, or work with equipment provided, financed or guaranteed by the co-contractor.

107. The criteria on the basis of which the employment relationship is presumed to be of one or the other nature can be supplemented or replaced by a Royal Decree with specific criteria for the sector(s), profession(s), category(s) of professions or professional activity(ies) concerned (Article 337/2, §3, Employment Relations Act).[91]

F. Commission for Regulation of the Employment Relationship

108. Initially, the Employment Relations Act provided for a Commission to regulate the employment relationship consisting of a normative and an administrative section. The normative division was[92] abolished by the 2012 amendment. This leaves the 'Administrative Commission for regulating the working relationship' (Article 329, Employment Relations Act).

---

91. *See* Royal Decree of 29 Apr. 2013 (the employment relationship between a security guard referred to in the Act of 10 Apr. 1990 regulating private and special security and his co-contractor), *Belgian Official Gazette* 14 May 2013; Royal Decree of 7 Jun. 2013 (the employment relationships existing in the context of the exercise of some real estate activities), *Belgian Official Gazette* 25 Jun. 2013; Royal Decree of 20 Jun. 2013 (the employment relationships existing in the context of the exercise of activities covered by the Joint Committee on Agriculture or the Joint Committee on Horticulture), *Belgian Official Gazette* 28 Jun. 2013.
92. Act of 25 Aug. 2012, *Belgian Official Gazette* 11 Sep. 2012.

109. The Administrative Commission, a governmental institution, has the task to take decisions regarding the qualification of a certain employment relationship (Article 338, Employment Relations Act). This task is what is called 'social ruling', along the lines of what exists in the tax field. The decisions are binding on the institutions represented in the Administrative Commission and on the social security funds referred to in Article 20 of Royal Decree 38 (Article 338, §4 of the Labour Relations Act).[93] They are, however, not binding upon courts. Courts will thus make their own assessment on the legal qualify. of a work relationship. Courts may overrule the decisions of the Administrative Commission.

§2. Types of Employment Contracts by Nature of the Work

I. Blue Collar and White Collar

A. Concept

110. The distinction between blue-collar workers and white-collar employees concerns a rather typical Belgian discussion. The Employment Contracts Act of 3 July 1978 defines the distinction as follows:

> The employment contract for manual workers is the contract under which an employee, a worker, undertakes, in return for remuneration and under the authority of an employer, to perform mainly manual work (art. 2, Employment Contracts Act). An employment contract for white-collar workers is a contract under which an employee, a white-collar worker, undertakes, in return for remuneration and under the authority of an employer, to perform intellectual work (art. 3, Employment Contracts Act).

111. As a worker, one is therefore either a blue-collar worker or a white-collar worker. The only criterion for determining whether a person is a worker or an employee in a specific case is the nature of the work performed. The legislator does not make it easy by referring to work that is *essentially* performed either as manual work or as intellectual work. The terminology used by the parties is not decisive.

112. The distinction between blue- and white-collar workers arose historically. However, the evolution of labour relations has made the distinction between manual labour and intellectual labour obsolete. It is generally no longer possible to make this distinction. It has led to interventions by the case law and the legislator, as will be explained below.

---

93. *See* Royal Decree of 11 Feb. 2013 on the composition and functioning of the chambers of the Administrative Commission for the regulation of the working relationship, *Belgian Official Gazette* 21 Feb. 2013; Royal Decree of 11 Feb. 2013 appointing the members of the Administrative Commission for the regulation of the working relationship, *Belgian Official Gazette* 21 Feb. 2013.

113. Although the distinction between blue-collar and white-collar workers mainly concerns dismissal law and the regulation of work incapacity, it also leads to important differences in collective labour law. Collective bargaining is often divided between blue-collar and white-collar workers. For example, blue- and white-collar workers may fall under a different joint committee, resulting in the application of different collective agreements even though they work in the same sector or in the same company. Blue-collar workers and white-collar workers are usually represented separately in the works council and the Committee for Prevention and Protection at Work (CPPW).

114. With the Act of 26 December 2013 on the introduction of a unitary status (Unified Status Act),[94] an important step was taken towards abolishing the distinction between blue-collar and white-collar workers. The 2013 Act is the result of intense negotiations with the social partners and is based on a compromise elaborated by the (then) Minister of Labour. The Unified Status Act largely intends to amend the Employment Contracts Act in its provisions regarding notice periods and the 'carenz day' (a non-paid day of work incapacity). The path taken to arrive at this 26 December 2013 law was long and with many hurdles.

B. Unconstitutionality and Unification Statute

115. As mentioned above, after the Second World War, the legislator strived for a gradual harmonisation of the status of blue- and white-collar workers. This did not go smoothly, and, in the meanwhile, doubts existed as to the compatibility of the different treatment of blue- and white-collar workers with the principle of equality contained in the Belgian Constitution.[95]

116. The Constitutional Court ruled on this subject for the first time in a judgment dated 8 July 1993. It concerned a judgment which dealt with preliminary questions in the context of disputes about the length of the notice period to be observed by the employer.[96] The Court considered that by basing the distinction between blue- and white-collar workers on the essentially manual or intellectual nature of their work, the legislator created a difference in treatment based on a criterion which, at present, could hardly justify its introduction in an objective and reasonable manner.[97] However, according to the Court, this finding did not imply that the legislator had also violated the principle of equality in the Belgian Constitution by not immediately and completely eliminating the distinction.[98] The fact that it would

94. *Belgian Official Gazette* 31 Dec. 2013.
95. Currently contained in Arts 10 and 11 of the Gw.
96. Constitutional Court 8 Jul. 1993, no. 56/93, *JTT* 1993, 389, note X. Heyden and *RBDC* 1994, 359, note S. Bredael.
97. Constitutional Court 8 Jul. 1993, no. 56/93, recital B.6.2.1. B.6.2.1.
98. *Ibid.*

be irresponsible to introduce such a distinction in the current context was not sufficient to justify its (immediate) abolition.[99] In 1978, the legislator had clearly opted for a gradual harmonisation, and not by a sudden abolition of the distinction between blue- and white-collar workers. Therefore, maintaining the distinction in the Employment Contracts Act of 3 July 1978 was, in the opinion of the Constitutional Court in 1993, not manifestly disproportionate to this objective.[100]

117. The judgment, however, gave a clear signal that something had to change. Different attempts were made to abolish the distinction between blue- and white-collar workers and to create a so-called 'unified status'. After the judgment, however, the legislator left the initiative for the further rapprochement of the statuses in the hands of the social partners. But they could not reach an agreement. In the meanwhile, the Constitutional Court confirmed its view in a judgment of 21 June 2001, which concerned the arbitrary dismissal of workers.[101]

118. An important shift came with a new judgment of the Constitutional Court. In a judgment dated 7 July 2011, the Constitutional Court set a tight deadline for abolishing the distinction between blue- and white-collar workers. The Court stated that the time to remedy the situation was not unlimited. The Constitutional Court held that the differences created by the legislator are in violation of Articles 10 and 11 of the Constitution.[102] However, the principle of legal certainty prompted the Constitutional Court to grant the legislator a final period of notice in which it could legislate. During a transitional period, which ended on 8 July 2013 at the latest, the effects of the unconstitutional legislative provisions (thus the old situation) would be maintained.

119. Under this pressure, the Unified Status Act came into existence and entered into force on 1 January 2014. The legislator was therefore too late in view of the Constitutional Court's above-mentioned deadline. Moreover, in its transitional provisions, this Unified Status Act maintains the distinction between blue- and white-collar workers with respect to the determination of the notice periods, in order to respect acquired rights from the past.

120. In a judgment of 18 December 2014, the Constitutional Court had to consider the issue again, this time in relation to Article 63 of the Employment Contracts Act (arbitrary dismissal). The Court held that this article was contrary to Articles 10 and 11 of the Constitution. However, the Court ruled that the effects of the contested regulation must be maintained – *in this case* until 1 April 2014 – in order to avoid the unconstitutionality resulting in considerable legal uncertainty to the detriment of the workers concerned in numerous pending and future cases.[103]

---

99. Constitutional Court 8 Jul. 1993, no. 56/93, recital B.6.3.1. B.6.3.1.
100. Constitutional Court 8 Jul. 1993, no. 56/93, recital B.6.3.2. B.6.3.2.
101. Constitutional Court 21 Jun. 2001, no. 84/2001, *Belgian Official Gazette* 17 Oct. 2001 and *RW* 2001-02, 271, note M. De Vos.
102. Constitutional Court 7 Jul. 2011, no. 125/2011, recital. B.3.1.
103. Constitutional Court 18 Dec. 2014, no. 187/2014.

121. In addition to the legislation, the social partners concluded (national) Collective Labour Agreement no. 109 in the NLC, which regulates the issue of justified motivation of dismissals, and this agreement came into force on 1 April 2014.

II. Sales Representatives

A. Concept

122. The law defines the employment contract for sales representatives as 'the contract under which an employee, the sales representative, undertakes, against remuneration, to seek out and visit clients with a view to negotiating and concluding business, under the authority, for the account and in the name of one or more clients' (Article 4, Employment Contracts Act).

123. It does not concern a third category of employees. The sales representative is always a white-collar employee. However, a number of special provisions apply to the employment contract for sales representatives, pursuant to Title IV of the Employment Contracts Act (Articles 87–107, Employment Contracts Act). These provisions offer additional protection to the sales representative.

124. In light of the debate on the unitary status between blue- and white-collar workers, the question arose as to whether a separate legal category of trade representatives was compatible with the constitutional principle of equality. The Constitutional Court had to address this question in a judgment of 10 July 2014. The Court concluded that the principle of equality had not been violated. According to the Court, the difference in treatment is based on an objective criterion and pursues a legitimate aim, namely the protection of the commercial agent against a tendency to evade labour legislation. The difference in treatment is also pertinent and proportionate according to the Court.[104]

125. The law originally excluded the insurance sector from the provisions. A person who locates and visits customers with a view to negotiating or concluding insurance contracts would therefore not be a sales agent according to the legal definition. However, in a judgment dated 18 February 1998,[105] the Court of Arbitration ruled that the exclusion of insurance brokers from the definition of commercial agent was contrary to the constitutional principle of equality.

126. A sales representative is an intermediary. He acts on behalf of his client (employer) and is not himself a party to the contracts that may be concluded between the client and the customer. The legal definition shows that a sales representative can be affiliated with several employers at the same time.[106]

---

104. Constitutional Court 10 Jul. 2014, no. 101/2014.
105. *JTT* 1998, 227.
106. *Parl.* Chamber 1977–78, 293/4, 6.

127. Only the person who carries out the described activities in a subordinate capacity can be a commercial representative. As with all employees, the presence or absence of a relationship of authority is a question of fact. However, the law creates a legal presumption. Notwithstanding any express provision of the contract or silence thereof, the contract concluded between the principal and the intermediary, whatever it may be called, shall be regarded as an employment contract for sales representatives, unless proof to the contrary is provided (Article 4, paragraph 2, Employment Contracts Act). Thus, sales representatives are presumed to work in a subordinate capacity, and are therefore employees. In the event of a dispute, it is up to the employer to prove the contrary. Not only the sales representative but also a third party, such as the National Social Security Office (NSSO), can rely on this legal presumption. When the NSSO contests the self-employed status of a representative, it does not have to prove the existence of an employer-employee relationship. It is up to the principal to prove the absence of an employer-employee relationship.[107]

III. Household Workers

128. The employment contract for household workers is the contract under which an employee, the domestic worker, undertakes, in return for remuneration and under the authority of an employer, to perform mainly domestic manual labour in connection with the housekeeping of the employer or his family (Article 5, Employment Contracts Act).

129. Title V of the Employment Contracts Act contains a number of specific provisions relating to the employment contract for servants.

130. It concerns a special category of blue-collar workers. According to the legal definition, a domestic servant mainly performs manual labour. A person who mainly performs intellectual work in connection with the household of the employer or his family is therefore not a domestic worker, but a regular white-collar employee.

IV. Students

131. The student employment contract is an employment contract concluded between a student and an employer by which the student undertakes to perform work for pay under the authority of an employer (Article 120, Employment Contracts Act).

132. Title VII of the Employment Contracts Act provides a number of special provisions for this category of employees.

107. Cass. 17 Nov. 1997, *JTT* 1998, 234 and 396.

133. Depending on the case, the student employment contract may be a contract for blue-collar or white-collar employees, and even a contract for sales representatives or a contract for household work (Article 121, paragraph 2, Employment Contracts Act).

134. The term 'student' is not defined in the law. The term is interpreted broadly. A student is someone who is following higher or university studies as well as someone following higher general, technical, artistic or vocational secondary education. It involves employment both outside and during school holidays.

135. In principle, the regulations concerning student work do not stipulate any age conditions, nor a minimum age. However, it is forbidden to let children work or allow them to work, or to carry out any activity outside the framework of their education or training (Article 7.1 Labour Code). In this context, children are minors under 15 years of age or still subject to full-time compulsory education (Article 6 Labour Code). Full-time compulsory education may last until the age of 16.

136. Notwithstanding any express provision, the contract concluded between an employer and a student, whatever name is given to it, is presumed to be an employment contract unless the contrary is proven (Article 121, Employment Contracts Act).

137. A student employment contract must be drawn up in writing for each student individually, no later than the time at which they enter employment (Article 123, Employment Contracts Act).

V. Homework and Telework

A. Concept

138. Homeworkers and teleworkers are employees who in principle work for their employer at a distance, usually (but not necessarily) from home. The regulations distinguish between homework and telework.

139. The Employment Contracts Act provides that Title VI regulates the employment of homeworkers who, for remuneration, perform work under the authority of an employer, at their place of residence or at any other place chosen by them, without being under the supervision or direct control of the employer (Article 119.1, §1, paragraph 1, Employment Contracts Act). Articles 119.3 to 119.12 do not apply to employees covered by the collective agreement on telework concluded within the NLC (Article 119.1, §2, Employment Contracts Act). The provisions on homework were introduced by the Act of 6 December 1996. Traditionally, homework has mainly involved manual workers, for example, in the textile and clothing industry. However, homework is increasingly being found in the service sector.[108]

140. Telework has two main legal regimes. CA no. 85 of 9 November 2005 applies to 'structural' telework, which is performed on a regular and non-occasional basis. The Workable and Agile Work Act[109] introduced a regulation for 'occasional' telework. This concerns telework that is performed occasionally and not on a regular basis. In light of the corona pandemic, the social partners in the NLC concluded CA no. 149 regulating the specific situation of telework during the pandemic.

141. It is conceivable (and in practice it is realistic) that an employee is only partly a homeworker or teleworker, and for the remainder is present in the enterprise. In such a case, he will fall under the special provisions for homework or telework and for work in the enterprise under the ordinary provisions.

B. Structural Telework

142. On 9 November 2005, in light of the European framework agreement on telework of 16 July 2002, National Collective Agreement No. 85 concerning telework was concluded in the NLC.

143. The collective agreement defines telework as a form of organisation and/or performance of work in which, with the use of information technology, within the framework of a contract of employment, work that could also be performed at the employer's company location is performed on a regular basis and not incidentally outside the company location (Article 2 CA no. 85).

144. The distinction between telework and homework is not always obvious. An important element in the definition of telework is that it involves the use of information technology. The distinction from mobile workers who use information technology is also not straightforward. For example, telework does not concern employees who use technology and whose mobility is a necessary part of the way the employment contract is executed (Article 2 CA no. 85). One might think here, for example, of IT professionals who visit their employer's clients.

145. Telework can be carried out at the home of the teleworker or at any other place chosen by the teleworker. Telework carried out in a satellite office of the employer, i.e., a decentralised room of the employer or a room made available to the employee by the employer, falls outside the scope of this agreement (Article 4 CA no. 85).

---

108. *Parl.St.* Chamber 1995–96, no. 232/1, 1.
109. Act of 5 Mar. 2017 on workable and agile work, *Belgian Official Gazette* 15 Mar. 2017.

C. *Occasional Telework*

146. Occasional telework is a form of organisation and/or performance of work under an employment contract in which, with the use of information technology, work that could also be performed at the employer's business location is carried out outside that location on an occasional and not regular basis (Article 23, Workable and Agile Work Act). Occasional telework may be carried out at the home of the occasional teleworker or at any other place chosen by the latter (Article 24, Workable and Agile Work Act).

147. According to the law, the employee is only entitled to occasional telework because of force majeure or personal reasons preventing him from performing his work at the employer's premises, as long as he performs a function and/or activity that is compatible with occasional telework (Article 26, Workable and Agile Work Act).

148. Furthermore, the employee must request occasional telework from his employer, and it must be based on mutual consent and a number of agreements to be made (Article 26, Workable and Agile Work Act).

D. *Corona-Telework*

149. In the course of the COVID-19 pandemic, legal uncertainty grew with regard to the application of the above-mentioned telework regimes. Those regimes not only make a distinction between structural and occasional telework but also start from the premise that telework is based on voluntary initiative of the parties and mutual consent. In light of the questions arising from the pandemic, and seen the fact that the government imposed or advised telework in many instances, the social partners in the NLC decided to adopt CA no. 149.

150. CA no. 149 was thus explicitly created with a view to responding to telework situations in the context of the corona pandemic. Moreover, CA no. 149 is only temporary. Article 17 stipulates that this collective labour agreement is concluded for a fixed period and will cease to apply on 31 December 2021. It was extended, however, until 31 March 2022.

§3. Types of Employment Contracts According to Their Duration

I. General

151. The distinction between a fixed-term and an employment contract for an indefinite period is a *summa divisio* in employment law. Article 7 of the Employment Contracts Act of 3 July 1978 states that the employment contract shall be concluded either for a fixed term or for a clearly defined work or for an indefinite period.

152. The distinction has a substantial impact on the legal regulation of the end of the employment contract. In practice, a fixed-term employment contract also creates a different expectation compared to a fixed-term contract. Moreover, the legislator still has a clear preference for the employment contract for an indefinite period of time, although the parties are, in principle, completely free to choose which employment contract they will enter into. The employment contract for an indefinite period of time is considered to be the externalisation of the security of employment that the legislator wanted to give to employment relationships. The term 'job security' is referring a set of rules of employment law with the common objective of ensuring that the employee retains his employment.

II. The Employment Contract for an Indefinite Period

A. Concept

153. In the case of an employment contract for an indefinite period of time, neither the duration of the contract nor the scope of the work has, in principle, been determined in advance. This does not mean that this contract cannot be terminated unilaterally. Nor does it grant lifetime employment. However, the end is uncertain, indefinite. The law expressly provides that an employment contract cannot be concluded for life (Article 7, Employment Contracts Act). However, clauses in an employment contract which, although they hinder the exercise of the right to unilateral termination, do not make it impossible to exercise that right are not contrary to public policy.[110] A clause in an employment contract which provides that the employer may never dismiss an employee except on serious grounds may nevertheless be null and void on grounds of public policy.[111]

154. An employment contract for an indefinite period is the most common contract in practice. It is also regarded by the legislator as the general rule or 'standard' for cooperation between employer and employee. When the conditions for realising another type of contract are not present, one is usually automatically dealing with an employment contract for an indefinite period of time.

B. Formalities

155. There are no formal requirements for the creation of an employment contract for an indefinite period of time. This contract can therefore be concluded by mere (oral) agreement of will between the employer and the employee. In practice, most contracts will be made in writing in order to create legal certainty and evidence of what has been agreed between the parties.

---

110. Cass. 16 Oct. 1969, *TSR* 1969, 355.
111. Cass. 31 Oct. 1975, *Arr.Cass.* 1975, 287; Cass. 30 Sep. 1991, *JTT* 1991, 479, *TSR* 1991, 343 and *RW* 1991–92, 777.

C. Termination

156. If the contract is concluded for an indefinite period of time, each of the parties has the right to terminate it by giving notice to the other party (Article 37, §1, paragraph 1, Employment Contracts Act; Article 32, 3°, Employment Contracts Act). In the law on dismissals, the termination of this contract is subject to many conditions and safeguards, such as respecting a notice period or justifying the dismissal. Of course, the employment contract for an indefinite period can also be terminated in other ways than by notice or dismissal (cf. Article 32, Employment Contracts Act; cf. Article 35, Employment Contracts Act).

III. The Employment Contract for a Fixed Period

A. Concept

157. The duration of the fixed-term employment contract must be clearly agreed when it is concluded. Either a duration or an end date is stipulated. One could also indicate a fixed event in the future that will result at the end of the contract. According to the Court of Cassation, a fixed-term employment contract necessarily presupposes that the contract mentions a specific day or an event which must occur at a specific time, after which the parties are released from their mutual obligations.[112]

158. It is clear from the Employment Contracts Act that one can enter into two types of fixed-term employment contracts:

- for a specified period;
- or for a clearly defined work (Article 7, Employment Contracts Act).

Stimulated by the European Union legislator, the Act of 5 June 2002 on the principle of non-discrimination in favour of fixed-term workers was adopted.[113] In Article 2, 2°, the Act defines a fixed-term employment contract as an employment contract, the end of which is determined by objective conditions such as the attainment of a specific date or the completion of a clearly defined task.

B. Formalities

159. Unlike the employment contract for an indefinite period of time, the conclusion of the employment contract for a fixed period is subject to strict formal requirements (Article 9, Employment Contracts Act):

(1) the agreement must be in writing;

112. Cass. 15 Apr. 1982, *JTT* 1982, 348, note M. Taquet and C. Wantiez.
113. *Belgian Official Gazette* 26 Jun. 2002.

(2) the document must be drawn up separately for each employee;
(3) the employment contract must be in writing before, or at the latest at the time when, performance of the contract begins.

This rule does not prevent the conclusion of a fixed-term employment contract without interruption following an already existing fixed-term employment contract with the same employer, as long as the second contract is not executed before its expiry date.[114] The fixed-term employment contract can therefore be concluded while a first employment contract is still in effect,[115] unless the employer wishes to avoid the mandatory provisions of the law by doing so.[116]

Furthermore, failure to comply with one of these rules does not render the employment contract null and void. It then automatically becomes an employment contract for an indefinite period of time (Article 9, paragraph 2, Employment Contracts Act).

C. Special Provisions

160. The Act of 5 June 2002 introduces a principle of equal treatment. It provides that, with respect to employment conditions, fixed-term employees may not be treated less favourably than comparable 'permanent' employees solely on the grounds that they are employed for a fixed term. An exception can only be made if the difference in treatment is justified by objective reasons (Article 4(1) of the Act of 5 June 2002). Where appropriate, their rights may be determined in proportion to their working time (Article 4(2) of the Act of 5 June 2002). The determination of seniority with regard to certain working conditions shall be made for fixed-term employees by the same criteria as for permanent employees, except when different periods of seniority are justified on objective grounds (Article 4, paragraph 3, Act of 5 June 2002).

161. The Act also provides that employers must inform fixed-term employees of vacancies in the undertaking to ensure that they have the same opportunity to secure permanent positions as other employees (Article 5(1) of the Act of 5 June 2002). This information may be provided by means of a general announcement in an appropriate place in the undertaking or establishment (Article 5, paragraph 2, Act of 5 June 2002).

D. Termination

162. The fixed-term employment contract ends automatically when the term expires (Article 32, Employment Contracts Act).

114. Cass. 17 May 1978, *RW* 1978–79, 903.
115. Cass. 22 Nov. 1979, *JTT* 1980, 75; Cass. 5 Nov. 1979, *JTT* 1980, 75.
116. Cass. Feb. 18, 1980, *TSR* 1980, 247.

163. If, after the expiry of the term, the parties continue to perform the contract, the same conditions apply to this contract as to an employment contract for an indefinite period (Article 11, Employment Contracts Act).

164. As a general rule, it is not possible to unilaterally terminate a fixed-term employment contract prematurely, except in case of an urgent reason (cf. Article 35, Employment Contracts Act). However, two important nuances need to be made here. First, since the Act of 26 December 2013 introduced a Unified Status, it is explicitly possible to terminate a fixed-term employment contract. Article 15 of the Unified Status Act added a new paragraph to Article 40 of the Employment Contracts Act. This allows each party to terminate the contract concluded for a fixed term or for a clearly defined work before its expiry without urgent cause during the first half of the agreed term and without allowing the period of notice to exceed six months, provided that the specific notice periods set out in Article 37/2 are observed (Article 40, §2, Employment Contracts Act).

Second, it is accepted that a party can 'breach' the fixed-term employment contract, in which case a (fixed) indemnity is due. If the contract is concluded for a definite period of time or for a clearly defined task, the party who terminates the contract without urgent cause before the expiry of the term is obliged to pay the other party an indemnity equal to the amount of the salary due until the expiry of the term, but not exceeding twice the amount of the salary corresponding to the duration of the notice period which should have been observed if the contract had been concluded without a time limit (Article 40, §1, Employment Contracts Act). A party who terminates the contract before its expiry, during the first half of the agreed term of the contract and without exceeding the period of six months, without urgent cause and without observing the notice period provided for in the first paragraph, shall be liable to pay the other party compensation equal to the remuneration corresponding either to the duration of the notice period provided for in the first paragraph or to the remaining part of that period (Article 40(2)(4) of the Law on Employment Contracts).

E. *Successive Contracts*

165. Successive employment contracts for a fixed term, without an interruption attributable to the employee, are only possible to a limited extent.

166. Successive employment contracts are considered to be (or become) employment contracts for an indefinite period of time, unless the employer can prove that these contracts are justified by the nature of the work or by other legal reasons (Article 10, Employment Contracts Act). Article 10 of the Employment Contracts Act establishes a legal presumption in favour of the employee, which can only be invoked by him.[117]

---

117. Cass. 2 Dec. 2002, *JTT 2003, 404,* Soc.Kron. *2003 (abridged), 167 and* RW *2003-01 (abridged), 183.*

167. The fact that the employer always needs a justification to conclude a successive employment contract with the same employee is a factor of uncertainty. The Act of 13 February 1998 therefore relaxed the possibility of concluding successive fixed-term employment contracts. Successive employment contracts for a fixed period can be concluded without additional formalities, but with a number of restrictions that can be referred to as the '4-3-2' rule:

- a maximum of four consecutive fixed-term employment contracts may be concluded;
- the duration of these contracts may not be less than three months at a time;
- the total duration of successive contracts may not exceed two years (Article 10bis, §2, Employment Contracts Act).

168. Even greater flexibility is possible with the prior consent of the Labour Inspectorate of the locality in which the business is established:

- more than four successive employment contracts for a fixed period can be concluded;
- however, the duration must be at least six months at a time;
- the total duration of successive contracts may not exceed three years (Article 10bis, §3, Employment Contracts Act).

169. The flexible regime, introduced by the Law of 13 February 1998, is only foreseen for fixed-term employment contracts and not for employment contracts for clearly defined work.

IV. The Replacement Agreement

170. A special type of contract is the replacement contract. This contract is concluded to replace an employee whose performance of the contract has been suspended, in other words to replace an absent employee.

171. An employee who replaces another employee may be hired under conditions that derogate as regards the duration of the contract and the notice period (Article 11ter, §1, Employment Contracts Act). However, the replacement must be for a person whose employment contract has been suspended for a reason other than lack of work for economic reasons, bad weather, a strike or a lockout (Article 11ter, §1, Employment Contracts Act).

172. This contract is somewhat in between the fixed-term contract and the indefinite contract. The duration is in fact uncertain. In deviation from the normally applicable notice periods, the replacement contract can be terminated when the replaced employee returns, with or without observance of a notice period. The intention of the replacement agreement is therefore that it lasts as long as the replaced employee is absent. However, the law stipulates that the duration of the replacement contract may not exceed two years (section 11b, §1, subsection 3, Employment Contracts Act).

173. The employment contract for replacement can also be terminated unilaterally before the replaced employee returns. In that case, however, the provisions that apply to the termination of an employment contract for an indefinite period of time apply. Therefore, the formalities and deadlines that apply to an open-ended employment contract must be respected.[118]

§4. Types of Employment Contracts According to Working Time

174. As regards the extent of working time, a distinction can be made between the employment contract concluded for full-time work and the employment contract concluded for part-time work.

I. Full-Time Employment

175. Full-time employment is still considered the most regular form of employment in Belgium. In principle, part-time work is understood as a percentage or fraction of full-time work. Full-time work is referred to in reference to the applicable working time in a normal average working week. The (full-time) weekly working hours are, however, not the same in every sector. For the legal full-time working week, reference has to be made to the Act of 10 August 2001 on the reconciliation of work and quality of life, in which the weekly limit for working time is set at thirty-eight hours.[119] This thirty-eight-hour week is seen as the general and average weekly working time limit. However, this can be departed from by collective agreement, and many sectors and companies have different working time regimes.

II. Part-Time Work

A. Sources

176. Part-time employment is regulated by several sources. The main provisions can be found in the Employment Contracts Act of 3 July 1978 (Article 11bis); the Labour Act of 16 March 1971; the Act of 5 March 2002 on the principle of non-discrimination in favour of part-time workers, as well as CA no. 35 of 27 February 1981 concerning certain provisions on part-time work.

---

118. Cass. 19 Jun. 1989, *JTT* 1989, 330, *Soc.Kron.* 1989, 339, *TSR* 1989, 347, *Pas.* 1989, I, 1149 and *Arr.Cass.* 1988–89, 1257.

119. Art. 2, §1 and §2 Act of 10 Aug. 2001 concerning the reconciliation of employment and quality of life, *Belgian Official Gazette* 15 Sep. 2001.

B. Concept

177. Part-time work is defined as work which is regularly and voluntarily performed for a shorter period than the normal period.[120] The normal period of work is then the working time of a full-time employee (Article 2 Act of 5 March 2002). The reference point is the normal working time in the enterprise or, where appropriate, in the sector (Article 3 of the Act of 5 March 2002).

C. Limits

178. For part-time work, there is primarily a minimum limit. The upper limit is full-time employment. But a one-third rule and a three-hour rule must be taken into account.

179. The weekly working time of the part-time employee may not be less than one-third of the weekly working time of the full-time employees who belong to the same category in the enterprise. In the absence of full-time employees who belong to the same category in the enterprise, the working time that applies in the same sector of activity must be observed (Article 11bis, paragraph 5, Employment Contracts Act). Furthermore, the duration of each working period may not be less than three hours (Article 21, paragraph 1 Labour Code). This rule applies to both full-time and part-time employees. However, it is particularly relevant for part-time employees. As a result, the work schedule of a part-time employee may not be shorter than three hours per day.

180. It must be noted that, under specific conditions, derogations from these 'minimum limits' may be granted in certain sectors or branches of activity or for specific categories of workers or works to which this limit cannot be applied (Article 11bis, paragraph 6, Employment Contracts Act).[121] This may be on the initiative of the government or of the social partners.

181. If the employment contract provides for a work schedule that is lower than what is prescribed by or pursuant to the applicable rules, the employer must pay a salary that is calculated on the basis of the minimum limit (Article 11bis, Employment Contracts Act).

---

120. *See* comments to Art. 1 CA no. 35.
121. *See* the Royal Decree concerning the derogations to the minimum weekly working time of part-time employees established by Art. 11bis of the Act of 3 Jul. 1978 on employment contracts, *Belgian Official Gazette* 30 Dec. 1992.

D. Formalities

182. The employment contract concluded for part-time work must:

- for each employee individually;
- be established in writing;
- at the latest at the time when the employee starts to perform his contract (Article 11bis, paragraph 1, Employment Contracts Act).

183. The document (the employment contract or an appendix) must state the agreed part-time working arrangements and work schedule (Article 11bis, paragraph 2, Employment Contracts Act).

E. Work Schedules

184. Part-time work may be organised according to a fixed or a variable work schedule (Article 11bis, paragraph 3. Employment Contracts Act).

185. In the case of a fixed work schedule, there is a fixed pattern in which the same working hours are always used, on either a daily or weekly basis, or over a longer cycle. By cycle is to be understood the succession of daily work schedules in a fixed order as determined by the employment regulations (Article 158, paragraph 2 Programme Law of 22 December 1989). This may therefore involve a fixed cycle over a period longer than one week, in which the pattern of working hours may vary from week to week, but in which the same pattern is repeated over a longer period. If the cycle is spread over more than one week, it must be possible to determine at any time when the cycle begins (Article 158, paragraph 1, Programme Law of 22 December 1989).

186. In the case of a variable work schedule, the basic weekly working time is set, but without specifying the days and/or hours of the work schedule in advance (Article 3, paragraph 1, CA no. 35). In that case, the employee must be informed in advance of his daily work commitments (Article 3, paragraph 2, CA no. 35 and Article 159 Programme Law of 22 December 1989). CA no. 35 provides that the advance notification procedure shall be determined by a collective agreement concluded within the competent joint committee (Article 3, paragraph 3, CA no. 35) and that, in the absence of such an agreement, the employee shall be informed of his schedule at least five working days in advance (Article 3, paragraph 4, CA no. 35). The Workable and Agile Work Act of 5 March 2017 slightly restated this principle. Notification of individual work schedules to the employee(s) concerned must be given to part-time employees at least five working days in advance in a reliable, appropriate and accessible manner. The period of five working days may be modified by a collective agreement declared generally binding by Royal Decree, but may not be less than one working day.[122]

187. The use of variable work schedules is a typical form of (internal) flexibility in the Belgian system. When a variable work schedule is applied, the weekly working hours must be observed on average[123] over a period of maximum one-quarter (i.e., a period of thirteen weeks). A collective agreement concluded in the joint committee or, failing that, the work regulations, can extend this period to a maximum of one year. It can also be extended by Royal Decree for employees and employers who are not subject to the Collective Agreements Act of 5 December 1968 (Article 11bis, paragraph 3, Employment Contracts Act).

188. For part-time work schedules, the work regulations are relevant (for a discussion of work regulations, *see* elsewhere in this monograph). The work regulations must state the start and end of the normal working day, the time and duration of the rest periods and the days of regular breaks.[124] Since the Workable Work Act, this no longer needs to be included separately for each (part-time) employment arrangement.[125]

F. Overtime Work

189. A part-time employee who works more than the agreed number of hours is not yet performing overtime within the meaning of the Labour Code of 16 March 1971. As a general rule, overtime according to that law is only work performed in excess of nine hours per day or forty hours per week (Article 29 Labour Code). However, account should be taken of CA no. 35, which defines 'additional hours' as hours which exceed the conventional working time of part-time employees without exceeding the normal working time laid down by law or collective agreement (Article 5, paragraph 2, CA no. 35). CA no. 35 leaves it to the joint committees to clarify under what conditions and to what extent additional hours may be worked (Article 5, paragraph 1, CA no. 35). Also, the King (i.e., the government) may equal some services of part-time employees, falling below the general limits of working time, with overtime (Article 29, §3 Labour Code).[126]

---

122. Art. 6, §1, 1°, para. 3, Act of 8 Apr. 1965 on labour regulations, *Belgian Official Gazette* 5 May 1965, inserted by Art. 56 of the Act of 5 Mar. 2017 on workable and agile work, *Belgian Official Gazette* 15 Mar. 2017.
123. That is, calculated in accordance with the provisions laid down in Art. 26bis, §1, para. 8 of the Labour Code.
124. Art. 6, §1, 1°, para. 1, Act of 8 Apr. 1965 concerning labour regulations, *Belgian Official Gazette* 5 May 1965.
125. Art. 56 Act of 5 Mar. 2017 on workable and agile work, *Belgian Official Gazette* 15 Mar. 2017.
126. *See* Royal Decree of 25 Jun. 1990 assimilating certain services of part-time employees to overtime, *Belgian Official Gazette* 30 Jun. 1990.

G. Equal Treatment

190. The principle of equal treatment between full-time and part-time workers is enshrined in several sources of law. The principle is based on a European directive.[127] In particular, with a view to the further realisation of this principle, the Act of 5 March 2002 on the principle of non-discrimination in favour of part-time workers was enacted. It provides that, in respect of employment conditions, part-time workers may not be treated in a less favourable manner than full-time workers in a comparable situation simply because they work part-time, unless the difference in treatment is justified by objective reasons. This law adds that, where appropriate, the rights of part-time workers may be determined in relation to their working time (*pro rata temporis*). Furthermore, according to this law, access to certain working conditions may be made conditional on a certain period of service, working time or remuneration, if this is justified on objective grounds (Article 4 of the Act of 5 March 2002).

191. The principle is also laid down in a similar way in CA no. 35 (Article 1bis CA no. 35). This CA lays down more detailed provisions on the pay of a part-time employee. A part-time employee must receive the same proportional remuneration as a full-time employee for equal work or work of equal value, regardless of the way in which the remuneration is paid (Article 9, paragraph 1, CA no. 35). All components of remuneration of the full-time employee must be applied to the part-time employee in proportion to his or her working time in the undertaking, according to the same standards, the same pay scales and the same award criteria, provided that he or she is employed under similar conditions and belongs to the same category of employees (Article 9, paragraph 2, CA no. 35).

192. Furthermore, the part-time employee is entitled to an average minimum monthly income which, in proportion to his/her working time in the company, is calculated proportionally to the average minimum monthly income of full-time employee, as it has been established in the collective agreement concluded within the competent joint committee or, failing that, within the NLC (Article 10 CA no. 35).

H. Priority to Full-Time Work

193. Upon request, a part-time employee must have priority to obtaining a full-time job that has become vacant, for which he may be eligible in so far as he meets the required qualifications (Article 4, paragraph 1, CA no. 35). A part-time employee who is interested in a full-time job must inform the employer or his employee's representative, who has the task of informing the interested employee of any vacant full-time job (Article 4, paragraph 2, CA no. 35; Articles 153–156 Programme Law of 22 December 1989).

127. Directive 97/81/EC, 15 Dec. 1997 concerning the Framework Agreement on part-time work concluded by UNICE, CEEP and the ETUC.

I. Equal Treatment

194. To prevent abuses and with a view to facilitating control, the necessary publicity must be given to the work schedule and the services of a part-time employee. A copy of the employment contract with the part-time employee signed by both parties showing the identity of the employee and the work schedule applicable to him must be kept in the place in the enterprise where the employment regulations can be consulted. There are also the obligations in the labour regulations and the advance 'posting' of the variable work schedule (Articles 157–159 Programme Law 22 December 1989).

§5. Triangular Employment Relationships

I. General

195. Temporary work and secondment of workers are well-known legal constructs in Belgian labour law. These forms of work create triangular employment relationships.

196. The main source is the Act of 24 July 1987 on temporary work, temporary agency work and the supply of workers to users. Reference should also be made to CA no. 108 concluded in the NLC.

197. The legislator has been fairly cautious when it comes to triangular employment relationships. Pursuant to Article 31, §1 of the Act of 24 July 1987, it is in principle forbidden, as an employer, to make employees who have been hired available to third parties who then use these employees and exercise over them any part of the authority that is normally vested in the employer. The law formulates two exceptions to this: temporary work on the one hand and authorised secondment of workers (putting workers at the disposal of a user) on the other hand.

198. Another concern of the legislator is that temporary work and secondment are forms of 'labour mediation', whereby supply and demand on the labour market are mediated via intermediaries in a commercial manner (in return for payment). Consequently, triangular employment relationships, such as temporary work, must also be viewed in the light of the rules on employment intermediation. This matter falls within the competence of the regions instead of under federal labour law.

199. Both the provisions on temporary work and those on secondment of personnel have somewhat been redesigned over the years, with a legislative intervention by an Act of 12 August 2000, which authorised posting in a more flexible way. The programme legislator of 27 December 2012 tried to remedy abusive effects arising therefrom. Also, with regard to temporary work, there has been some legal development. First of all, the Belgian legislator wanted to transpose the obligations of the European Temporary Work Directive (Directive No. 2008/104/EC) with the Act of 9 July 2012. In addition, the legislator intervened since temporary work, originally aimed at accommodating peaks or the temporary replacement of employees, was in practice increasingly used as a recruitment channel (which went against the ratio and the text of the old legislation). With the introduction of the 'inflow' motive in the Act of 24 July 1987 (introduced by the Act of 26 June 2013[128]), this practice was recognised and given a legal foundation as of 1 September 2013. The implementation modalities of the Law of 24 July 1987, which in the meantime had been scattered among CA no. 36 and CA no. 58, were on this occasion regrouped in the new national CA no. 108 of 16 July 2013.

II. Temporary Work

A. *Concept*

200. A contract for temporary work is defined as a contract under which a temporary worker undertakes, in return for pay, to perform an approved form of temporary work for a user (Article 7, 2° of the Act of 24 July 1987).

201. There is a legal and irrebuttable presumption that the agreement organising temporary work is an employment contract (Article 8, paragraph 1 of the Act of 24 July 1987).

202. Temporary employment involves three parties.

(1) Temporary work agency: the company whose activity consists in hiring temporary workers in order to place them at the disposal of users with a view to carrying out permitted temporary work (Article 7, 1° Law of 24 July 1987).
(2) Temporary worker: an employee who undertakes through a temporary work contract to be put at the disposal of one or more users (Article 7, 3° Law of 24 July 1987).
(3) The user: the natural or legal person to whom, on the basis of an agreement with the temporary work agency, the temporary employee is posted for permitted temporary work and who exercises authority over this temporary employee that normally accrues to the employer.

203. In the case of temporary work, it is permitted that the employer (the temporary employment agency) delegates its authority to a user (Article 31, §1 of the Act of 24 July 1987).

128. Act 26 Jun. 2013 amending the Act of 24 Jul. 1987 on temporary work, temporary agency work and the provision of workers for users, as regards the contract of temporary work, *Belgian Official Gazette* 16 Jul. 1987, entry into force 1 Sep. 2013.

B. Permitted Temporary Work

204. Temporary workers may only be employed to perform 'permitted' temporary work. Temporary work agencies may only supply temporary workers to users in defined circumstances. Users may only employ temporary workers in the same circumstances (Article 21 of the Act of 24 July 1987). If these conditions are not met, the user and the temporary worker will be considered to be linked by a contract of employment for an indefinite period (Article 20, 2° Law 24 July 1987).

205. Temporary work is (only) allowed for the following purposes:

- replacing a permanent employee; or
- meeting a temporary increase in work; or
- ensuring the execution of an exceptional work (Article 1, §1 of the Act of 24 July 1987); or
- filling in a vacant position with a view to recruiting someone permanently (Article 1, 1bis of the Act of 24 July 1987). This form of temporary employment concerns the so-called inflow motive.

C. Inflow Motive

206. The 'inflow motive' is highly regulated and has to meet specific conditions set by the law. The aim of this motive should be using temporary workers with a view to later recruitment by the user of an employee for an indefinite period. The aim of the 'intake' motive is to give the user company an opportunity to become acquainted with the qualifications and skills of the temporary worker and to give the temporary worker an opportunity to become acquainted with the job and the user company's work environment.[129]

207. CA no. 108 lays down a specific rule to be observed: no more than three attempts are allowed for a maximum period of six months per (vacant) position, within a period that may not exceed a total of nine months (Article 26, §1 CA no. 108). A user is, however, not obliged to use the same temporary employment agency for each of the three attempts.

In this context, Article 9bis of the Act of 24 July 1987 obliges the user to inform the temporary work agency of the number of temporary workers previously supplied to (potentially) fill a certain vacancy. The temporary work agency must include this information in the temporary work contract. In this way, a temporary worker who is hired under the entry motive can verify how many candidates preceded him with a view to filling the vacancy in question.

129. Cf. commentary on Art. 24 CA no. 108; Bill of the Act of 8 Apr. 2013 amending the Act of 24 July 1987 on temporary work, and the provision of workers for the benefit of users, as regards the contract of temporary work, *Parl.* Chamber 2012–13, no. 53K2740/1, 29–30.

208. In principle, a user who permanently employs a temporary agency worker must do so on the basis of an employment contract for an indefinite period (Article 20b, paragraph 1 of the Act of 24 July 1987; Article 31 CA no. 108).

D. Prohibited Temporary Work

209. In the past, the employment of temporary workers was prohibited in certain sectors or for certain professional categories. However, these prohibitions have been gradually abolished. In practice, however, a limitation on the use of temporary agency work is sometimes provided for through collective agreements.

210. In some cases of temporary work, an agreement is necessary with the trade union delegation at the enterprise. Temporary workers may not be employed in the event of a refusal or lack of such agreement, which can be necessary in the event of the temporary replacement of an employee whose employment contract has been terminated and in case of a temporary increase in work (Article 19, paragraph 2, CA no. 108).

211. A temporary work agency may not assign temporary workers to do work for a user (or keep them at work there) in the event of a strike or lockout (Article 19, paragraph 1, CA no. 108).

E. Duration

212. In the case of temporary work, the approach of the law is that the work performed with the user is of a temporary nature. It is therefore assumed that the employment contract for temporary work is concluded for a fixed period of time, or for a clearly defined task, or to replace a permanent employee (Article 2 and 8, §1, paragraph 2 of the 24 July 1987 Act). The legislator has opened up the possibility to organise temporary work on the basis of a contract for an indefinite period (cf. Article 8ter Act of 24 July 1987), but this requires strict conditions and needs further detailed measures to be taken through collective agreements in the joint committee for temporary work.

213. In the context of temporary work, however, successive fixed-term contracts of employment may be concluded with the same employee. In such case, the parties are not deemed to have entered into a contract for an indefinite period of time (Articles 3 and 8, §1, paragraph 2 of the Act of 24 July 1987). Furthermore, unless otherwise agreed, the first three working days are regarded as a probationary period. Until the expiry of this period, either party may terminate the contract without notice or compensation (Articles 5 and 8, §1, paragraph 2 of the Law of 24 July 1987).

214. The possibility to conclude successive fixed-term contracts has the potential of abusing temporary work and hinder job security of workers on the labour market. The legislator addressed the widespread use of so-called daily contracts, which only give a guarantee of temporary work for one day, but which may lead to a chain of daily contracts over a longer period with the same employee. The Act of 26 June 2013 inserted an Article 8bis in the Act of 24 July 1987 to regulate the use of successive daily contracts for temporary work. Successive daily contracts with the same user are (only) permitted if the user can demonstrate the need for flexibility for the use of such successive daily contracts. The user must demonstrate the need for flexibility if and insofar as the volume of work at the user is dependent on external factors or the volume of work fluctuates significantly or is linked to the nature of the assignment (Article 33, §3 CA no. 108).

It must be noted that not only daily contracts are used in temporary work but also (consecutive) weekly contracts are applied in practice. The legislator has, however, not specifically addressed the issue of other short-term contracts than 'daily contracts'.

F. Formalities

215. The law requires that two different writings be made with respect to the temporary employment contract.

216. First, an intention to conclude a temporary employment contract must be established in writing by both parties, for each temporary worker individually, no later than the time at which the temporary worker first enters into the service of the temporary employment agency. Second, the employment contract for temporary work must be concluded in writing at the latest at the time when the temporary worker commences his employment (Article 8, §2 of the Law of 24 July 1987). The first document, which records the intention to conclude a temporary employment contract, does not need to be renewed each time a temporary worker concludes a contract with the same temporary employment agency to perform temporary work for a user. The second document, the actual employment contract, is drawn up each time a temporary agency worker works for a user company. The applicable wage and employment conditions are then included in this document.

217. The law has a specific sanction. If the temporary employment contract has not been signed at the latest when the temporary worker starts working, the provisions of a permanent employment contract apply. However, this sanction does not apply if there is an electronic contract and a number of conditions are met (Article 8 of the Act of 24 July 1987).

G. Content of the Employment Contract

218. The temporary employment contract must state the name of the user, the reason, as well as, where appropriate, the duration of the contract and the reason for the replacement, the professional qualifications of the temporary worker, the place of work and working hours, the stipulated wages and allowances to which the temporary worker is entitled (Article 9 of the Act of 24 July 1987).

It is assumed that the absence of any mention of this in the document renders the contract null and void (Article 31, §1 and §2 of the Act of 24 July 1987), so that the user and the temporary worker are considered to be linked by a contract of employment for an indefinite period from the start of the performance of the work (Article 31, §3 of the Law of 24 July 1987).

A number of mandatory details are added to this by means of collective labour agreements (including those of the NLC and the temporary work sector).

219. Contractual clauses which would prohibit the temporary worker from committing himself directly to an employment with a user are regarded as null and void (Article 16 of the Act of 24 July 1987). This means that it is not possible to prohibit the temporary worker from transferring and directly contracting with the user. In practice, it regularly happens that temporary workers become employees of the user after their period of temporary work. Practice also learns that temporary work agencies ask for a compensation or a fee in case of such a transfer. According to the case law, a clause in the contract between the temporary work agency and the user whereby the user undertakes to pay a compensation or fee to the temporary employment agency if it engages the temporary worker before the end of a minimum period is possible and not considered contrary to the principle laid down in Article 16 of the Law of 24 July 1987.[130]

H. Wages and Conditions

220. Temporary agency work provides for a so-called pay-ratio rule. The law provides that the temporary worker's pay may not be lower than that to which he would have been entitled if he had been employed under the same conditions as a permanent worker by the user company (Article 10(1) of the Act of 24 July 1987).

This rule may, however, be deviated from if equivalent benefits are granted by a collective agreement concluded in the joint committee for temporary employment and declared generally binding by the government (Article 10, paragraph 2 of the Act of 24 July 1987).

221. As of 5 August 2012, the legislator brought the Act of 24 July 1987 into line with the European Temporary Work Directive (2008/104/EC).[131] The inserted Article 10bis stipulates that during the period in which the temporary worker works for the user company, he/she has the right, under the same conditions as the permanent workers of that user company, to access the company facilities or services present in the user company, such as canteens, childcare and transport facilities, unless the difference in treatment is justified by objective reasons.

130. Ghent 15 Feb. 2010, *DAOR* 2010, p. 96, 496, note A. Van Bever.

131. Act of 9 Jul. 2012 transposing Directive 2008/104/EC of the European Parliament and of the Council of 19 Nov. 2008 on temporary agency work, *Belgian Official Gazette* 26 Jul. 2012, *err. BS* 17 Aug. 2012.

222. In addition, the temporary work agency may be fully or partially exempted from the obligations relating to maintaining the normal wage, as provided for in the event of suspension of the implementation of the employment contract, insofar as a collective agreement concluded in the joint committee for temporary employment and declared universally binding by the government has imposed this obligation on the Social Security Fund for Temporary Employees (Article 11 of the Act of 24 July 1987).

223. Pursuant to the European Temporary Agency Work Directive (2008/104/EC),[132] the user is also responsible, for the period during which the temporary agency worker works for him, for applying the provisions on combating discrimination in general and equal treatment of men and women, maternity protection and protection of nursing mothers, as applicable at the place of work (Article 19, paragraph 2 of the Act of 24 July 1987). Finally, the user must inform temporary workers employed by him of any vacant posts in his company (Article 20bis of the Law of 24 July 1987).

I. Termination

224. The temporary work agreement ends automatically at the end of the term, or at the time at which the work described in advance is performed. In the case of a replacement employment contract, this may be terminated without notice upon the return of the employee who has been replaced.

225. The law regulates the situation of premature termination, a unilateral termination taking place before the predefined term. If the contract has been concluded for a definite period or for a clearly defined work, the party who terminates the contract unilaterally before the expiry of the term and without urgent cause is obliged to pay the other party an indemnity equal to the amount of the salary which remained due until the expiry of the term, but not exceeding twice the amount of the salary corresponding to the duration of the notice period which should have been observed if an employment contract without a time limit had been concluded (Article 14, paragraph 1 of the Act of 24 July 1987). If the contract was concluded in order to replace a permanent employee for a non-determined period, the temporary employment agency that unilaterally terminates the contract before the end of the replacement period without urgent reasons is obliged to pay the temporary employee compensation equal to the gross pay for three months (Article 15, paragraph 1 of the Act of 24 July 1987).

226. The above compensation is not payable if the employment contract is not fulfilled through the fault of the user until the period has expired, if the temporary work agency provides the temporary worker with an alternative job for the period

132. Act of 9 Jul. 2012 transposing Directive 2008/104/EC of the European Parliament and of the Council of 19 Nov. 2008 on temporary agency work, *Belgian Official Gazette* 26 Jul. 2012, *err. BS* 17 Aug. 2012.

still to run, guaranteeing him the same pay and equivalent working conditions (Article 14, paragraph 2 of the Law of 24 July 1987).

227. The temporary worker himself may terminate the contract, subject to seven days' notice, if he has entered into a (regular) employment relationship (Article 15, paragraph 2 of the Act of 24 July 1987).

J. Agency and User

228. The temporary employment agency concludes a contract with the user for the provision of a worker. In principle, this is a contract under civil law. In practice, it is often referred to as a 'service level agreement'. However, the Act of 24 July 1987 contains special rules concerning this agreement.

229. The contract between the temporary employment agency and the user must be made in writing within seven working days of the date on which the temporary worker starts work (Article 17, §1 of the 24 July 1987 Act). This agreement must also contain a number of statements (Article 17, §1 of the 24 July 1987 Act).

230. The temporary worker must receive written notification of the content of the agreement between the temporary agency and the user within two working days of the start of his employment (Article 17, §2 of the Law of 24 July 1987).

231. The temporary work agency remains the employer of the temporary worker. The agency must therefore observe all the obligations under employment law that normally apply to employers. This means, among other things, that the agency is responsible for paying the wages of the temporary employee.

232. The user has the temporary worker at his disposal and exercises authority over the temporary worker. The law has therefore imposed a number of obligations under employment law on the user. As long as a temporary worker works for him, part of the employer's obligations under social legislation rest with the user. Moreover, the temporary employment agency may only post temporary workers to users who undertake to comply with these obligations. In particular, the user is responsible for applying the provisions of the legislation on the regulation and protection of work in force at the place of work. During the period in which the temporary worker works for the user, the user is responsible for applying the provisions of the legislation on the regulation and protection of work that apply at the place of work (Article 19, paragraph 1 of the Act of 24 July 1987). These include provisions relating to: working hours, public holidays, Sunday rest, work by women, work by young people, night work, labour regulations, monitoring the performance of part-time workers, the health and safety of workers (Article 19, paragraph 2, Act of 24 July 1987). A separate royal decree regulates in particular the health and safety of temporary workers.[133]

233. Any user of temporary workers is obliged to refuse to provide the services of any temporary work agency that it knows is not complying with the obligations imposed by the law (Article 12b of the Act of 4 August 1996). For its part, each temporary work agency is required to refuse to post its temporary workers to a user of whom it has knowledge that the latter is failing to comply with his legal obligations (Article 12c Act of 4 August 1996).

234. For the application of legal provisions based on the number of employees employed by a company, the temporary workers supplied to a user are taken into account when calculating the staff employed by that user (Article 25, paragraph 1, Act of 24 July 1987). However, this does not apply to temporary workers who replace permanent employees (Article 25, paragraph 2, Act of 24 July 1987). The principle is important, among other things, for the establishment of a works council or a CPPW. The precise method of calculating the average for temporary workers employed by a user is laid down by more specific regulations (Article 25, paragraph 3 of the Law of 24 July 1987).

III. Secondment

A. Concept

235. In the case of secondment of workers, a triangular employment relationship is created in a very similar way as with temporary work. However, it does not concern temporary work. It is an other situation in which an employer hires out his employee to one or more third parties, who use the employee and exercise over him a part of the authority that normally belongs to the employer. In short, an employer hires out employees to a user.

236. Unlike temporary work, the activity of secondment is not in principle an ordinary activity of the employer's company in question. There are three actors:

(1) the employer: the enterprise that makes an employee available to a user;
(2) the seconded worker: the worker who undertakes to be put at the disposal of one or more users (Article 7, 3° of the Law of 24 July 1987);
(3) the user: the natural or legal person to whom a worker is seconded under a contract with the provider (employer) and who exercises over this posted worker authority which normally belongs to the employer.

---

133. Royal Decree of 15 Dec. 2010 establishing measures on the well-being at work of temporary agency workers, *Belgian Official Gazette* 28 Dec. 2010.

B. Prohibition

237. Pursuant to Article 31, §1 of the Act of 24 July 1987, it is in principle prohibited, as an employer, to hire out employees to third parties who use these employees and exercise over them any part of the authority normally vested in the employer. According to the Court of Cassation, this prohibition is of public order. Consequently, an agreement that violates this prohibition is absolutely null and void.[134]

238. The legislator has, nevertheless, provided for a number of exceptions. We will mainly discuss three of them, one of which, however, is not a real exception.

239. The first exception relates to consent. An employer may, in addition to his usual activity/activities, post his employees to a user for a limited period if he has obtained the prior consent of the social inspection officer (Article 32, §1 of the Act of 24 July 1987). The prior consent of the competent official may in principle only be granted following an agreement between the user and the trade union delegation representing the staff of the business or, where there is no such delegation, the employees' organisations represented on the joint committee to which the business belongs. In the event of disagreement by the trade union delegation, this agreement can be granted by the competent joint committee (Article 32, §3 of the Act of 24 July 1987).

240. A second exception concerns a specific situation. The law provides that prior consent is not required when a permanent employee, who appears to be linked to his employer by virtue of his original contract of employment, is exceptionally made available to a user: a) in the context of cooperation between the undertakings of the same economic and financial entity; or b) for the short-term execution of specialised tasks requiring specific professional skills[135] (Article 32, §1, paragraph 2 of the Act of 24 July 1987). In such cases, the user must inform the competent official of the social inspection at least twenty-four hours in advance (Article 32, §1, paragraph 3 of the Act of 24 July 1987).

241. A third exception is not a real exception, but rather a limitation of the prohibition of secondment. The prohibition to second employees only applies to the hiring out of an employee to a user with the delegation of authority. This means that a secondment without delegation of authority is not prohibited. In addition, the posting of self-employed employees is not subject to the prohibition either. Primarily with a view to making it more flexible, the legislator inserted a provision limiting the scope of the prohibition.[136] There are two main contexts, explained hereinafter.

---

134. Cass. 15 Feb. 2016, No. C.14.0448.F.

135. A collective labour agreement concluded within the National Labour Council can specify the concepts of short-term execution and specialised tasks requiring specific professional skills (Art. 32, §1, para. 2, Act of 24 Jul. 1978).

136. Introduced by Art. 181 Act of 12 Aug. 2000 containing social, budgetary and other provisions, *Belgian Official Gazette* 31 Aug. 2000.

242. First, the law stipulates that, for the application of the prohibition on secondment, compliance by the third party with the obligations imposed on him as regards well-being at work does not constitute the exercise of any part of the employer's authority (Article 31, §1, paragraph 2 of the Act of 24 July 1987).[137]

243. Second, the law provides that, for the application of the prohibition set out in Article 31, §1 of the Act of 24 July 1978, instructions given by the third party to the employees of the employer in execution of a written agreement between the third party and the employer do not constitute an exercise of any part of the authority of the employer, provided that this written agreement explicitly and in detail determines which instructions exactly can be given by the third party to the employees of the employer, that this right of instruction of the third party does not in any way undermine the authority of the employer and that the actual implementation of this agreement between the third party and the employer is fully in line with the explicit provisions of the aforementioned written agreement (Article 31, §1, paragraph 3 of the Act of 24 July 1987).[138] If, in accordance with the provisions of the paragraph 3 of Article 31, §1, an agreement is concluded between a third party and an employer stipulating the instructions which, in execution of that agreement, may be given by the third party to the employees of the employer, the third party shall inform its works council without delay. In the absence of a works council, the information referred to in this paragraph is provided to the CPPW and, failing that, to the members of the trade union delegation (Article 31, §1, paragraph 4 of the Act of 24 July 1987).[139]

244. This latter 'exception' is seen in practice as a high degree of flexibility, which makes many situations of secondment possible.

C. *Special Conditions*

245. The conditions and the duration of the secondment must be set out in a document signed by the user, the employer and the employee (Article 32, §2, paragraph 1 of the Act of 24 July 1987). However, the employee's written agreement is not required if tacit consent is customary in the sector where the employee is employed (Article 32, §2, paragraph 1 of the Act of 24 July 1987). The document must be drawn up before the start of the secondment (Article 32, §2, paragraph 2 of the Act of 24 July 1987).

246. The contract that binds the worker and his employer remains in force during the period of secondment; however, the user becomes jointly and severally liable for the payment of social security contributions, salaries, allowances and benefits arising therefrom (Article 32, §4, paragraph 1 of the Act of 24 July 1987). Under no circumstances may these wages, allowances and benefits be lower than those

137. Amended by Program Act 27 Dec. 2012, *Belgian Official Gazette* 31 Dec. 2012.
138. *Ibid.*
139. *Ibid.*

received by employees performing the same duties in the company of the user (Article 32, §4, paragraph 3 of the Act of 24 July 1987). As with temporary employment, a pay-ratio rule applies here too. Like in the case of temporary work, the user is also responsible for applying the provisions of the legislation on the regulation and protection of work applicable at the place of work (Article 32, §4, paragraph 2 of the Act of 24 July 1987).

247. For the enforcement of the legal provisions, penal provisions apply as well as civil sanctions.

248. A contract with secondment in contravention of the provision of the Act of 24 July 1987 is null and void from the beginning of the performance of the work for the latter (Article 31, §2 of the Act of 24 July 1987).[140] Where a user has work carried out by employees who have been made available to him in contravention of Article 31, §1 of the Act of 24 July 1987, the user and the employees are deemed to be linked by a contract of employment for an indefinite period from the start of the work (Article 31, §3, paragraph 1 of the Act of 24 July 1987). However, the employee(s) concerned may terminate the contract without notice or compensation. The user and the person who provides employees to the user in contravention of Article 31, §1 of the Law of 24 July 1987 are jointly and severally liable for the payment of social security contributions, wages, remuneration and benefits arising from the contract (Article 31, §4 of the Law of 24 July 1987).[141]

IV. (Sub)contracting

249. Contracting and subcontracting are legal concepts that are very similar to secondment when it comes to situations where products or services are carried out for a client using labour. However, they are related to civil law and, in principle, not to labour law. In practice, the undertakings may make personnel available to a user, without delegating any of the employer's authority to that user. This makes the situation different from a secondment, whereby the authority of the employer is transferred to the user. In the event of (sub)contracting, the employees of the (sub)contractor continue to work under the authority of their own employer. They will perform work(s) for a client of their employer, but without working under the authority of the principal.

250. With (sub)contracting, employees of different companies may be present at the same workplace. In such cases, the employers of such workers must cooperate in the implementation of occupational safety and health measures and coordinate their action accordingly. This follows from the well-being legislation in labour law (Article 7 of the Act on Wellbeing of Workers of 4 August 1996).

---

140. *See also* Cass. 8 Oct. 2018, AR S.14.0006.N-S.14.0059.N/1.
141. *Ibid.*

§6. FORMATION OF THE EMPLOYMENT RELATIONSHIP

I. Validity Conditions

A. Competence

251. In the Belgian system, from the age of 18 years old, an individual has full legal capacity. A minor (until 18 years old) thus has limited capacity with regard to entering into an employment contract. The rule is that minors may conclude an employment contract only with the express or tacit authorisation of their father, mother or guardian. If the authorisation is refused, it can be granted by the juvenile court at the request of the public prosecutor's office or a family member (Article 43 Employment Contracts Act of 3 July 1978).

252. The lack of authorisation of the parent or guardian only gives rise to the relative nullity of the employment contract. This nullity can therefore only be invoked by the minor or his legal representative.[142]

253. When employing minors, the prohibition of child labour will play a role. Some exceptions are allowed under strict conditions, and the protective provisions regarding the employment of young workers must be taken into account (cf. Articles 6–10*bis* and 30–34*ter* Labour Code of 16 March 1971). With regard to child labour, children are understood to be minors under the age of 15 or minors who are still subject to full-time compulsory education (Article 6 Labour Code 16 March 1971).

254. Any spouse has the right to engage in an occupation without the consent of the other spouse. However, if the other spouse considers that this would be seriously detrimental to his or her moral or material interests or to those of his or her minor children, he or she has the right to appeal to the Court of First Instance and, in urgent cases, to the president of that court (Article 216 Old Civil Code).

B. Consent

255. Article 1108 of the Old Civil Code provides that agreements, in order to be valid, require the consent of each of the parties. This also applies to employment contracts.

256. No consent is valid if it is given by mistake, under coercion or obtained by fraud (section 1109 of the Old Civil Code). Article 1110 of the Old Civil Code also refers to error of will. A mistake in the misrepresentation on the part of a contracting party with respect to one of the elements of the contract may lead to the nullity of the contract, at least if it occurs at the time of the conclusion of the contract and

142. Labour Court Liege 1 June 1984, *TSR* 1984, 396.

concerns a core element of the contract itself. It should be noted that the fact that consent is given by an economically weak person does not in itself constitute a legal problem of valid consent.[143]

C. *Valid Object and Cause*

257. The object of every contract is something that a party undertakes to give, or that a party undertakes to do or not to do (Article 1126 of the Old Civil Code). For the employee, the object of the employment contract is to perform the work about which the parties have an agreement; for the employer, the obligation is the provision of the work and the payment of wages.

258. The cause of the contract is the purpose for which the contract is concluded. An obligation entered into without cause, or with false cause, or with unlawful cause, cannot have any effect under civil law (Article 1131 of the Old Civil Code). A cause is unlawful if it is prohibited by law, or if it is contrary to morality or public order (Article 1133 of the Old Civil Code).

D. *Consequences of Nullity in Employment Contracts*

259. A specific provision has been enacted to regulate the consequences of nullity in employment contract law. It is provided that the nullity of the contract cannot be invoked in respect of the rights arising for the employee under the Employment Contracts Act when work is performed:

- pursuant to a contract, on the ground that it infringes the provisions which govern employment relations;
- in gambling rooms (Article 14, Employment Contracts Act).

A similar provision appears in the Act of 12 April 1965 on the protection of wages (Article 47 Act 12 April 1965).

II. Recruitment and Selection

A. *Concept*

260. Recruitment and selection are part of the pre-contractual phase in the conclusion of the employment contract. This is the phase which covers all the activities and negotiations carried out between two parties with a view to concluding an employment contract.

---

143. Cass. 2 May 1969, *Pas.* 1969, I, 781.

261. Recruitment and selection are often mentioned in one breath. Yet they are different activities in human resources management. National CA no. 38, the most important source of law on recruitment and selection, defines recruitment as 'all the activities carried out by or on behalf of the employer with regard to advertising a vacancy' (Article 2, paragraph 4 CA no. 38). As for the concept of selection, CA no. 38 defines this as 'the totality of the distinct steps carried out by or on behalf of the employer, with a view to recruiting staff' (Article 2, paragraph 5, CA no. 38).

262. The person who goes through the recruitment and selection process is referred to as a job applicant or candidate employee. CA no. 38 defines the job applicant as 'the natural person who applies for a job in response to an offer of employment with the aim of being hired for the offered position' (Article 2, paragraph 3, CA no. 38). Applying for a job should be seen in a broader context than simply applying for an existing job. It is obvious that employment contracts are also concluded as a result of an unsolicited application, or through channels other than job offers. In principle, CA no. 38 can be considered to apply when a job applicant aims to be considered for a recruitment decision.

B. Obligations

263. CA no. 38 is a source of law which explicitly regulates the activities of recruitment and selection. However, not all the provisions of this collective agreement are enforceable in the same way.

264. Legally, CA no. 38 is divided into two parts. CA no. 38 was concluded in the NLC. Articles 1 to 6 (which is Chapter III relating to employer obligations in connection with recruitment and selection) and Article 19 were declared universally binding.[144] As a consequence, these are legally enforceable obligations. On the contrary, Chapter IV 'only' contains recommendations or standards of behaviour. They may, nevertheless, function as interpretative guidelines of other legal norms and, in this way, they could be enforced through a general duty of care resulting from Article 1382 or 1134(3) of the Old Civil Code.

265. Employment discrimination law is discussed elsewhere in this monograph. However, also CAO no. 38 includes a non-discrimination provision. The employer is held to be obliged to respect the principle of equal treatment for job applicants, as laid down in CA no. 95 of 10 October 2008 which concerns specifically equal treatment of employees during all phases of the employment relationship.

266. CA no. 38 provides that costs of examinations and tests, carried out as part of a selection procedure, shall be borne by the employer (Article 3 CA no. 38). The purpose of this article is to prevent applicants from having to pay for tests and examinations themselves while carried out as part of the selection procedure.

144. Royal Decree 11 Jul. 1984, *Belgian Official Gazette* 28 Jul. 1984.

267. If an applicant, who benefits from unemployment insurance benefits, takes part in a selection test, the employer is obliged, at the applicant's request, to provide proof of the date and time of the candidate's participation and, where applicable, the reason why he has not been hired (Article 4 CA no. 38).

268. It may happen that the applicant sends the employer certain documents in support of his application together with his letter of application, for which he has incurred a number of costs, such as, copies of diplomas, certificates, publications, references, photographs and the like. If the applicant is rejected, the employer must keep these documents available for a reasonable period of time, as they may be useful to the applicant in subsequent applications (Article 5 and Commentary on Article 5 of Collective Labour Agreement no. 38).

269. The employer may not ask applicants to produce certified copies of diplomas, certificates, attestations and other documents. However, employers may ask applicants to provide a legible copy of the original document. In the event of doubt as to the veracity of the copy submitted or sent, the employer may ask the applicant to produce the original document (Article 6 CA no. 38).

C. Recommendations

270. As referred to above, CA no. 38 includes a number of recommendations or rules of good conduct. Under this section, the following principles are mentioned.

271. The employer must provide applicants with sufficient information regarding the job offered (Article 8, paragraph 1, CA no. 38).

272. The job advertisement must contain the following information: the nature of the job; the requirements for carrying out the job; the place where the job is to be performed, unless this cannot be established beforehand or if it concerns jobs that are not tied to a specific place of employment; where appropriate, the intention to establish a recruitment reserve; the manner in which applications can be made (Article 8, paragraph 2, CA no. 38). The information is designed to allow the applicant to receive the necessary information to form a picture of the offered position and to be able to make a decision responsibly (commentary on Article 8 CA no. 38).

273. The selection procedure must be conducted within a reasonable period of time (Article 15 CA no. 38). Applicants who meet the job requirements specified in the job offer, but whose application is not accepted, shall be informed in writing by the employer within a reasonable period of the decision taken with regard to them (Article 9 CA no. 38). This provision is of course open to interpretation.

274. If the selection procedure includes a productive practical test, this test may not last longer than is necessary to test the applicant's ability (Article 16 CA no. 38).

275. CA no. 38 stipulates that the applicant's privacy must be respected during the selection procedure. This implies that questions regarding the candidate's private life are only justified if they are relevant due to the nature and conditions of performance of the vacant position (Article 11 CA no. 38). This applies not only to the employer but also to the persons who participate in the selection work on his behalf, such as psychologists and doctors (commentary on Article 11 CA no. 38). The right to privacy is also contained in other sources of law, including Article 22 of the Constitution. Also, the 2016 European General Data Protection Regulation (GDPR) will be applicable to most recruitment and selection procedures. The GDPR is directly applicable and enforceable in the Belgian legal system.

276. In accordance with CA no. 38, the applicant is required to participate in good faith in the selection procedure. This includes that the applicant provides all necessary information on professional and educational history, in so far as this relates to the nature and conditions of performance of the vacant position (Article 13 CA no. 38). This can be linked to the civil law obligations concerning contractual negotiations, according to which the person entitled to information must be informed of all elements that a normal person in the same circumstances would consider important.

277. The offering of fictitious jobs for advertising reasons is expressly prohibited (Article 18 CA no. 38). When announcing a job offer, it must be clear that a job offer is actually made and available (commentary on Article 18 CA no. 38).

D. Medical Examinations

278. Medical examinations are often carried out in the context of recruitment. Given the sensitivity of these examinations in terms of personal integrity, privacy and possible discrimination, medical examinations are subject to strict conditions and regulations.

279. First of all, there is the Act of 28 January 2003 on medical examinations.[145] This act provides that biological tests, medical examinations or oral information gathering with a view to obtaining medical information about the state of health or pedigree of an employee or candidate employee may not be performed for reasons other than those related to the employee's current fitness for and the specific characteristics of the open position (Article 3, §1, paragraph 1, Medical Examination Act). The main purpose of this law is to regulate a number of specific medical examinations. It seeks to ban predictive genetic testing or HIV testing[146] and to avoid that occupational medicine would too easily lead to HIV testing.[147]

145. Act of 28 Jan. 2003 on medical examinations carried out within the framework of employment relationships, *Belgian Official Gazette* 9 Apr. 2003.
146. *Parl.*Senate BZ 1999, no. 2-20/1, 2.
147. *Parl.*Senate BZ 1999, no. 2-20/1, 3 (referring to occupational medicine).

280. The regulation of medical examinations of employees cannot be dissociated from the principles of occupational medicine. These principles are based on the Wellbeing of Workers Act of 4 August 1996 and Wellbeing Codex which contains more specific and detailed provisions.

281. Occupational medicine has essentially a preventive task. The following objectives apply to the health surveillance of employees and candidate employees:

- promote and maintain the health of workers by preventing risks;
- promote employment opportunities for all, in particular by proposing suitable working methods to the employer, suggesting adaptations to the workplace and looking for suitable work, including for employees with a reduced capacity to work;
- avoid employing workers in tasks which, owing to their state of health, they would not normally be able to carry out.

282. In principle, the employer only subjects employees (or prospective employees) to an occupational health examination if they occupy a safety position or a position involving specific risks (cf. Article I.4-3.-§1 and I.4-25 Wellbeing Codex). The health assessment of a candidate employee can take place before the employment contract is concluded, but only insofar as this health assessment is the last step in the recruitment and selection procedure and if the employment contract, subject to the decision of the prevention advisor occupational physician, would be effectively concluded. The health surveillance makes it possible to determine the unfitness of the employee, given the job-related characteristics.

E. Prohibition of Discrimination

283. The ban on discrimination is not only important in recruitment and selection. The prohibition of discrimination also plays a role in determining terms and conditions of employment or in the termination of an employment contract. For this reason, the equal treatment legislation will be dealt with under a separate heading in this monograph.

F. Employment Services

284. In the context of the conclusion of an employment contract, it is also important to consider the role of employment (intermediation) services and private employment agencies. This plays a role not only in forming employment relationships but also, more generally, in the functioning of the labour market.

285. Employment services are traditionally a public service. In the federal context of Belgium, the issue is a regional matter. Each region has its employment service body, offering employment mediation services as a public service. However, there is also private employment mediation and, thus, many private employment agencies are active. The recognition of this private employment mediation services has, however, only come step by step. It accelerated when, in 1997, a new Convention was adopted in the ILO framework, namely Convention 181 on private employment agencies.

286. An important principle in labour mediation is the prohibition of payment by the employee. In the Flemish Region, the Decree of 10 December 2010 stipulates that the employment agency can under no circumstances request or receive any remuneration from the employee (Article 5, 9° Decree 10 December 2010). This principle is also upheld in the Law of 24 July 1987 with regard to temporary work. Under no circumstances may a financial contribution be demanded from the temporary agency worker, either directly or indirectly (Article 24, paragraph 2 of the Act of 24 July 1987).

§7. Proof of Employment Contract

287. The conclusion of an employment contract does not, in principle, require that the contract be in writing. However, the existence and the contents of an employment contract are easier to prove when the contract is concluded in writing. In the absence of a written document, witness evidence is allowed, regardless of the value of the dispute (Article 12, Employment Contracts Act).

288. An originally written employment contract can subsequently be amended by an oral agreement.[148] The content of the orally amended employment contract can be proven by witnesses or presumptions, even if the original employment contract was established in writing.[149]

289. For certain employment contracts or certain clauses to be valid, a written document is required. A written document is required, for example, for the conclusion of an employment contract for a definite period of time. Clauses, such as the non-competition clause (about which more below), should also be agreed upon in writing.

---

148. Cass. 4 May 1987, *RW* 1987-88, 477, *Soc.Kron.* 1987, 272, *JTT* 1987, 406, *TSR* 1987, 305, *Arr-.Cass.* 1986-87, 1157 and *Pas.* 1987, I, 1021.
149. Cass. 28 May 1979, *RW* 1979-80, 1186 and 2113.

Chapter 2. Rights and Obligations of the Parties

§1. General

290. The rights and obligations of the parties to the employment contract are regulated in a multitude of sources. Based on the principle of freedom of contract, the employer and employee are free to determine their mutual rights and obligations. Section 1134 of Old the Civil Code applies, so that the contract becomes the law of the parties and for the parties.

291. Nevertheless, contractual freedom is limited in labour law. In this field, there are many statutory provisions of mandatory law. These are generally intended to provide the employee with (minimum) protection and to structure employment relations. Moreover, there are also many collective agreements (concluded at national, sectoral or company level) which regulate employment conditions. In principle, collective agreements take precedence over individual agreements (Article 51, Collective Labour Agreement Act) and thus also limit individual freedom of contract.

292. The Law on Employment Contracts of 3 July 1978 regulates many of the rights and obligations of the parties. It also regulates specific clauses. However, this law is not the only mandatory statutory source of employment regulation. Different other acts will thus be referred to in the chapters and sections below. It does not take away that the Law on Employment Contracts of 3 July 1978 stands very central in regulating the individual employment relationship.

§2. Mutual Respect and Esteem

293. As far as the obligations of the parties are concerned, the employment contract starts with a provision concerning mutual respect. The law provides that both the employer and the employee owe each other respect and esteem. Furthermore, according to the law, during the execution of the contract, they must observe and enforce decency and good morals (Article 16 of the Law on Employment Contracts).

294. While this provision is formulated as an open normen, it should be noted that it has not yet seen any strong independent development. Nevertheless, it can be seen as a translation of the duty of good faith, which any of the parties to a contract owe each other (following Article 1134, paragraph 3 of the Old Civil Code).

§3. LIABILITY

I. General

295. The legislator has introduced a special regime regarding the civil liability of the employee. It concerns a form of limited immunity. Only in a limited number of situations, the employee is liable for damages as a result of errors or faults committed during the execution of the employment contract. The regime is contained in Article 18 of the Law on Employment Contracts.

296. According to the Constitutional Court, the limitation of the worker's liability is justified 'by the legislator's concern to protect the worker against any damage caused by his occasional or minor shortcomings during the performance of his contract of employment, taking into account the increased risk implied by any professional activity and the fact that the workers perform their activity for the benefit of their employer and under his authority'.[150]

297. In addition to the regulation of Article 18, a number of other obligations of the employee should be taken into account.

The employee is obliged to return to the employer the working tools and unused raw materials entrusted to him in good condition (Article 17, 5° Law on Employment Contracts). However, the employee is not responsible for damage or wear due to regular use of the equipment, nor for its accidental loss. Once he has received the work, he is no longer responsible for the defective work (Article 19 Law on Employment Contracts). In addition, the employer is liable for the defective work due to the poor quality of the raw materials, data, tools or equipment supplied by him (Article 22, Employment Contracts Act).

II. Limited Liability

298. If, in the performance of his contract, the employee causes damage to the employer or to third parties, he shall be liable only for his fraud and for serious fault (Article 18, paragraph 1, Employment Contracts Act). In the case of minor fault, the employee is only liable if such fault occurs habitually, rather than accidentally (Article 18, paragraph 2, Employment Contracts Act). Only in these cases can the employee be obliged to pay the damage.[151]

299. A commonly occurring minor fault is a fault which, although slight, occurs repeatedly. The fault need not necessarily be of the same kind each time. A habit is shown by a repetition of faulty actions which indicate a certain state of mind of the employee.

---

150. *See* Constitutional Court 29 .ember 2006, no. 185/2006, B.5.
151. Cass. 22 Feb. 1989, *RW* 1989–90, 83.

300. The person who suffers damage because of the fault of the employee may be the employer himself, or a third party, like a customer of the employer, a supplier, a casual passer-by, etc.

301. Under penalty of nullity, no derogation from the employee's limitation of liability may be made, unless, and only as far as liability towards the employer is concerned, by a collective agreement declared generally binding by the King (Article 18, paragraph 3, Labour Contracts Act).

III. Employer's Liability

302. The reduced liability of the employee does not affect the liability of the employer. Based on Article 1384 of the Old Civil Code, the employer remains liable for damage caused by his employee even when, in view of Article 18 of the Law on Employment Contracts, the employee himself is not liable.[152] A third party can thus bring an action against the employer on the basis of Article 1384 of the Civil Code, even if the employee himself is not liable for it (under Article 18, Employment Contracts Act).

303. The employer may deduct from the salary the indemnities and compensation due to him pursuant to this liability regime (so only if the employee is liable) under the conditions as stipulated in Article 23 of the Act of 12 April 1965 on the protection of employees' salaries (Article 18, paragraph 4 of the Act on employment contracts). Pursuant to Article 23 of the Act of 12 April 1965, the total of these deductions may not exceed one-fifth of the salary due on each payment (usually monthly), after deduction of the tax deductions and social security contributions.

§4. Regulated Clauses

304. As referred to above, the parties to the employment contract have a relatively wide margin of negotiation and freedom of contract. However, many clauses which the parties may envisage to include in the employment contract are regulated by the Employment Contracts Act. It means that the parties can freely decide to include these clauses, but the (minimum) terms and conditions of these clauses will be set or determined by the law.

I. Aggravating Clauses

305. Article 6 of the Employment Contracts Act contains the so-called prohibition of aggravating clauses. It provides that all clauses contrary to the provisions of

152. Cass. 18 Nov. 1981, *RW* 1982–83, 859.

Employment Contracts Act and its implementing decrees are null and void, insofar as they are intended to reduce the rights of the employee or to increase his obligations.

306. The scope of this rule is limited. It only concerns terms that violate the provisions of the Employment Contracts Act (and its implementing decrees). In other words, Article 6 has no autonomous or overall substantive meaning in labour law. It can only receive meaning in substance if another article of the Law on Employment Contracts is read (and violated) in conjunction with it. Article 6 concerns, as it were, a minimum protection for the employee. When this protection is provided by the Employment Contracts Act, it cannot be lowered, or in other words, the employee's rights contained in the Law on Employment Contracts cannot be reduced, nor can his obligations be increased.

II. Marriage and Maternity

307. Clauses providing that marriage and maternity would terminate the contract are null and void (Article 36, Employment Contracts Act).

III. Pension Clause

308. Clauses providing that reaching the statutory or conventional retirement age would terminate the contract are null and void (Article 36, Employment Contracts Act).

IV. Prohibition of Lifelong Bonding

309. An employment contract cannot be concluded for life (Article 7, Employment Contracts Act). This rule has already been explained above and is an elaboration of the provisions of section 1780 of the Old Civil Code.

V. Arbitration Clause

310. An arbitration clause is a clause whereby the employee and the employer undertake to submit any disputes arising from the application of the contract to an arbitrator (or arbitration panel).

311. In order to protect employees and allow them to keep free access to courts, such clauses are prohibited as a general rule as standard clauses in employment contracts (Article 13 of the Act on Employment Contracts). Clauses having the same purpose in work regulations (Article 10 of the Act of 8 April 1965) or in a collective agreement (Article 9 of the Act of 5 December 1968) are also null and void.

312. There is an important nuance. The prohibition of an arbitration clause shall not prevent the conclusion of an arbitration agreement in respect of disputes after they have arisen. In other words, employees cannot be bound to arbitration beforehand, but can conclude an arbitration agreement with the employer after a dispute has arisen, for that concerned dispute.

313. Furthermore, an arbitration clause is allowed, under limited conditions, for a specific category of white-collar workers with a high responsibility in the company (Article 69, Employment Contracts Act).

VI. Modification Clause

314. A clause by which the employer reserves the right to unilaterally change the terms and conditions of the employment contract is, in principle, null and void (Article 25, Employment Contracts Act).

315. However, the Court of Cassation assumes that this nullity only applies to terms that are intended to modify essential elements of the employment contract.[153]

316. A more extensive discussion of this clause is dealt with in the context of the doctrine of 'implicit dismissal' and the unilateral amendment of employment conditions (*see* the section on employment termination).

VII. Training Clause

317. A training clause is understood to mean the clause by which the employee, who follows a training at the expense of the employer during the running of his employment contract, undertakes to repay to the employer part of the training costs if he would leave the company before the end of an agreed period (Article 22bis, §1, paragraph 1, Employment Contracts Act).

318. A training clause is only possible under limited conditions. For example, the law states that the clause must be set out in writing, for each individual employee, at the latest when the training intended by the clause concerned starts (Article 22bis, §2, paragraph 1, Employment Contracts Act). Moreover, it can only be determined within the framework of an employment contract concluded for an indefinite period (Article 22bis, §2, paragraph 2, Employment Contracts Act). The Act also contains a number of specific conditions (Article 22bis, §3, §4 and §5, Employment Contracts Act). For example, the training clause shall have no effect when the employment contract is terminated by the employer without severe cause, or by the employee with severe cause.

153. Cass. 14 Oct. 1991, *RW* 1991–92, 809.

VIII. Non-compete Clause

319. A non-competition clause is one whereby the employee undertakes not to carry on similar activities after leaving the company, either by running a business himself or by joining a competing employer, and whereby he has the possibility of damaging the company which he has left by using the knowledge he has acquired in that company, whether in the industrial or commercial field, for himself or for a competing company (Article 65, §1, Employment Contracts Act).

320. The non-competition clause is discussed below in the context of the employee's non-compete obligations.

IX. Delcredere Clause

321. The 'delcredere clause' is specifically regulated for sales representatives. It concerns a clause in the employment contract which makes the sales representative liable for the insolvency of the client which he has brought to the company. Except in the case of gross negligence or fraud, this clause will however only apply for the amount equal to the commission that was paid in respect of client's unrecoverable claims. In addition, any 'delcredere clause' must be in writing (Article 107, Employment Contracts Act).

X. Trial Clause

322. A trial clause is a clause which provides for a trial period, i.e., a period of time during which it can be assessed whether the employment contract should continue or not after the end of that period.

323. In the past, a special regime applied for employment termination during the period of application of a trial clause. However, the Unified Status Act (*see* elsewhere in this monograph) abolished these provisions, with the exception of the contract for the employment of students and the contract for temporary work. The legislator justified the abolition of the regulation of the trial clause period by the fact that the new notice periods are relatively short during the employee's first year of employment.

324. The probationary period is maintained for contracts for temporary work and contracts for the employment of students. With regard to the employment contract for temporary work, it should be noted that Article 5 of the Act of 24 July 1987 stipulates that, unless there is a contrary agreement, the first three working days are considered to be a probationary period. Until the end of that period, either party may terminate the contract without notice or compensation. If a temporary worker is employed by the same user in the same job, at the same work location by means of successive temporary employment contracts, successive probationary periods are prohibited (Article 5 of the Act of 24 July 1987).

325. With respect to the student employment contract, its regime is inspired by that of the temporary work contract. The first three working days are considered to be a probationary period. Until the end of this period, each of the parties may terminate the contract without notice or compensation (Article 127, Employment Contracts Act).

§5. Employee Obligations

I. Employee Obligations

326. Article 17 of the Employment Contracts Act contains a number of obligations for the employee. They are explained below.

II. Performing Work

327. According to the law, every employee is obliged to perform his work carefully, honestly and accurately, at the time, place and in the manner as agreed (Article 17, 1°, Employment Contracts Act). The employee is thus not only obliged to perform the agreed work. He must also perform the work carefully, honestly and accurately.

III. Following Orders and Instructions

328. The employee is obliged to act in accordance with the orders and instructions given to him by the employer, or the employee's agents or representatives, with a view to executing the contract (Article 17, 2°, Employment Contracts Act).

329. The employer has the power to direct and supervise the work. With this, the legislator actually confirms the authority of the employer.

IV. Confidential Information

330. The employee is obliged, both during and after the termination of the contract, to refrain from unlawfully obtaining, using or disclosing[154] a business secret[155] of which he may become aware in the course of his employment, as well as from disclosing secrets relating to personal or confidential matters of which he may become aware in the course of his employment (Article 17, 3°, a), Employment Contracts Act).

154. Within the meaning of Art. XI.332/4 of the Economic Code.
155. Within the meaning of Art. I.17/1, 1°, of the Economic Code.

331. Section 309 of the Criminal Code, furthermore, provides for the punishment of 'he who maliciously or fraudulently discloses to others secrets of the factory in which he has been employed or is still employed'. Similarly, Article 458 of the Criminal Code makes the violation of professional secrecy a criminal offence. This may also apply in the employment relationship, particularly where the relationship is between the employee and the employer's suppliers, customers, patients, etc.

V. (Non-)competition

332. The employee is obliged, both during and after the termination of the contract, to refrain from engaging in acts of unfair competition (Article 17, 3°, b), Employment Contracts Act). This should be read in conjunction with the provisions on non-competition clauses (Articles 65 and 86, Employment Contracts Act). This issue will be elaborated below in a specifically dedicated section to non-compete obligations.

VI. Safety

333. In accordance with Article 17, 4° of the Employment Contracts Act, the employee must refrain from doing anything that may harm his own safety or that of his fellow workers, his employer or third parties.

334. As further explained, the employer also has obligations in relation to safety, health and, more broadly, well-being at work.

VII. Work Tools and Raw Materials

335. In accordance with Article 17, 5°, the employee must return to the employer the working tools and unused raw materials entrusted to him in good condition. The employee is, however, not liable for damage or wear due to regular use, nor for accidental loss (Article 19 Act on Employment Contracts).

§6. Employer Obligations

I. Provide Work

336. The employer is obliged to employ the employee in the agreed manner, at the agreed time and place, in particular, if the circumstances so require and in the absence of any provision to the contrary, by providing the assistance, tools and materials necessary for the execution of the work (Article 20, 1° Act on Employment Contracts).

337. The law itself stipulates ('subject to contrary provision') that it is somewhat possible to deviate from this rule, meaning that it can be agreed that the employee uses his own tools.[156]

II. Health and Safety

338. The employer is obliged to act with due care to ensure that work is performed under proper conditions regarding the employee's safety and health and that first aid can be provided in the event of an accident. To this end, a first aid box must be permanently available to the staff (Article 20, 2°, Employment Contracts Act).

339. This obligation is further concretised and supplemented by the Act of 4 August 1996 on the well-being of employees in the performance of their work (the Wellbeing of Workers Act). This Act constitutes the general framework setting out general principles, prevention principles and bodies (such as prevention services or prevention advisers and the CPPW). This law is accompanied by a series of implementing decrees. These are included in a 'Codex on Wellbeing at Work' (Wellbeing Codex).[157]

340. The Wellbeing of Workers Act applies in the first instance not only to employees and employers (Article 2, §1, paragraph 1, Wellbeing of Workers Act) but also to 'persons who, other than under an employment contract, perform work under the authority of another person' (Article 2, §1, paragraph 2, Wellbeing of Workers Act). Assimilation means, *inter alia*, that civil servants who are employed by government agencies under the terms of a statute fall within the scope of the Act.

III. Paying Wages

341. The employer is obliged to pay the employee's salary in the agreed manner, time and place (Article 20, 3°, Employment Contracts Act).

342. Reference should be made to specific legislation, namely the Act of 12 April 1965 on the protection of employees' wages (discussed below). It should also be taken into account that many wage provisions are laid down in collective agreements.

IV. Accommodation

343. A specific provision relates to the situation in which the employer would provide accommodation. The employer is obliged to provide the employee with

---

156. Cass. 9 Sep. 1991, *JTT* 1992, 30, *TSR* 1991, 414, *Soc.Kron.* 1992, 58 and *RW* 1991–92, 848.
157. Ministerial circular of 28 Sep. 1993, *Belgian Official Gazette* 5 Oct. 1993.

proper accommodation and healthy and sufficient food if he has undertaken to provide him with board and lodging (Article 20, 4°, Employment Contracts Act).

V. Religion and Civil Duties

344. The employer is obliged to give the employee the necessary time to fulfil his duties of religion, as well as his civil obligations arising from the law (Article 20, 5° Law on Employment Contracts). This obligation should also be linked to the legislation combating discrimination on the basis of religion or belief (*see* further in relation to the Act of 10 May 2007). Civil duty means duties as a guardian, or a member of a jury of a court (in certain criminal law cases there is trial by jury).

VI. Reception

345. The employer is obliged to devote the necessary care and attention to the reception of employees and of young employees in particular (Article 20, 6°, Employment Contracts Act). The reception obligations of the employer are further elaborated in CA no. 22. of 26 June 1975.[158]

VII. Storage of Work Tools and Objects

346. The employer is obliged to take reasonable care of the tools that belong to the employee, as well as the personal items that the employee is required to deposit; under no circumstances may the employer refuse to return the tools or personal items (Article. 20, 7°, Law on Employment Contracts). The employee's personal items may include items such as clothing and bicycles.

VIII. Language

347. A particular set of obligations refer to the use of languages in employment and labour relations. It is connected with the federal structure of the country and the existence of language communities (Dutch-speaking and French-speaking).

348. Article 129, §1 of the Constitution stipulates that the parliaments of the Flemish and French Communities regulate by law the use of languages as regards the 'social relations' between the employer and the personnel, as well as the documents and records of the companies as prescribed by the law and by the regulations.

---

158. Royal Decree of 9 Sep. 1975, *Belgian Official Gazette* 8 Oct. 1975.

349. On this basis, a series of language regulations were drawn up. As far as the Dutch language area is concerned, the Flemish decree regulating the use of languages for the social relations between employers and employees, as well as for the legally prescribed documents and records of companies, abbreviated as the Language Decree, applies. Pursuant to[159] Article 5, §1 of the Language Decree, the language to be used, in Flanders, in social relations between employers and employees, as well as for the legally prescribed documents of undertakings and for all documents intended for employees, should be Dutch. Because of the possible restriction on the free movement of employees in the European Union, the Language Decree has been amended following a ruling by the Court of Justice.[160] Since then, in addition to a Dutch version of documents, a legally valid version in another language can be drawn up, subject to strict conditions, for individual employment contracts with a cross-border character.[161]

350. In the other regions, a different arrangement applies. The coordinated laws of 18 July 1966 on the use of languages in administrative matters[162] apply for the Brussels-Capital Region, the municipalities with facilities and the German-language region. For the French-speaking regions, the Decree of 30 June 1982 on the protection of the freedom of use of the French language in social relations between employers and their staff, as well as of acts and documents of enterprises imposed by the laws and regulations, applies.[163]

159. *Belgian Official Gazette* 6 Sep. 1973.
160. CJEU 16 Apr. 2013, C-202/11, *Anton Las v. Psa Antwerp NV.*
161. Decr.Flemish Parl. 14 Mar. 2014 amending Arts 1, 2, 4, 5, 12 and 16 of the decree of 19 Jul. 1973 regulating the use of languages for social relations between employers and employees, as well as the documents and records of enterprises required by law and regulations, *Belgian Official Gazette* 22 Apr. 2014, ed. 2.
162. *Belgian Official Gazette* 2 Aug. 1966.
163. *Belgian Official Gazette* 27 Aug. 1982.

Chapter 3. Remuneration and Benefits

§1. CONCEPT

351. Wages are one of the constitutive elements of an employment contract. However, in Belgian employment law, there is no single concept of what constitutes remuneration. The concept of remuneration or 'pay' is defined differently depending on the applicable legislation. However, the respective wage concepts of the Employment Contracts Act of 3 July 1978 and of the Wage Protection Act of 12 April 1965 are the most important ones.

352. The Employment Contracts Act talks about the employee's remuneration in several places. This Act also uses numerous wage limits to determine the rights and obligations of the parties. The determination of the indemnity in lieu of notice (compensation for breach of contract) is also based on the employee's wages. However, the Employment Contracts Act does not provide itself a definition in any of its provisions. Therefore, the Court of Cassation has provided a definition. According to the Court of Cassation, remuneration is the consideration for the work performed in the execution of an employment contract.[164]

353. The remuneration for work may consist of *money* but may also consist of *benefits in kind (benefits 'in natura')*. For example, the personal benefit of being able to use a company car for private purposes constitutes remuneration for the employee.[165] The same applies to a contribution that the employer pays into a group insurance scheme for the benefit of the employee.[166]

354. Another important act concerns the Wage Protection Act of 12 April 1965. This act, as is clear from the title, aims to protect the wages of the employee. Article 2 of this Wage Protection Act expressly defines what constitutes wages. This definition is also relevant for social security since the contributions to the social security system (for employer and employee) are based on the wages paid to employees.

355. The Wage Protection Act understands as 'wages':

1° the wages in money to which the employee is entitled by virtue of his employment at the expense of the employer;
2° tips or service money to which the employee is entitled by virtue of his employment or custom;
3° benefits in kind to which the employee is entitled by virtue of his employment, at the expense of the employer (Article 2, paragraph 1, Wage Protection Act).

164. Cass. 20 Apr. 1977, *RW* 1979–78, 1871, concl. Adv. Gen. H. Lenaerts; Cass. 2 Apr. 1978, *RW* 1977–78, 2441, concl. Adv. Gen. H. Lenaerts.
165. Labour Court Brussels 19 Jan. 1977, *Med.VBO* 1978, 726; Labour Court Brussels 31 Jul. 1979, Med.*VBO* 1980, 2377.
166. Labour Court Brussels 8 Mar. 1977, *Med.VBO* 1977, 3743; Labour Court Brussels 22 May 1978, *JTT* 1979, 340; Labour Tribunal Brussels 7 Apr. 1995, *JTT* 1995, 369.

356. The Wage Protection Act excludes a number of elements from the definition of pay. For the application of this law, compensation paid directly or indirectly by the employer is not considered as pay:

(a) as vacation pay;
(b) which must be considered as a supplement to the compensation due as a result of an accident at work or an occupational disease;
(c) which must be considered as a supplement to the benefits granted for the different branches of social security (Article 2, paragraph 3, 1°, Wage Protection Act).

357. Neither are payments in cash or in shares or participation certificates made to employees in accordance with the Act of 22 May 2001 on employee participation in the capital and profits of companies (Article 2, paragraph 3, 2°, Wage Protection Act) regarded as pay.

358. The concept of pay in the Wage Protection Act differs from that in the Employment Contracts Act. For example, a severance payment does not constitute pay within the meaning of the Act on Employment Contracts because it does not constitute consideration for the work performed, but it does constitute pay within the meaning of Article 2 of the Wage Protection Act, as it constitutes a benefit in money to which the employer is entitled under the employment relationship, although it is not granted in consideration for the work performed (but rather as compensation for employment termination).[167]

§2. Right to Remuneration

I. Source

359. The right to remuneration arises primarily from the agreement between the employee and the employer to perform work in return for remuneration. However, the level of pay does not depend solely on the individual employment contract. Collective agreements also determine the wages of employees (such as minimum wages, premiums, etc.). In many cases, the law also provides for a right to remuneration or even additional premiums, such as for wages in the event of overtime work.

360. The right to wages or benefits (such as a premium) may even be based on 'usage' as a source of labour law. According to the Court of Cassation, in order for a usage within the framework of the employment contract to be a source of rights, an existing practice for granting a benefit must be demonstrable as well as being characterised by a degree of generality and continuity.[168]

167. *Cf.* Cass. 9 Oct. 1978, *RW* 1978–79, 2162.
168. Cass. 19 Jan. 2004, AR S.030073.N.

361. Wage claims may also arise from a unilateral undertaking by the employer. For example, an end-of-year bonus determined in accordance with work performed by employees may be considered as a unilateral undertaking entered into by the employer and will then constitute pay for the worker.[169]

II. No Work, No Pay

362. In Belgian labour law, there is a principle which can be summarised as 'no work, no pay'. This means that, in principle, an employee only acquires the right to remuneration to the extent that he performs work for it.

363. In line with this, the Court of Cassation stated that although pay is the consideration for work performed in execution of an employment contract, the right to that consideration in itself is not characteristic of the concept of pay. But the right is a necessary consequence of performing work under the employment contract.[170] It is therefore incompatible with the very nature of the employment contract and with the concept of pay to consider that there is no entitlement to pay in so far as it relates to benefits granted in consideration of work carried out under a contract of employment.[171]

III. Level of Pay

364. The amount of the wages is in principle a matter for the parties. They determine the wages in the individual employment contract. However, in doing so, they must take into account what is provided for in (usually sectoral) collective agreements, which usually contain wage scales with minimum wages linked to employees' jobs or functions. Many collective agreements also contain mechanisms for indexing wages. It means that wages will increase automatically, according to an agreed formula, when the consumer prices in the country increase. This wage indexation mechanism is a typical feature that applies to many workers in the Belgian system.

365. Minimum wages applicable in Belgium are essentially fixed by collective agreements concluded at both national and sectoral levels. National CA no. 43 of 2 May 1988 (for workers aged 18 or over) and CA no. 50 of 29 October 1991 (for workers aged under 21) are the most important as regards national minimum wage arrangements. But sectoral and company level collective agreements are the dominant sources.

366. The setting of pay levels needs, of course, to take into account the applicable 'wage norm' set under the country's wage policy, discussed hereinafter.

---

169. Cass. 18 Dec. 1974, No. 1404, *TSR* 1975, 79.
170. Cass. 11 Sep. 1995, AR S.940041.N.
171. Cass. 11 Sep. 1995, AR S.940041.N.

§3. WAGE POLICY

367. From the above, it is clear that the social partners (trade unions and employers' organisations) are in principle the main actors in determining (minimum) wages in the private sector. Furthermore, the parties themselves can negotiate individually, within the confines and respect of the applicable collective agreements. Wage setting at minimum level is, in other words, largely based on a tradition of social concertation. However, Belgium knows a so-called (and much discussed) guided wage policy. The free determination of wages must take account of a number of limits.

368. Over the years, the government has introduced a 'wage norm'. This finds its current legal basis in the Act of 26 July 1996 on the promotion of employment and the preventive safeguarding of competitiveness. As the title of this act suggests, the 'wage norm' aims to be respected throughout the country in order to preserve the competitiveness of the economy.

369. The 'wage norm' concerns a mechanism whereby a (maximum) margin for the development of wage costs in the country is established every two years, taking into account the development of wage costs in neighbouring countries (mainly Germany, France, the Netherlands). The wage norm is expressed in a 'percentage', and functions as benchmark indicating how much wages can be increased in the (next) relevant period (of, in principle, two years). As a rule, the (nationally organised) social partners (trade unions and employers' organisations) determine the country-wide applicable wage norm. However, they do so within the procedures and margins laid down in the law. If the social partners do not reach an agreement, the government may impose the nationally applicable wage norm.

370. Since 2015, the government increasingly interfered in wage setting, mainly to moderate the evolution of wages in the country. It did so through specific interventions. With the Act of 28 April 2015, the government set a maximum margin of wage cost development for the years 2015 and 2016.[172] The maximum margin was even set at 0% for the year 2015 (meaning no wage increases) and at 0.5% of the gross wage bill for the year 2016. Since this is of course a strong intervention of the government in the free wage formation, these measures passed a review by the Constitutional Court in light of the Constitution guaranteeing the right to collective bargaining.[173] In later phases, a national collective agreement (no. 119) again set the wage norm. The maximum margin for the development of wage costs at 1.1% for the period 2017–2018.[174]

371. For the period 2019–2020, the social partners did not come to a final agreement, and only a draft IPA (Interprofessional Agreement) was made by the major

172. *Belgian Official Gazette* 30 Apr. 2015.
173. Constitutional Court 13 Oct. 2016, no. 130/2016; Constitutional Court 1 Dec. 2016, no. 152/2016.
174. Collective Agreement No. 119 establishing the maximum margin for wage cost development for the period 2017–2018 (RD of 13 May 2017, *Belgian Official Gazette* of 24 May 2017).

social partners. The 'wage norm' of 1.1% was subsequently set by Royal Decree.[175] Indexations (and baremic increases) remained however guaranteed. The latter issue is important since the government has also interfered in the so-called index mechanism (indicated above). The government imposed an 'index jump' with the Act of 23 April 2015 on improving employment.[176] It meant that no indexation of wages (and social benefits) could take place, while the index normally functions as a method to make sure that purchasing power of workers evolves with the increase of living expenses. The index mechanism was temporarily (de facto until the end of April 2016) disabled by the law.

372. For the period 2021–2022, the social partners, again, did not reach an agreement. The wage norm was laid down by Royal Decree (RD of 30 July 2021) implementing the Act of 26 July 1996 on the promotion of employment and the preventive safeguarding of competitiveness. Article 1 of this Royal Decree sets the 'wage norm' for the period 2021–2022 at 0.4%. Also here, indexations and baremic increases remain guaranteed.

§4. Equal Pay for Equal Work

373. In Belgium, there is no 'overall' principle of equal pay for equal work. In principle, an employer can agree and apply different wages with employees, even though the jobs are the same or similar. One could call this an issue of personnel policy. However, the equal pay principle is especially significant in discrimination law. Traditionally, the principle of equal pay has been linked to discrimination between men and women (e.g., on the basis of Article 157 TFEU, the EU's Treaty framework). The Discrimination Acts of 10 May 2007 add a number of other discrimination grounds to this.

374. The Act of 22 April 2012 on the fight against the gender pay gap should be mentioned.[177] The law aims at eliminating the pay gap (including pay and employee benefits) between men and women by, among other things, including it as a fixed topic in the social dialogue. Employers who normally employ at least fifty employees on average are obliged to draw up an analysis report on the remuneration structure of the female and male employees within the enterprise and to communicate it to the works council or, in its absence thereof, to the CPPW (i.e., the committee responsible for well-being at work). This consultation body can then decide whether an action plan should be drawn up on the basis of this analysis report. Employers who employ at least fifty workers are also offered the possibility of appointing a mediator from among their staff. The mediator supports the establishment of the action plan and the progress report, and acts as a confidential adviser to employees who believe they are subject to unequal treatment as regards gender-based remuneration. Finally, all employers are required to break down pay data in the social

175. RD of 19 Apr. 2019, *Belgian Official Gazette* 24 Apr. 2019.
176. *Belgian Official Gazette* 27 Apr. 2015.
177. *Belgian Official Gazette* 28 Aug. 2012.

balance sheet of the enterprise according to the gender of employees, unless no more than three employees are employed.[178]

§5. PROTECTION OF REMUNERATION

375. The Wage Protection Act of 12 April 1965 is an important instrument in Belgian labour law when it comes to the protection of wages or remuneration. It provides for a number of provisions aimed at guaranteeing the free disposal of the employee over his/her pay. It also guarantees the effective payment of wages.

376. Under Article 1, the Wage Protection Act applies not only to employees and employers but also to all persons who, otherwise than under a contract of employment, perform work for pay under the authority of another person, and those who employ them. Thus, the provisions also apply, except where more favourable provisions are made, to persons employed under a civil servant statute.[179]

377. The employer is prohibited from restricting in any way the employee's freedom to dispose of his wages as he sees fit (Article 3, Wage Protection Act).

378. The employee has the right to receive from the employer the remuneration due to him (Article 3bis, Wage Protection Act).

379. The legislator has a preference over payment in the applicable currency. Pay in cash (payment may also be electronically wired to the employee's bank account) must be paid in the currency that is legally accepted in Belgium when the employee performs his activity there (Article 4 Wage Protection Law). Belgium is a European Union country applying the Euro as its official currency.

380. Part of the wages may be paid *in kind*. This is possible if this method of payment is customary or desirable in view of the nature of the industry or profession concerned (Article 6(1)(1), Wage Protection Act). The benefit in kind must, however, be estimated in writing and may not, in principle, exceed one-fifth of the total gross salary (Article 6(1)(2) and (3), Wage Protection Act). In addition, benefits in *kind* may only be provided as remuneration (Article 6(2)(1), Wage Protection Act) if they relate to:

(1) housing;
(2) gas, electricity, water, heating and fuel;
(3) the enjoyment of a land;
(4) food used at the place of work;
(5) tools, service or work clothes and their upkeep, in so far as the employer is not obliged to provide or maintain them by law or regulation;

178. RD 25 Apr. 2014 on the mediator in the fight against the gender pay gap, *Belgian Official Gazette* 21 May 2014.
179. Cass. 14 Mar. 2004, *RW* 2004–05, 534.

(6) material or equipment necessary for the work, which at the expense of the employee in accordance with his employment or use.

381. Payments *in kind* may not include spirits or products which are harmful to the health of the employee and his family (Article 6, §2(2), Wage Protection Act). In addition, the employer may not seek to make a profit from the payment in *kind* (Article 6, §3, Wage Protection Act).

382. The salary must be paid at regular intervals, at least twice a month, at an interval of no more than sixteen days, except for the salary of employees, which must be paid at least once a month (Article 9, paragraph 1, 1°, Wage Protection Act).

383. In principle, the employer must always pay the salary in full. He may only make the legally permitted deductions from the gross salary. For example, the Wage Protection Act stipulates that the following deductions may be made from the employee's pay (Article 23(1), Wage Protection Act):

(1) deductions made under tax and social security legislation and under private or collective agreements on supplementary social security benefits;
(2) fines imposed under the work regulations;
(3) the compensations and indemnities resulting from the liability of the employee (cf. Article 18, Employment Contracts Act);
(4) cash advances paid by the employer;
(5) the guarantee provided for the fulfilment of the employee's obligations.

384. The total amount withheld may not exceed one-fifth of the salary *in specie* due at each payment, after deductions made pursuant to tax legislation, social security legislation and private or collective agreements on supplementary social security benefits (Article 23, paragraph 2, Wage Protection Act).

However, this limitation does not apply if the employee has committed fraud or has voluntarily terminated his employment before settlement of the compensation and indemnities due on the grounds of liability (Article 23(3), Wage Protection Act).

385. The Wage Protection Act is enforced with criminal sanctions. The employer, his employee or his agent who has not paid the employee's salary or has not paid it on the due date can be criminally sanctioned. The Court of Cassation has stated that both non-payment of wages and non-timely payment of wages are punishable.[180]

180. Cass. 21 Nov. 2017, P.17.0070.N/1.

Chapter 4. Working Time and Time Off

§1. General

386. Working time is one of the essential components of the working conditions of the parties to the employment contract. Working time is, however, not (fully) freely agreed in the individual employment contract. Laws and collective agreements provide for daily and weekly limits to working time, and many other specific aspects of working time are regulated.

387. The Labour Act of 16 March 1971[181] contains the basic rules on working time for employees (cf. Chapter III. of this act relates to working and rest times). The Labour Act uses the term 'working time' (cf. section 2).

§2. Scope of the Labour Act

388. The Labour Act applies to employees and employers (Article 1, paragraph 1, Labour Act), as well as to persons who, other than under a contract of employment, perform work under the authority of another person and the person who employs them (Article 1, paragraph 2, 1° and 2°, Labour Act).

389. The Act also contains a number of exclusions or limitations. The provisions on working hours (cf. Chapter III, Labour Act) do not apply to:

- persons employed by the state, the provinces, the municipalities, the public institutions falling under them and the institutions of public utility, unless they are employed by institutions that exercise an industrial or commercial activity or by institutions that provide medical, prophylactic or hygienic care (Article 3, §1, 1°, Labour Act);
- persons working in a family business in which normally only relatives by blood, marriage or foster children work under the exclusive authority of the father, mother or guardian (Article 3, §1, 3°, Labour Act);
- sailing personnel of fishing companies (Article 3, §1, 5°, Labour Act);
- household workers (Article 3, §3, 2°, Labour Act);
- sales representatives (Article 3, §3, 3°, Labour Act);
- employees appointed by the King (i.e., the government) who exercise a leading function or hold a position of trust (Article 3, §3, 1°, Labour Act).

390. Also, homeworkers are excluded from the legal provisions concerning working time limits (Article 3bis, Labour Act).

181. Labour Act 16 Mar. 1971, *Belgian Official Gazette* 30 Mar. 1971.

391. With regard to this last category of employees, i.e., leading and trusted personnel (Article 3, §3, 1°, Labour Act),[182] a Royal Decree of 10 February 1965 further defines[183] these employees. It concerns, among others, positions such as directors, vice-directors, persons who exercise actual authority and who are responsible for the entire company or a major subdivision thereof, private secretaries, persons in charge of control or inspection missions or technical assignments. The scope of this is not limited to commercial or industrial undertakings.[184] What is 'trusted personnel' may be a matter of interpretation. A position involving trust does not imply that the function concerned entails an autonomous power of decision.[185] But a responsibility for final decisions will certainly contribute to such qualification.[186] The list provided in the 1965 Royal Decree is obviously outdated. It is therefore generally interpreted in an evolutionary manner, without disregarding the limitative nature of the list.

392. In addition, the provisions of Chapter III, section 1 of the Labour Act, which relate to Sunday rest, do not apply to:

- sailing personnel employed on water transport projects, with the exception of employees who are bound by an employment contract for inland waterway boatmen (Article 3, §2, 1°, Labour Act);
- employees employed in educational institutions (Article 3, §2, 2°, Labour Act).

393. A special arrangement applies to doctors, veterinary surgeons, dentists, medical specialists in training and student trainees who are preparing to practise the professions of doctor, veterinary surgeon and dentist (Article 3b Labour Code). The Labour Code of 16 March 1971 already excluded these professions from its scope, which was at odds with the European Working Time Directive 2003/88/EC of 4 November 2003. By means of the Act of 12 December 2010, the legislator aimed to bring about conformity with the European legislation.[187] According to this law, the weekly working time of these employees may not exceed an average of forty-eight hours over a reference period of thirteen weeks. Furthermore, the working time may not exceed an absolute limit of sixty hours during each working week. Any period of work between twelve and twenty-four hours must be followed by a minimum rest

182. This is an imperative legal provision within the meaning of Art. 51 of the Collective Agreements Act: Cass. 10 Jan. 2000, AR S.990127.N.
183. *Belgian Official Gazette* 12 Feb. 1965.
184. Cass. 21 May 2007, AR S.06.0015.N.
185. Cass. 29 Mar. 2010, AR S.09.0034.N, *NB Arbeidsrecht* 2010/6.
186. For example, an employee held in a leadership position or a position of trust is an employee whose job is to monitor transactions regarding purchases and inventories, make final decisions regarding purchases, and purchasing managers cannot make purchases without his approval, according to Cass. 11 Sep. 2017, No. S.15.0064.N-S.15.0111.N.
187. Act of 12 Dec. 2010 determining the working hours of doctors, dentists, veterinary surgeons, candidate doctors in training, candidate dentists in training and student trainees preparing to practise these professions, *Belgian Official Gazette* 22 Dec. 2010.

period of twelve consecutive hours. Subject to strict conditions, however, an additional period of up to twelve hours per week may be worked to ensure, among other things, standby duty at the workplace. An individual written agreement from the employee is required in that case.

§3. Concept of Working Time

394. Working time or working hours is the time during which the staff is at the disposal of the employer (Article 19, paragraph 2, Labour Act).

395. While this seems a simple definition, it is open to discussion, certainly when issues of availability or on-call services arise.

396. For certain categories and at the request of the competent joint committee, the King can determine the time during which the staff is at the disposal of the employer, as, for example, in the transport sector (Article 19, paragraph 3, Labour Code).

397. The question arises as to when exactly an employee is available to the employer. For example, what does one do with being 'available' or 'standby'? Similarly, simply being present in the company does not imply that one is available to the employer. That is, in principle, the case when one takes a break.

398. The matter is strongly influenced by the case law of the Court of Justice of the European Union, which interprets the concept of working time on the basis of the European Working Time Directive.[188] According to the case law of the Court of Justice, 'on-call' duty initially appeared to be regarded as working time only if it was accompanied by physical presence at the workplace.[189] In the *Jaeger* judgment, the Court of Justice specified that on-call duty, where a doctor is required to be physically present in the hospital, must be regarded in its entirety as working time within the meaning of the European Working Time Directive, even if the person concerned is permitted to rest at his place of work during the periods when his services are not required.[190]

399. However, a new debate arose in relation to on-call duty or standby duty at home. In the past, the Belgian Court of Cassation assumed that periods of on-call duty, during which the employee must be permanently available to answer a call from the employer, but during which his physical presence at the workplace is not required, are not considered as working time within the meaning of Article 19 of the Labour Act. According to the Belgian Court, the fact that the freedom of movement of the worker during on-call duty is limited, because he must stay within a certain radius of the workplace in order to reach it within a certain time, did not alter

188. Now Directive 2003/88/EC.
189. CJEU 3 Oct. 2000, No. C-303/98.
190. CJEU 9 Sep. 2003, No. C-151/02.

this conclusion.[191] This view implied that only the time during which the worker is effectively called in would be actually working time.[192] The Belgian Constitutional Court also addressed the issue and ruled that the time during which firefighters must be on standby, but are not required to be at the workplace, does not count as working time within the meaning of the law.[193] However, the Belgian case law was contradicted by the Court of Justice in the *Matzak* judgment of 21 February 2018.[194] In this judgment, the Court ruled that home-based standby duty performed by a worker, whereby he is obliged to respond to calls from his employer and be ready within eight minutes, so that his ability to undertake other activities is very much reduced, must be classified as 'working time'.

400. Another issue is whether an employee's travel on the instructions of his employer, for example, to visit a client, constitutes working time. In principle, business trips are part of the normal activities and will constitute working time. Commuting (home-work-home), however, is in principle not working time. According to the *Tyco* judgment of the Court of Justice of the European Union,[195] the time spent daily by employees without a fixed or usual place of work, on the journey between their place of residence and the location of the first and last customer designated by their employer, should be classified as 'working time'.

§4. Rest Periods

401. Employees are entitled to rest periods. It must be noted that rest periods do not only concern breaks that interrupt periods of work during a given day but also concern the periods between two working days.

402. The law states that employees may not work for more than six hours without interruption (Article 38quater, §1, paragraph 1, Labour Act). Young employees[196] may not work for more than 4.5 hours without interruption (Article 34, paragraph 1, Labour Act). After this period of work, a rest period must be provided (Article 38c(2), Labour Act). The duration and the arrangements for granting this break are laid down in a collective agreement or, for employers not covered by a collective agreement, are determined by a Royal Decree (Article 38c(2), Labour Act). In the absence of such a collective agreement or Royal Decree, the employee shall be granted at least a 15-minute break at the latest when the duration of the work reaches six hours (Article 38c, §3, Labour Act).

---

191. Cass. 10 Mar. 2014, AR S.13.0029.N.
192. Cass. 18 May 2015, AR S.13.0024.F.
193. Constitutional Court 3 Mar. 2016, no. 35/2016.
194. CJEU 21 Feb. 2018, no. C-518/15.
195. CJEU 10 Sep. 2015, no. C-266/14.
196. Youthful employees are minors who are 15 years of age or older and who are no longer subject to full-time compulsory education (Art. 2, para. 1, Labour Code).

403. In addition, in principle, employees are entitled to at least eleven consecutive hours of rest within each twenty-four-hour period between stopping and resuming work (Article 38ter, §1, Labour Act).

§5. Working Time Limits

404. In principle, working hours are limited, per week and per day. The daily limit is eight hours (Article 19, paragraph 1, Labour Act).

405. For the weekly limit, one should refer to the Act of 10 August 2001 on reconciling employment and quality of life. The weekly limit is set at thirty-eight hours.[197] The weekly limit can also be fixed by collective agreement, or in the absence of such agreement, in the company's work regulations.[198]

406. These are, in principle, maximum limits. They may therefore be reduced (Article 28, §1, Labour Act). The daily limit may, however, also be increased. The daily limit may be increased to nine hours if the working time regulation per week includes one half-day, one full day or more than one rest day, except for Sundays (Article 20, §1, Labour Act). It can be increased to ten hours for employees who cannot return to their place of residence or stay every day because of the distance from the place of work (Article 20, §2, Labour Act).

407. In order to meet the need for more flexibility, the possibility of using flexible working arrangements has been provided for. This means that the basic working time is calculated on the basis of an average weekly working time, viewed over a reference period which is fixed by the legislator at one year[199] (Article 20bis, Labour Act). Through this 'annualisation' of working time, a company can thus deal more flexibly with peaks and troughs, without having to pay for additional overtime.[200] There are, however, a number of conditions. The flexible working arrangement must be provided for by the company's work regulations or by a collective agreement (Article 20bis, §1, paragraph 1, Labour Act). The applicable working hours must be specified in the work regulations (Article 20bis, §1, paragraph 3, Labour Act). A number of limits also apply (Article 20bis(1)(2), Labour Act). For example, a daily working time limit of nine hours and a weekly working time limit of forty-five hours must be observed (Article 20bis, §1, paragraph 2, 3°, Labour Act).

197. Art. 2, §1 and §2 Act of 10 Aug. 2001 concerning the reconciliation of employment and quality of life, *Belgian Official Gazette* 15 Sep. 2001.
198. Art. 2, §1 Act of 10 Aug. 2001 concerning the reconciliation of employment and quality of life, *Belgian Official Gazette* 15 Sep. 2001.
199. Introduced by s. 2 Workable and Agile Work Act of 5 Mar. 2017, *BS* 15 Mar. 2017.
200. Cf. Art. 29 Labour Code.

408. The Labour Act also refers to 'shift work' (working in 'shifts'). With shift work, the daily and weekly limits may be exceeded (Article 22, 1°, Labour Act). In this case, working hours may never exceed eleven hours per day or fifty hours per week (Article 27, §1, Labour Act).

409. For 'continuous work', i.e., for the execution of work that, by its nature, may not be interrupted, the maximum limits may also be exceeded (Article 22, 2°, Labour Act). In this case, the working hours are always limited to twelve hours per day and fifty hours per week. However, the weekly working time may be increased to fifty-six hours if the daily working time does not exceed eight hours (Article 27, §2, Labour Act).

410. Finally, a Royal Decree may allow the daily and weekly limits to be exceeded in the industries, categories of enterprises or branches of enterprises where these limits cannot be applied (Article 23, Labour Act).

411. Except in the case of continuous work, an occurring or threatening accident, or urgent work on machines, the working time may never exceed eleven hours per day or fifty hours per week, even if the different provisions are applied simultaneously (Article 27, §1, Labour Act). Still, except for schemes involving night work, a Royal Decree may allow the fifty-hour limit to be exceeded in those industries, categories of companies or branches of companies in which this limit cannot be applied (Article 27, §3, Labour Act).

§6. OVERTIME

412. Overtime is defined as work performed in excess of nine hours per day or forty hours per week or in excess of the lower limits set by a collective agreement or by Royal Decree in implementation of Article 28 of the Labour Act (Article 29, §2, Labour Act).

413. A Royal Decree may assimilate to overtime some services of part-time employees, which do not reach the normal limits for overtime (Article 29, §3 Labour Code). This was done by the Royal Decree of 25 June 1990 on the assimilation of certain services of part-time employees to overtime.[201]

414. In general, overtime work is discouraged by various conditions, including the obligation to pay 'overtime pay', i.e., an allowance for overtime work (Article 29, §2, paragraph 2, Labour Act). Overtime is paid at an amount that is at least 50% higher than the ordinary wage. This increase shall be 100% for overtime worked on Sundays or rest days granted pursuant to the legislation on paid holidays (Article 29(1), Labour Act).

201. *Belgian Official Gazette* 30 Jun. 1990.

415. A collective agreement may allow the overtime allowance due to be converted into an additional 'recovery rest period'. Under such an agreement, every hour of overtime worked, which must be paid with a 50% allowance, is entitled to at least half an hour of recovery rest, whereas every hour of overtime worked, which must be paid with a 100% allowance, is entitled to at least one hour of recovery rest (Article 29, §4, Labour Act).

416. When the maximum limits have been lowered by virtue of a collective labour agreement, the questions as to whether overtime pay should be paid must be answered taking into account the maximum limits as established by that collective agreement. The same applies to the determination of recovery rest (Article 28, §4, Labour Act).

417. The Workable and Agile Work Act of 5 March 2017 introduced the possibility of performing 'voluntary overtime'. According to Article 25bis, §1 Labour Act, on the initiative of the employee and with his agreement, the working time limits can be exceeded by a maximum of hundred hours per calendar year. On the basis of national CA no. 129, the social partners increased this to 120 hours per calendar year. By a collective agreement declared generally binding by Royal Decree, this number of hours can even be increased to a maximum of 360 hours. Of course, voluntary overtime is only possible to the extent that the employer also wishes these hours to be worked.[202]

§7. Recovery Rest

418. In most cases where working time limits are exceeded, recovery rest must be provided. This means that the excess work is compensated with time off.

419. The granting of recovery rest often results from respecting the average working time calculated over a certain reference period. It is then ensured that, in the event of excess hours being worked at one time, less hours are worked at another time, so that the average working time is not exceeded at the end of the reference period.

§8. Night Work

420. A departure point of principle is that workers may not perform night work. Night work is defined as work performed between 20:00 in the evening and 6:00 in the morning (Article 35, §1 and §2, Labour Act).

---

202. Art. 25bis, §1 Labour Code, inserted by Art. 4 Workable and Agile Work Act of 5 Mar. 2017, *Belgian Official Gazette* 15 Mar. 2017.

421. However, there are numerous exceptions to the general prohibition of night work. For example, in so far as this is justified by the nature of the work or the activity, night work is possible in hotels, restaurants, off-licences, newspaper companies, travel agencies, companies that sell fuel for motor vehicles on a small scale, companies that operate car parks, companies that produce, process or transport gas, electricity or water; in establishments or by persons providing medical, prophylactic or healthcare, agricultural work, work that, by its nature, cannot be interrupted, transport work, loading and unloading, pharmacies, photography and film studios, radio and television distribution and broadcasting, artisanal bakeries and pastryshops, educational and housing establishments, supervisory work and monitoring, cleaning, necessary repairs and maintenance, for the provision of all logistical and support services relating to electronic commerce[203] (Article 36, Labour Act). In addition, a Royal Decree may, if necessary and under conditions, shall determine, authorise night work in certain industries, undertakings or professions or for the performance of certain works (Article 37, §1, Labour Act).

422. CA no. 46 of 23 March 1990 was concluded in the NLC concerning support measures for shift work involving night work and other forms of night work.

§9. Sundays and Holidays

423. In principle, it is forbidden to work on Sundays (Article 11, Labour Act). But there are numerous exceptions to this rule. Certain activities may be performed on Sundays insofar as the normal operation of the business does not allow them to be performed on another day of the week, such as 1° supervision of the business premises; 2° cleaning, repair and maintenance work, insofar as this work is necessary for the regular continuation of the business, as well as the work outside production which is necessary for the regular resumption of the business on the following day; 3° work performed in order to deal with an accident which has occurred or is threatening; 4° urgent work on machines or equipment and work which is required by an unforeseen necessity; 5° work to prevent damage to raw materials or products. The work referred to here may be performed by employees of the company as well as by other employees. The provisions are without prejudice to the laws on mines, quarries and graves, coordinated by the Royal Decree of 15 September 1919 (Article 12, Labour Act).

424. Workers may also be employed on Sundays in the companies or for the performance of works designated by a Royal Decree (Article 13, Labour Act).

425. The law also provides for a number of cases in which Sunday working is possible, subject to a number of conditions. Thus, employees may be employed on

203. The latter concerns the relaxation of night work in e-commerce, as inserted by Art. 79 of the Workable and Agile Work Act of 5 Mar. 2017, *Belgian Official Gazette* 15 Mar. 2017; *see also* Arts 55–65 (introduction of working arrangements involving night work and Sunday work in e-commerce) Programme Act 25 Dec. 2017, *Belgian Official Gazette* 29 Dec. 2017.

Sundays from 8 a.m. to noon in retail establishments other than those already exempted, unless a Royal Decree has imposed municipal or other restrictions. In seaside resorts, climatic health resorts and tourist centres, employees may work in retail shops and hairdressing salons on Sundays, provided that, in application of this section, Sunday employment for each individual employee is limited to thirty-nine Sundays per calendar year (Article 14, Labour Act).

426. The regulations on public holidays are contained in the Act of 4 January 1974 on public holidays (the Public Holidays Act) and the Royal Decree of 18 April 1974.[204] Here, too, an employee may, in principle, not be employed on ten public holidays per year (Article 4, Public Holidays Act). An employee may, however, be employed on a public holiday if Sunday work is permitted by or under the Labour Act (Article 10, paragraph 1, Public Holidays Act).

427. The ten statutory public holidays in Belgium are: 1 January (New Year's day); Easter Monday; 1 May (Labour Day); Ascension Day; Pentecost Monday; 21 July (Belgian National Holiday); Assumption of Mary; 1 November (All Saints' Day); 11 November (Armistice Day); 25 December (Christmas).[205] If a public holiday coincides with a Sunday or an ordinary day of inactivity, it is replaced by an ordinary day of activity (Article 6, Public Holidays Act).

§10. New Working Arrangements

428. A specific form of working time flexibility exists in Belgian labour law. The Act of 17 March 1987 on the introduction of 'new working arrangements' in companies[206] was introduced to allow for the flexibilisation of working time. The law allows not only to calculate working time limits on the basis of an average but also to exceed the legal limits of eleven hours per day and fifty hours per week (Article 27, Labour Act). However, this is on the condition that a maximum working time of twelve hours per day is observed and recovery rest is granted (cf. Article 26bis, §1, Labour Act).[207] Within the conditions of the law, the work performance does not, in principle, give rise to additional overtime pay.[208] In addition, it is possible to derogate from the ban on Sunday work, the ban on night work, or the ban on working

204. *Belgian Official Gazette* 31 Jan. 1974; Royal Decree 18 Apr. 1974 determining the general arrangements for implementing the Act of 4 Jan. 1974 on public holidays, *Belgian Official Gazette* 24 Apr. 1974.
205. Art. 1 RD 18 Apr. 1974 determining the general arrangements for implementing the Law of 4 Jan. 1974 on public holidays, *Belgian Official Gazette* 24 Apr. 1974.
206. *Belgian Official Gazette* 12 Jun. 1987.
207. Art. 2, 3° New Working Arrangements Act.
208. Art. 3 New Working Arrangements Act.

on public holidays.[209] The 'new working arrangements' can only be introduced subject to an information and negotiation procedure. National CA no. 42[210] further provides for the modalities.

§11. Right to Disconnect

429. In 2018, a 'right to disconnect' was introduced in Belgian labour law.[211] It is not formulated as an individual right to disconnect. The law provides that the employer must organise consultation in his company about disconnection from work and from the use of digital communication tools. It is related to the company's policy regarding whether an employee can be reached (or must be available) outside of his normal working hours via, for example, mobile phones, smartphones or computers. The consultation should ensure respect for rest periods, holidays and other leave of the employees and to safeguard a work-life balance.

§12. Holidays and Leave

430. In addition to the absences due to illness or work accidents and in addition to the regulations regarding work (or rest) on Sundays and public holidays, labour law contains a number of other relevant rules and agreements regarding absence or leave.

431. Thus, according to Article 30, §1 of the Employment Contracts Act, the employee has the right to be absent from work, with retention of his normal pay, on the occasion of family events, for the fulfilment of civic obligations or civilian assignments and in the event of an appearance before a court of law. In addition, there are many other regulations, agreements or arrangements that are provided for in collective agreements. For example, there are systems such as time credit, parental leave, paid educational leave, leave for compelling reasons and so on. As the names suggest, these leave systems are often linked to specific situations or motives.

432. An important ground for absence is the entitlement to time off. Therefore, annual leave should be mentioned. Holidays are regulated by the (coordinated) Acts of 28 June 1971 on the annual leave of employees (abbreviated to 'Holiday Act')[212]

209. Art. 2 New Working Arrangements Act.
210. CA no. 42 of 2 Jun. 1987 concerning the introduction of new working arrangements in undertakings, amended by CA no. 42bis of 10 Nov. 1987, declared universally binding by the Royal Decree of 18 Jun. 1987 and the Royal Decree of 14 Jan. 1988 respectively, *Belgian Official Gazette* of 26 Jun. 1987 and 3 Feb. 1988.
211. Act of 26 Mar. 2018 on strengthening economic growth and social cohesion (Arts 15–17), *Belgian Official Gazette* 30 Mar. 2018.
212. *Belgian Official Gazette* 30 Sep. 1971.

and the Royal Decree of 30 March 1967 determining the general arrangements for implementing the Acts on the annual leave of employees (abbreviated to 'Holiday Decree').[213]

433. In accordance with Article 2 of the Holiday Act, employees, employed full-time or part-time, are entitled to annual holidays in proportion to their performance. In principle, an employee (in a regular full-time system) is entitled to twenty days of holiday per year. This is therefore a total period of four weeks. Part-time employees exercise their holiday entitlement pro rata. Modalities, such as payment of wages and holiday allowance during this period, are also regulated by the Holiday Act.

434. According to Article 63 of the Holiday Decree, the holidays, or the holiday period, are determined either collectively or individually. A holiday period can be determined at sector level for an entire category of employees, or at company level through consultation. In the absence of such a collective agreement, holidays are taken by individual agreement between the employer and the employee.

435. The execution of the employment contract is suspended during the employee's annual leave. This concerns both the days on which the company is closed due to a collective holiday and the days on which the employee takes his/her own annual holiday (Article 28, 1°, Employment Contracts Act).

§13. Parenting

436. The situation of parenthood, and pregnancy preceding it, is surrounded by many safeguards and rights.

437. In the case of pregnancy and childbirth, a system of maternity leave applies (Article 39, Labour Act). An employee is entitled to fifteen weeks of maternity leave. In the case of multiple births, this period is seventeen weeks, but it can be extended to nineteen weeks. The employee may not work from the seventh day preceding the presumed date of birth until the expiry of a nine-week period starting on the day of birth. The prenatal leave therefore lasts at least seven days and the postnatal leave at least nine weeks. The remaining weeks can be moved around.

438. A pregnant employee, who has informed the employer of her condition, is entitled to be absent from work, on full pay, for the time necessary to attend prenatal examinations, where these cannot take place outside working hours. To be entitled to pay, the employee must notify the employer in advance of her absence. If a collective agreement or the work regulations so require, or failing that at the employer's request, the employee must provide the employer with a medical certificate justifying her absence (cf. Article 39bis, Labour Act).

---

213. *Belgian Official Gazette* 6 Apr. 1967.

439. There is protection against dismissal under Article 40 of the Labour Act. Except for reasons unrelated to the physical condition caused by the pregnancy or the childbirth, an employer who employs a pregnant employee may not take any action intended to terminate unilaterally the employment relationship from the moment he is informed of the pregnancy until one month after the end of the post-natal rest period. It is for the employer to prove that such grounds exist. At the employee's request, the employer must inform her of this in writing. If the reason invoked in support of the dismissal is not in accordance with the legal requirements, the employer must pay the employee a fixed allowance equal to her gross salary for six months, without prejudice to the other allowances owed in the event of termination of the employment contract. Of course, the provisions relating to equal treatment and non-discrimination, which are described elsewhere, should also be mentioned in this context.

440. Under Article 30, §2 of the Employment Contracts Act, fathers or co-parents are entitled to be absent from work for fifteen days, for births since 1 January 2021 and for twenty days for births as from 1 January 2023.[214]

441. The legislator also provides for adoption leave. An employee is entitled to adoption leave of a maximum of six consecutive weeks if the child is under 3 years at the time the leave starts and a maximum of four weeks in other cases. In order to exercise the right to adoption leave, such leave must commence within two months of the child's registration as a member of the employee's family in the population register or in the foreigner's register of the municipality where he or she resides (Article 30ter, Employment Contracts Act).

442. An employee who meets the requirements has the right to take parental leave until the child for whom the leave is taken has reached the age of 12. This leave system also applies in the case of parenthood after adoption.[215] Parental leave is based on European legislation.[216]

214. Inserted through Art. 63 of the Programme Act of 20 Dec. 2020, *Belgian Official Gazette* 30 Dec. 2020.
215. RD 29 Oct. 1997 declaring universally binding Collective Agreement No. 64 of 29 Apr. 1997, concluded in the National Labour Council, establishing a right to parental leave, *Belgian Official Gazette* 7 Nov. 1997; RD 29 Oct. 1997 establishing a right to parental leave in the context of a career break, *Belgian Official Gazette* 7 Nov. 1997.
216. Directive No. 96/34/EC of 3 Jun. 1996 on the framework agreement on parental leave concluded by UNICE, CEEP and the ETUC, OJ L 19 Jun. 1996, p. 145, 4.

Chapter 5. Work Incapacity and Other Interruptions

§1. Concept

443. When one speaks of the suspension of the employment contract, this refers to the suspension of the execution of the employment contract. It means that the mutually assumed obligations of the parties are suspended. For the employee, it means a suspension of the obligation to perform the work; for the employer, it means a suspension to provide the work and to pay the salary.

444. Suspension of the employment contract may occur for various reasons: due to 'force majeure'; due to a legal provision which defines a particular situation as a cause for suspension (e.g., incapacity for work); by mutual agreement of the parties (e.g., 'unpaid leave' or sabbatical leave); legitimate cases of suspension recognised by case law (e.g., strike).

445. The consequences of many suspension situations are regulated by laws, royal decrees, collective agreements, etc. Some of them will be dealt with later on. It is useful to point out three general consequences at this point:

(1) because in case of suspension of the employment contract, its execution is suspended, it means that the parties remain bound by the rights and obligations resulting from the employment contract, such as the duty of respect and esteem, non-competition, confidential information and so on;
(2) suspending the employee's obligation to perform work generally implies suspending the employer's obligation to pay the wages. There are exceptions to this (continued payment of wages in the event of illness, holidays, etc.), but these are expressly provided for by law, a collective agreement, or in some other way;
(3) as soon as the ground for suspension disappears, the performance of the employment contract resumes in principle without any further formal requirements, and the parties resume the full performance of their obligations as agreed.

§2. Force Majeure

446. Article 1148 of the Old Civil Code states that no damages shall be due if the debtor has been prevented by force majeure or accident from giving or doing what he was bound to do.

447. Force majeure is a sudden, unforeseeable and insurmountable event,[217] occurring entirely independently of the will of the party invoking it,[218] which renders the performance of the obligation impossible and is not attributable to the fault of the debtor. Circumstances hindering the performance of the contract do not constitute force majeure.[219]

448. In reciprocal contracts, such as employment contracts, force majeure, which prevents a party from fulfilling its obligations, results in either the suspension or termination of the contract by operation of law, depending on whether or not the obstacle allows the contract to be performed.[220]

449. The legislator explicitly refers to force majeure with respect to employment contracts, and also makes a distinction between force majeure which has a suspensive effect *and* force majeure which has a terminating effect. The Employment Contracts Act of 3 July 1978 provides that force majeure suspends the execution of an employment contract if its effects are temporary (Article 26, Employment Contracts Act). Article 32, 5°, of the Employment Contracts Act, on the contrary, provides that the obligations arising from the contracts governed by this Act can (also) be terminated by force majeure.

Whether force majeure is suspensive or terminative is a question of fact. However, the Court of Cassation suggests that the notion of 'temporary' in Article 26 of the Employment Contracts Act is opposed to 'permanent'. Thus, a case of force majeure with very long-lasting consequences only has a suspensive effect on the execution of the employment contract. For a force majeure event to be terminating, it must in principle make the performance of the obligations definitively impossible.[221]

The distinction is obviously important. In the case of terminating force majeure, both parties are definitively relieved of their obligations, and the employment contract terminates without further formality, and without the parties being liable to each other for notice or compensation in lieu of notice.

450. In light of this, specific case law with regard to work incapacity should be mentioned. The Court of Cassation has stated in a number of judgments that a temporary incapacity for work of the employee as a result of illness or an accident, irrespective of its duration, does not constitute a case of force majeure leading to the termination of the employment contract. On the other hand, permanent incapacity to work, which makes it definitively impossible for the employee to perform the stipulated work, does constitute a case of terminating force majeure (terminating the employment contract).[222] However, this jurisprudence is under pressure, *inter alia*

---

217. Cass. 9 Oct. 1986, *RW* 1987–88, 778.
218. Cass. 28 Nov. 1984, *Pas.* 1985, I, 390.
219. Cass. 9 Dec. 1976, *Arr.Cass.* 1977, 404, *RW* 1977–78, 695 and *Pas.* 1977, I, 408; Cass. 10 Jan. 1994, *JTT* 1994, 209, *RW* 1994–95, 51, *Arr.Cass.* 1994, 17 and *Pas.* 1994, I, 13.
220. Cass. 13 Jan. 1956, *Pas.* 1956, I, 460 (S).
221. Cass. 10 Jan. 1994, *JTT* 1994, 209 (S).
222. Cass. 5 Jan. 5, 1981, *RW* 1980–81, 2401; Cass. 21 Apr. 1986, *TSR* 1986, 372; Cass. 13 Feb. 1989, *RW* 1988–89, 1298; Cass. 13 Mar. 1989, *RW* 1989–90, 46 and *JTT* 1989, 331.

in view of the employer's 'reintegration obligations' in work incapacity law as well as due to anti-discrimination provisions (*see* further on Article 34, Employment Contracts Act).

§3. Pandemic

451. During the COVID-19 (corona) pandemic, the government took a lot of different measures in order to secure and manage the sanitary situation of the country. Also, employers have taken different measures, based on governmental advice or on protocols issued by the government or the social partners.[223] Different measures were related to the health and safety context at work. The government introduced telework, besides social distancing and other measures, as one of the instruments to reduce physical contact in the (working) population. The social partners in the NLC adopted a specific national collective agreement concerning 'corona'-related telework, CA no. 149. The purpose of this collective agreement was to regulate the situations of telework that were imposed or advised by the government during the pandemic.

452. Many of the government's measures were issued on the basis of legislation that existed before the pandemic. In this context, discussions came up with regard to the legal basis for some of the measures. Therefore, the government introduced a new bill before the Parliament, which subsequently adopted the so-called Pandemic Act of 14 August 2021.[224] It concerns an act on administrative policy measures during an epidemic emergency. The Pandemic Act enables the government to take the necessary measures in the event of an epidemic emergency, in all kinds of societal spheres, including the determination of the conditions of work organisation, subject to the measures taken pursuant to Act of 4 August 1996 on the well-being of workers (discussed elsewhere in this monograph). The Social Penal Code was amended to allow for the enforcement of future measures in this context.

§4. Guaranteed Daily Wage

453. As a general rule, if the performance of the employment contract is suspended due to force majeure, there is no right to remuneration. In principle, a right to remuneration arises only to the extent that the employee performs work. Nevertheless, for a number of situations, the legislator has provided for a right to wages, even when no work is done. A 'guaranteed daily wage' is an example of this.

454. The 'guaranteed daily wage' concerns an entitlement to pay for a full working day, even if an employee is unable to work on that day, or only a part of that day, due to circumstances beyond his control. The scheme is set out in Article 27 of

223. Cf. F. Hendrickx, S. Taes & M. Wouters, *Covid-19 and Labour Law in Belgium*', 11(3) European Lab. L. J. 276–285 (2020).

224. *Belgian Official Gazette* 20 Aug. 2021.

the Employment Contracts Act. The law distinguishes between two hypotheses: 1° entitled to guaranteed daily pay is the employee who, while commuting to work, arrives late or not at the place of work, provided that the delay or absence is due to a cause which occurred on the way to work and which is independent of the employee's will (Article 27, paragraph 1, 1°, Employment Contracts Act); 2° also entitled to a full day of wages is a worker who, outside the case of a strike, is prevented from (continuing to) working due to a cause beyond his control (Article 27, paragraph 1, 2°, Employment Contracts Act).

§5. Work Incapacity

I. Concept

455. Incapacity for work refers to the situation where an employee, due to illness or accident, is unable to perform the contractually agreed tasks.

456. It should be noted that the 'work incapacity' in Belgian labour law is not completely similar to the concept of 'work incapacity' or 'disability' understood in Belgian social security law, which provides for sickness benefits. In social security, reference is usually made to a well-defined 'degree' of incapacity. In labour law, the main standard is whether the employee can or cannot perform the agreed work.[225] Someone who is party suitable for work but not fully for the work that he must perform under the employment contract is unfit for work within the meaning of labour law (the Employment Contracts Act), but not necessarily for social security law.[226] The difference between labour law and social security law can lead to the rare case, though not purely theoretical, that an employee remains without protection.

457. Work incapacity must be the result of an illness or accident. A specific regime applies to accidents at work or occupational diseases, which are subject to separate regulations. For work accidents and professional diseases, reference can be made to the Act of 10 April 1971 on work accidents and the coordinated Acts of 3 June 1970 on occupational diseases. These Acts are complemented with additional and more specific regulations through specific Acts and Royal Decrees.

458. Work incapacity, other than work accidents or occupational diseases, however, relates to all kinds of illnesses or accidents with which one can be confronted as a human being. The legal regime for this general situation of work incapacity will be dealt with hereinafter.

225. Labour Court Liege 19 Sep. 1991, *Soc.Kron.* 1992.
226. *Cf. Parl.* Chamber 1959—60, no. 414/1, 1.

II. Obligations

459. The incapacity of the employee to perform his work suspends the execution of the contract of employment (Article 31, §1, Employment Contracts Act). It means that the employee is (temporarily) released from his obligation to work. In other words, incapacity for work is a legitimate situation of absence from work. The legislator has, nonetheless, created an obligation for the employer to continue to pay wages (at least for a certain period).

460. If the employee is unfit for work, he must as soon as possible inform his employer (Article 31, §2, paragraph 1, Employment Contracts Act). The employee must usually also submit a medical certificate to the employer. This is the case if a collective agreement or the company's work regulations prescribe this, or in the absence of such a provision, at the request of the employer (Article 31, §2, paragraph 2, Employment Contracts Act). Except in cases of force majeure, the employee shall send or hand in the medical certificate at the company, within two working days from the day of incapacity or from the day of receipt of the request, unless a different period has been set by collective agreement or by the work regulations.

461. The medical certificate is generally issued by the employee's doctor and must state the fact of the incapacity for work, its probable duration and whether or not the employee may leave his home (Article 31(2)(2), Employment Contracts Act). Thus, the employer does not have the right to have any knowledge about the nature of the illness (or accident) that caused the employee's incapacity for work. This information is covered by the medical practitioner's professional secrecy and is protected by the employee's privacy. The employee may, of course, disclose it to the employer on his or her own initiative, but is under no obligation to do so. This principle has created much discussion in light of the COVID-19 pandemic. As a principle, employers have had no right to know whether their employees were infected during the pandemic. What is allowed, however, is that the responsible corporate practitioner, to which every employer must be linked, may receive information on infections of employees. But, this corporate practitioner is bound by professional secrecy.

462. Article 61, 2° Law on the Statute of Unions has inserted in Article 31 of the Law on Employment Contracts a paragraph 3/1. This section establishes the sanction for failure to notify the employer, failure to submit the medical certificate (within the time limit) and failure to comply with the medical control (in connection with control). The sanction consists of the loss of the guaranteed salary (sick pay), preceding the notification, presentation or control.

III. Sick Pay

463. During the period of work incapacity, the employee is entitled to a wage guarantee (sick pay), at the expense of the employer. It amounts to the full or partial continued payment of wages, depending on whether the employee is a white-collar worker or a blue-collar worker.

464. The guaranteed salary (sick pay) is in principle granted for a limited period (collective agreements can, however, extend the statutory period). After this period, an employee is in principle fully covered by social security protection (sickness and invalidity insurance) and/or a private insurance formula.

465. For the regulation of sick pay, Articles 52 and 53 of the Employment Contracts Act for blue-collar workers, Articles 70, 71 and 73 of the Employment Contracts Act for white-collar workers, and two national collective agreements are particularly relevant (CA no. 12bis of 26 February 1979; CA no. 13bis of 26 February 1979). The provisions of these collective agreements are not applicable if there are agreements within the joint committee that contain equivalent or more favourable provisions.

466. As regards the amount of sick pay and its duration, a distinction must be made between blue-collar and white-collar workers.

467. The overview looks as follows:

Blue Collar		
Day 1–7	100% wage to be paid by the employer	no supplement
Day 8–14	60% of the wages to be paid by the employer	+25.88% supplement to be paid by the employer
Day 15–30	60% wage related social security benefit (by public social security fund)	+25.88% supplement to be paid by the employer

White Collar		
Day 1–7	**100% wage** to be paid by the employer	no supplement
Day 8–14	**100% wage** to be paid by the employer	no supplement
Day 15–30	**100% wage** to be paid by the employer	no supplement

468. Certain short-term–white-collar workers follow the regime of the blue-collar workers. Furthermore, after the thirty days of wage guarantee, the social security system takes over and provides for sickness benefits, in principle related to 60% of the wages of the employee.

IV. Medical Control

469. In order to justify his absence and to be entitled to a guaranteed salary, the employee must certify his incapacity for work. As indicated above, this is done by submitting a medical certificate, which is drawn up by the employee's (own) medical practitioner. However, if the employer doubts the veracity of the work incapacity (and thus has a suspicion of fraud), he has the possibility to control it. The control is performed by a 'control doctor' assigned (and paid) by the employer.

470. Obviously, such control of the employee's work incapacity is a delicate matter. The legislator has therefore issued a regulation. This was done by the Act of 13 June 1999 on 'control medicine'. Also, the provisions of Article 31 of the Employment Contracts Act are important.

471. The employee may not refuse to see or be examined by a medical officer authorised and paid for by the employer. Unless the person who issued the medical certificate to the employee considers that his state of health does not allow him to travel to another place, the employee must present himself to the 'control doctor' on request. The employee's travel expenses are borne by the employer (Article 31, §3, paragraph 1, Employment Contracts Act).

472. The control doctor shall verify whether the employee is actually incapacitated for work, verify the probable duration of the incapacity for work and, where appropriate, other medical data in so far as they are necessary for the control; all other findings shall remain subject to professional secrecy (Article 31, §3, paragraph 1, Employment Contracts Act).

473. The control doctor performs his task in accordance with the provisions of Article 3 of the Act of 13 June 1999 on control medicine (Article 31, §3, paragraph 3, Employment Contracts Act).

474. Article 61, 3° of the Unified Status Act introduced a special regime (Article 31, §3, of the Unified Status Act). It is provided that a collective agreement or a work regulation may determine a daily period of up to four consecutive hours between 7 am and 8 pm, during which the employee must be at the disposal of the control doctor at his place of residence or at a communicated other place of residence.

475. It is possible that the control doctor and the general practitioner treating the employee come to opposite conclusions regarding the employee's incapacity for work. A dispute may then arise, as the employer may withhold the guaranteed salary (Article 31, §4, Employment Contracts Act) or may impose other sanctions (such as disciplinary sanctions). The law provides for disputes of a medical nature arising between the employee and the control doctor to be settled by arbitration. The decision resulting from this arbitration procedure is final and binding on the parties (Article 31, §5, paragraph 1, Employment Contracts Act). All this is without prejudice to the competence of the courts (Article 31, §5, paragraph 1, Employment Contracts Act).

V. Reintegration

476. In spite of – but also partly in response to – the case law of the Court of Cassation concerning the termination of force majeure in the context of permanent work incapacity, the legislator has made efforts to introduce the notion of 'reintegration'.

477. The Codex on Wellbeing provides for a procedure regarding the reintegration of workers who are incapacitated due to illness or disability. The aim of this reintegration process is to provide the disabled employee with temporary modified or alternative work pending the return to his/her agreed work, or definitively to provide him/her with modified or alternative work if the employee is definitively unfit to perform his/her agreed work.[227] This reintegration process is legally framed by Article 34 of the Employment Contracts Act, which stipulates that the incapacity for work resulting from illness or accident, which makes it definitively impossible for the employee to perform the agreed work, can only end the employment contract on grounds of force majeure after the end of the reintegration process of the employee concerned.

227. Book I, Title 4, Ch. VI, Wellbeing Codex of 28 Apr. 2017, *Belgian Official Gazette* 2 Jun. 2017.

Chapter 6. Discrimination

§1. General

478. Employment discrimination has become a very important component of labour law. After focusing initially on gender, new sets of legislation have arisen over the years, with a widening of the scope of equality law. The influence of European Union law is apparent.

479. Belgian anti-discrimination law is, in fact, strongly influenced by European Union law. At the European level, anti-discrimination law has continued to evolve. Whereas at first it only concerned discrimination based on sex, and nationality in free movement law, new EU powers led to the Racial Discrimination Directive and the Framework Directive. The Racial Discrimination Directive introduced the principle of equal treatment irrespective of racial or ethnic origin into broad areas of social life, including employment and vocational training.[228] The Framework Directive covers a wide range of 'new' grounds of discrimination, such as religion or belief, disability, age and sexual orientation.[229]

480. The Belgian (federal) labour discrimination law forms a 'triptych' (or rather a 'quadriptych') of Acts of 10 May 2007. This regulation replaced the anti-discrimination laws of 25 February 2003. The 2003 legislation first implemented EU law, but was partially annulled by the Constitutional Court[230] on 6 October 2004, on the grounds that the legislation itself infringed the prohibition of discrimination by selecting specific grounds for discrimination, while there was no objective and reasonable justification for the fact that people discriminated against on other ground, such as political opinion or language, could not enjoy the protection of non-discrimination law. Because of this, new legislative initiatives led to the Act(s) of 10 May 2007.[231] Rather than a single law, three separate instruments (in fact four) were adopted: in addition to a 'general' Anti-Discrimination Act (ADA) of 10 May 2007, the Act of 10 May 2007 combating discrimination between women and men was adopted, as well as the Act of 10 May 2007 amending the Act of 30 July 1981 punishing certain acts inspired by racism or xenophobia. The same date also saw an Act to adapt provisions of the Code of Procedure.[232]

481. This gives the following statutory overview:

- Act of 10 May 2007 on combating certain forms of discrimination;
- Act of 30 July 1981 punishing certain acts inspired by racism or xenophobia (as amended by the Act of 10 May 2007);
- Act of 10 May 2007 on combating discrimination between women and men;

---

228. Dir. EC Council, No. 2000/43, 29 Jun. 2000, *OJ L* 19, 19 Jul. 2000, p. 180, 22.
229. Dir. EC Council, No. 2000/78, 27 Nov. 2000, *OJ L* 2 Dec. 2000, p. 303, 16.
230. *Belgian Official Gazette* 16 Oct. 2003, 50353.
231. *Belgian Official Gazette* 30 May 2007.
232. All published in *Belgian Official Gazette* 30 May 2007.

- Act of 10 May 2007 adapting the Code of Procedure to legislation on combating discrimination and punishing certain acts inspired by racism or xenophobia.

482. In addition, there are some important national collective agreements that contain the prohibition of discrimination:

- CA no. 38 of 6 December 1983 concerning the recruitment and selection of employees (cf. Article 2bis);
- CA no. 25 of 15 October 1975 concerning equal pay for male and female employees;
- CA no. 95 of 10 October 2008 concerning equal treatment during all phases of the employment relationship.

483. Equal treatment principles should also be taken into account in a number of special regulations in labour law. There is, for example, the Act of 5 March 2002 on the principle of non-discrimination in favour of part-time workers and the Act of 5 June 2002 on the principle of non-discrimination in favour of fixed-term workers.

484. This provides the following overview of discrimination grounds in Belgian labour law:

- following the EU Directives: sex; race; ethnic origin; religion or belief; disability; age; sexual orientation;
- following the Acts of 10 May 2007 (including Act of 30 July 1981 on racism): sex; so-called race; colour; descent or national or ethnic origin; social origin; age; sexual orientation; civil status; birth; property; religion or belief; political opinion; syndical conviction, language, present or future health condition; disability; physical or genetic characteristic;
- following CA no. 38 and CA no. 95: age; sex; marital status; history of illness; race; colour; ancestry or national or ethnic origin; political or philosophical belief; membership of a trade union or other organisation; sexual orientation; disability.

§2. Statutory Protection

I. General

485. Below, a closer look will be taken at the Act of 10 May 2007 to combat certain forms of discrimination (the ADA). Much of this Act also applies to the other Acts as the three substantive ADAs have a similar scope and systematics. As a rule, what is said about the ADA also applies to the other acts. However, where special emphasis should be placed, explicit reference is made to the Act of 10 May 2007 to combat discrimination between women and men (the Gender Discrimination Act (GDA)) and the Act of 30 July 1981 to punish certain acts inspired by racism or xenophobia, as amended by the Act of 10 May 2007 (the Racism Discrimination Act (RDA)).

486. As the ADA itself states, its aim is to establish a general framework for combating discrimination, on a limited (but large) number of grounds: age, sexual orientation, civil status, birth, property, religion or belief, political opinion, syndical conviction, language, current or future state of health, disability, physical or genetic characteristic or social origin (Article 3 ADA).

The discrimination ground 'trade union membership' was added to the law later.[233] In doing so, the legislator reacted to a judgment of the Constitutional Court of 2 April 2009,[234] in which the Court criticised the fact that the ADA uses a so-called closed list of protected criteria, but without including trade union membership in that list. As a result, the legislator inserted the words 'trade union affiliation' in Articles 3 and 4, 4° of the Act of 10 May 2007, so that discrimination on the basis of membership or belonging to a trade union or of trade union activity is covered by these articles.

II. Scope

487. The ADA has a broad scope of application. The Act applies to all persons in the public sector as well as in the private sector, including public authorities (Article 5, §1).

With regard to matters, the Act states that it covers (Article 5, §1):

(1) access to and supply of goods and services which are available to the public;
(2) social protection, including social security and healthcare;
(3) the social benefits;
(4) supplementary social security schemes;
(5) the employment relationship;
(6) the mention of it in an official document or in a report;
(7) membership of or involvement in an employers' or employees' organisation or any organisation whose members are engaged in a particular occupation, including the benefits provided by such organisations;
(8) access to and participation in, as well as any other exercise of, economic, social, cultural or political activity open to the public.

488. The ADW broadly applies to employment relationships (Article 5, §1, 5° ADA). Under the Act, 'employment relations' are defined as (Article 4, 1 ADA) those relations which include, but are not limited to, employment, conditions of access to employment, terms and conditions of employment, and severance arrangements, and this in both the public and private sectors; for both paid and unpaid work, work done under internship agreements, apprenticeship agreements, vocational training agreements and starter job agreements or work on a self-employed basis; for all levels of the occupational hierarchy and for all branches of activity; irrespective of the statutory or contractual arrangements of the person carrying out the work.

233. Art. 107 Act of 30 Dec. 2009 containing various provisions, *Belgian Official Gazette* 31 Dec. 2009.
234. GwH 2 Apr. 2009, No. 64/2009.

III. Mechanism

489. The ADW is based on the principle of non-discrimination. The Act states that any form of discrimination is prohibited (Article 14 ADA). It also defines what constitutes discrimination: direct discrimination, indirect discrimination, instructions to discriminate, intimidation and a refusal to make reasonable adjustments for the benefit of a person with a disability (Article 14 ADA).

490. As is well known, the ADA is based on an exhaustive list of protected criteria. Thus, Article 3 of this Act states that its purpose is to create a general framework for combating discrimination on the basis of the specified grounds.

491. However, the existence of protected criteria does not necessarily mean that the use of one or more of these criteria is always prohibited. A distinction based on the protected grounds must, however, be justified.

492. In making a direct distinction on the basis of the protected criteria, the Act applies in principle an 'open' system of justification.

Article 7 ADA provides: 'Any direct discrimination based on one of the protected criteria constitutes direct discrimination, unless this direct discrimination is objectively justified by a legitimate aim and the means of achieving that aim are appropriate and necessary.'

This open system of justification is, in principle, applicable, with the exception of the situations referred to in Article 8 of the ADA (referring to specific grounds). In fact, this general system is the same justification test that is used in the context of justifying an indirect distinction (*see* Article 9 ADA).[235]

493. In a number of situations involving direct discrimination, a more 'closed' system of justification (and thus a stricter test) applies. This is the case for the matters listed in Article 8 ADA. There is stricter protection of direct discrimination on grounds of age, sexual orientation, religion or belief, or disability can only be justified on the basis of essential and determining occupational requirements.

Under Article 8(2) of the ADA, a substantial and determining occupational requirement can be said to exist only if:

- a particular characteristic, related to age, sexual orientation, religion or belief, or disability, is essential and determining because of the nature of the particular occupational activities concerned or the context in which they are carried out; and
- the requirement is based on a legitimate aim and is proportionate to the aim pursued.

The courts will examine in each specific case whether a certain characteristic constitutes a substantial and determining occupational requirement (Article 8, §3 ADA).

235. *Parl.* Chamber 2005–06, No. 2722/001, 47.

494. For indirect discrimination, the Act states that any indirect distinction based on one of the protected criteria constitutes indirect discrimination (Article 9 ADA) unless the apparently neutral provision, criterion or practice underlying that indirect discrimination is objectively justified by a legitimate aim and the means of achieving that aim are appropriate and necessary; or, unless, in the case of indirect discrimination on the grounds of disability, it is shown that no reasonable accommodation can be made.

495. In preparing the legislation in Parliament, the legislator made it clear in any case that the justification (the 'legitimate objective') cannot relate to discriminatory motives. Thus, the willingness to accommodate a discriminatory preference of customers or other employees cannot be accepted as a legitimate objective.[236]

496. As far as gender-based discrimination is concerned, also there the principle is that a direct distinction based on gender can only be justified on the basis of an essential and determining occupational requirement (Article 13, §1 and §2 GDA). However, the GDA adds that a Royal Decree, deliberated on in the Council of Ministers, determines the situations in which a particular characteristic constitutes a genuine and determining occupational requirement within the meaning of this provision (Article 13, §3 GDA). Currently, the Royal Decree of 8 February 1979 determining the cases in which gender can be mentioned in the conditions for access to a job or a professional activity still applies.[237] It provides that in the conditions for access to a job or a professional activity for which gender is a determining condition, gender can only be mentioned in the following cases:

1° positions or professional activities of: actor, dramatist, singer, dancer, and of artist called upon to perform a male or female role; a mannequin who needs to dress in order to represent garments; a model for painters, sculptors, photographers and beauty salons;
or
2° employment or professional activities exercised in countries which are not Member States of the European Union and the exercise of which is reserved to a particular gender by local legislation and customs.

IV. Positive Action

497. The legislation provides that a direct or indirect distinction based on one of the protected criteria never gives rise to a finding of discrimination if this direct or indirect distinction involves a measure of positive action (Article 10, §1 ADA). A positive action measure can only be implemented if a number of following conditions are met (Article 10, §2 ADA):

– there must be an apparent disparity;

236. *Parl.* Chamber 2005–06, No. 2722/001, 49.
237. *Belgian Official Gazette* 16 Feb. 1979.

- the elimination of this inequality should be identified as an objective to be promoted;
- the positive action measure must be of a temporary nature and must disappear once the objective pursued has been achieved;
- the measure of positive action should not unduly restrict another's rights.

498. The law instructs the government to determine by Royal Decree the situations in which and the conditions under which a measure of positive action can be taken (Article 10, §3 ADA). The regulatory framework for positive action in the private sector was provided by the Royal Decree (RD) of 11 February 2019 laying down the conditions for affirmative action.[238] Article 3 of this RD defines positive actions as specific measures to prevent or compensate for disadvantages related to the protected criteria, as mentioned in the anti-discrimination laws, with a view to ensuring full equality in practice. The intention of the RD is to support positive actions with a positive action plan. This positive action plan is in principle established by collective agreement or by act of accession according to an established model in which the conditions concerning positive actions are laid down. However, the RD stipulates that companies can also initiate positive action in other forms than a collective agreement or through an act of accession. Pursuant to Article 7 of the RD, the positive action plan must be submitted for approval to the Minister to whom work belongs. This seems to refer only to the positive action plans in a collective agreement or act of accession. In case of a positive action plan in another form, it is only foreseen to inform the Minister (cf. Article 9 of the RD).

V. Age Discrimination

499. The ADA also provides for a number of special justifications with regard to a distinction based on age. These justifications exist specifically for employment relationships and supplementary social security schemes.

500. The law provides that, in the field of employment relations and supplementary social security schemes, a direct distinction based on age does not constitute discrimination if it is objectively and reasonably justified by a legitimate aim, including legitimate employment policy objectives, the labour market or any other comparable legitimate aim, and the means of achieving that aim are appropriate and necessary (Article 12, §1 ADA). With this provision, the legislator wishes to implement the provisions of Article 6.1 of the European Framework Directive 2000/78/EC. This article allows Member States to provide in certain cases for the justification of discrimination based on age in horizontal relations.

238. *Belgian Official Gazette*, 1 Mar. 2019.

VI. Identity-Based Organisations

501. The ADA provides exception in relation to identity-based organisations. Thus, the law states that, for public or private organisations, the basis of which is religion or philosophy of life, a direct distinction based on religion or philosophy of life with regard to the professional activities of this organisation does not constitute discrimination if, due to the nature of the activities or the context in which they are carried out, the religion or philosophy of life constitutes an essential, legitimate and justified occupational requirement in view of the basis of the organisation (Article 13 ADA).

Under this provision, no other direct distinction can be justified on the basis of another protected criterion, unless this is done in application of another provision of this title (Article 13 ADA).

502. Provided that the provisions of this Act are otherwise observed, this Act shall not affect the right of public or private organisations whose foundation is based on faith or philosophical belief to require from persons working for them an attitude of good faith and loyalty to the foundation of the organisation (Article 13 ADA).

§3. Enforcement

503. The ADA has both a civil and a criminal section. The focus is clearly on the civil law part, which, among other things, offers the possibility of instituting an injunction procedure and obtaining compensation.

504. The ADA provides for the nullity of contradictory terms and of clauses waiving the protection of the law (Article 15 ADA). This nullity provision, imposed by the European legislator, concerns not only discriminatory provisions in individual employment contracts or other individual agreements but also collective agreements, documents drawn up unilaterally, company regulations and the like.

505. The law provides that, in case of discrimination, a complaint can be filed, either in the company with the Labour Inspectorate, or with the Centre for Equal Opportunities (called 'Unia') (Article 17, §3 ADA). A legal action remains of course possible. In the event of a complaint, the person concerned by the complaint is protected against adverse measures (Article 17 ADA). The protection also applies to witnesses.

506. The legislator has provided for compensation for the victim of discrimination. In the event of discrimination, the victim may claim compensation in accordance with contract or tort law (Article 18, §1 paragraph 1 ADA). The victim can choose between claiming lump sum compensation or compensation for the damage actually suffered. In the latter case, the victim must prove the extent of the damage suffered (Article 18, §1 paragraph 2 ADA). The ADA provides that, if the victim claims moral and material damages due to discrimination in the framework of the employment relationship or the supplementary social security schemes, the lump sum compensation for material and moral damages is equal to the gross remuneration for six months (Article 18, §2, 2° ADA).[239]

507. The ADA provides for the possibility to receive an injunction order. The victim of an alleged discrimination (as well as interest groups) can file a case with the president of the competent court with the request to order the cessation of discriminatory practices. The procedure is conducted as in summary proceedings (Article 20, §1 ADA).

239. Art. 18, §2, 1° and 2° of the Act of 10 May 2007 on combating certain forms of discrimination does not violate Arts 10 and 11 of the Constitution, according to Constitutional Court judgment of 7 Jun. 2018, no. 70/2018, so that the fact that an employer who has committed discrimination must pay significantly higher compensation in respect of an employee than any other person who has committed discrimination does not violate the principle of equality.

Chapter 7. Employment Termination

§1. Introduction

I. Employment Security

508. The termination of the employment relationship is a much-debated topic in labour law in Europe, also in Belgium. It is obviously related to the importance attached to job security, or broader employment security, and the functioning of the labour market.

509. Job security is still an important value in Belgian labour law. The Belgian legislator created many rules to guarantee job security. These statutory regulations are, moreover, often supplemented by job security regulations in collective agreements.

II. Methods of Termination

510. A central provision is Article 32 of the Employment Contracts Act of 3 July 1978. It provides that, subject to the general modes of extinction of contractual obligations, the obligations arising from the employment contract take an end:

(1) by the expiry of the term;
(2) by completion of the work for which the agreement was concluded;
(3) by the will of one of the parties, when the agreement has been entered into for an indefinite period of time, or in case of an urgent reason for termination;
(4) by the death of the employee;
(5) due to force majeure.

The reference to 'the general modes of extinction of obligations' implies that the modes of termination under civil law (other than those mentioned) in principle also apply to the employment contract. Therefore, the employment contract can also be terminated by a judicial dissolution (which, however, rarely arises) or by the mutual consent of the parties.

511. Every reciprocal contract, such as an employment contract, contains a tacit resolutive clause (Article 1184 Old Civil Code). This means that, in the event of a breach of contract, a court may, in principle, order the contract to be performed or rescinded. This method of termination is practically non-existent in employment contracts. The mandatory performance *in kind of* employment contracts is virtually impossible, considering the freedom of employment and the freedom of dismissal of the parties. Furthermore, judicial dissolution is time-consuming, and the rules of employment termination offer more effectiveness and certainty. Nevertheless, judicial dissolution is possible,[240] except for employee representatives or candidates for their position in the Works Council or the CPPW (Article 2, §6 Act 19 March 1991).

512. However, there are limitations to the methods of termination under civil law that have to do with the autonomy and functions of employment law. One example is the express resolutive condition (Article 1183 Old Civil Code). The application is practically not evident in employment relations. An express resolutive condition in an employment contract is null and void if it has the effect that the contract can be terminated exclusively by the will of one of the parties without taking into account the mandatory rules on dismissal prescribed by the Employment Contracts Act.[241] Only few exceptions in which a termination clause may exist mainly applies in cases where the employee no longer fulfils certain clear (e.g., legal) conditions to carry out his duties. One may think of the continued possession of a driver's licence as a condition for performing the job of a driver.

513. Pursuant to Article 32, 4° of the Employment Contracts Act, the employment contract ends upon the death of the employee. This conclusion is also implied by the assumption that the employment contract is always concluded *intuitu personae* of the employee. In case of death, no further formalities, deadlines or indemnities are required. The death of the employer does not, in principle, terminate the contract. If the employer is a legal person (a corporation), the issue will be resolved depending on the solutions of corporate law or, in case of economic difficulties or bankruptcy, of commercial law. If the employer is a natural person, the employer's decease leads to the end of the employment contract only when the contract was concluded *intuitu personae* on the side of the employer. In this case, the judge will fairly assess whether there are grounds for compensation for the employee (Article 33, Employment Contracts Act).

III. Unilateral Termination

514. In many cases, the employment contract is terminated at the initiative of one of the parties. In Belgian employment law, a number of concepts should be distinguished.

515. In Belgian labour law, the concept of dismissal refers to the unilateral legal act by which one party to the employment contract notifies the other of its intention to terminate the employment contract.[242] It is not a purely theoretical concept, but

240. Cass. 25 Feb. 1991, *JTT* 1991, 194; Labour Court Brussels 17 Jan. 1992, *JTT* 1993, 149.
241. Cass. 18 Jan. 1993, *JTT* 1993, 141.
242. Cass. 23 Mar. 1981, *Arr.Cass.* 1980–81, no. 419, p. 817 and *JTT* 1981, 240, note M. Taquet and C. Wantiez; Cass. 12 Sep. 1988, *Arr.Cass.* 1988–89, 23, 47; Cass. 14 Oct. 2002, *Arr.Cass.* 2002, no. 537, p. 2172; Cass. 19 May 2008, *Arr.Cass.* 2008, no. 302, p. 1239 and *RABG* 2009, 157, note V. Dooms.

one that is applied in case law. It is accepted that a dismissal terminates the contract with immediate effect and that the termination is irrevocable. A dismissal is, in principle, not subject to any formality.

516. It follows from this that each party to the employment contract can at any time unilaterally terminate the contract and thus impose the end of the employment contract on the other party. In other words, the employment contract will be definitively terminated as a result of the expression of the will by one of the parties, regardless of the answer to the question of whether the dismissal was lawful or regular. This, in Belgian labour law, is also referred to as the 'power to dismiss'. It is the recognised power of each party to unilaterally terminate the employment contract by mere expression of will, even in disregard of legal rules that limit or exclude the right to unilaterally terminate the employment contract. The other party is bound by this unilateral expression of will, in the sense that it will have to undergo the change in its legal situation that occurs as a result of the exercise of the right to dismiss by the other party. The exercise of the power of dismissal with disregard for any applicable rules of law can obviously lead to the obligation to pay damages to the other party. This indemnity is usually fixed. However, the Court, whether ruling on the merits or in summary proceedings, cannot order the employer to reinstate an employee.[243] Only in a very limited number of cases, the legislator has provided for the possibility for reinstatement, but even then the employer cannot be obliged to actually proceed to reintegrate the employee. Refusal to reintegrate leads, in those foreseen cases, merely to higher damages.[244]

517. The 'power to dismiss' is, therefore, not the same as the 'right to dismiss'. In most cases, the employment contract can only be *lawfully* terminated when formalities and a term of notice are respected, and a lawful motivation exists. The 'power to dismiss' merely allows a party to unilaterally terminate the contract anyway, without respect for the legal conditions.

§2. Unified Status

518. For almost a century, dismissal law has been dominated by the distinction between blue- and white-collar workers. As mentioned above, both the legislator and the social partners strived for a gradual harmonisation of the status of blue- and white-collar workers over the years, but it was not until major court cases came out that the legislator took care of legal reform.

243. Cass. 20 Jun. 1988, *RW* 1988–89, 678.
244. *See*, *e.g.*, Arts 14–19 of the Act of 19 Mar. 1991 on special rules for dismissal of staff representatives of works councils and committees for safety, health and improvement of the workplace and of candidate staff representatives.

I. Rulings of the Constitutional Court

519. As explained above, in a judgment of 7 July 2011, the Constitutional Court found that there was a violation of Articles 10 and 11 of the Constitution due to the statutory differences in treatment between blue-collar and white-collar workers with regard to the duration of the notice period. The Constitutional Court concluded that Articles 52, §1, paragraphs 2–4, and 59 of the Employment Contracts Act violated Articles 10 and 11 of the Constitution. However, the principle of legal certainty prompted the Constitutional Court to grant the legislator a final period of extension in which to legislate. During a transitional phase, which ended on 8 July 2013 at the latest, the effects of the unconstitutional legislative provisions were maintained.

520. In the midst of this development, a draft interprofessional agreement (IPA) for the period 2011–2012 was signed on 18 January 2011 within the so-called Group of 10, an informal body of the top negotiators of the major trade union and employers associations in Belgium. This draft agreement held out the prospect of a package of measures that fitted in with a phased rapprochement between the statuses of blue- and white-collar workers. The draft interprofessional agreement was not finally approved by all the parties concerned (why it remained a draft). Nevertheless, the government took the draft agreement as the basis for a bill that led to the Law of 12 April 2011, which is therefore known as the 'IPA Act'.[245] However, this IPA Act did not offer a fundamental reform and still maintained the distinction between blue- and white-collar workers.

521. Seen the judgment of the Constitutional Court in 2011, the general expectation was that the legislator would take new measures by 8 July 2013, the deadline of the Court. This soon proved to be a vain hope. The social partners and the government did not reach an agreement, and the 8 July 2013 deadline passed without any new legislation. However, intensive negotiations took place between the social partners and the Federal Minister of Labour. A compromise came out, and the basis for legal unification of the statutes was laid.

522. The compromise proposal was finally submitted in the autumn of 2013. This led to the 'Act of 26 December 2013 on the introduction of a unified status between blue and white collar workers with regard to notice periods and the carenz day and accompanying measures' (the Unified Status Act), which was published in the *Belgian Official Gazette* on 31 December 2013. The Unified Status Act is largely intended to amend the Employment Contracts Act of 3 July 1978 in its provisions concerning notice periods.[246]

245. Act of 12 Apr. 2011 adapting the Act of 1 Feb. 2011 extending the crisis measures and implementing the Interprofessional Agreement, and implementing the government's compromise on the draft interprofessional agreement, *Belgian Official Gazette* 28 Apr. 2011, ed. 2 (abbreviated IPA Act).

246. Explanatory Memorandum to the bill of 21 Nov. 2013 concerning the introduction of a unitary status between blue- and white-collar workers with regard to notice periods and the carenzdag and accompanying measures, *Parl.St.* Chamber 2013–14, no. 53K3144/001 (hereinafter 'Explanatory Memorandum'), 4.

II. Entry into Force

523. The new dismissal law entered into force on 1 January 2014 and became, in principle, applicable with respect to dismissals as from 1 January 2014. It means that it applies to all existing and running employment contracts as well as to newly concluded employment contracts concluded as from that date.

524. The Act, however, provides for a transitional arrangement. The terms of notice already acquired under the old legislation before the entry into force of the new legislation would not be affected. It implies that the notice periods to be observed by employees whose employment contract started before 1 January 2014 are calculated on the basis of the sum of two parts. The first part is calculated on the basis of the seniority acquired on 31 December 2013. The second part is calculated on the basis of the seniority acquired as from 1 January 2014. Therefore, the 'old' dismissal provisions of the Employment Contracts Act still have to be taken into account for quite some time. The transitional regime will be discussed in more detail below. It should already be noted here that this transitional rule does not simplify the dismissal law.

525. Since the legislator was actually too late, seen the deadline (8 July 2013) of the judgment of the Constitutional Court, the question arose as to how to look to dismissals after the deadline but before the Unified Status Act came into force (i.e., between 8 July 2013 and 31 December 2013). In a judgment dated 21 January 2016, the Constitutional Court basically gave more leeway, until 31 December 2013 seen the otherwise existing considerable legal uncertainty.[247]

526. The main points of the Unified Status can be summarised as follows.

(1) The Unification Statute Act amends the Employment Contracts Act of 3 July 1978. Thus, the Employment Contracts Act remained fully in place. It should be noted that, despite the ambitions expressed in the title of the 'Unified Status' Act, the Employment Contracts Act still contains the distinction between blue- and white-collar workers. Article 2 (blue-collar workers) and Article 3 (white-collar workers) of the Employment Contracts Act have not been abolished. As a result of the transitional rules on dismissal for current employment contracts, a distinction will still have to be made between blue-collar workers and white-collar employees.

(2) The provisions of the Employment Contracts Act relating to the notice periods for blue- and white-collar workers, including those introduced by the aforementioned 'IPA Act', are abolished. New provisions (such as Article 37/1 to 37/11) aim at harmonising the dismissal rules of all employees and employers. The new provisions lay down the general rules including new harmonised notice periods. As mentioned above, a transitional arrangement will apply, as a result of which the old (abolished) dismissal provisions will continue to apply for some time.

247. Constitutional Court, 21 Jan. 2016, no. 10/2016.

(3) The general outlook of dismissal law is maintained. Articles 32 and 37 of the Employment Contracts Act remain in force. Article 35 of the Employment Contracts Act is not affected either, so that dismissal for serious cause remains possible at all times. The Unified Status Act also does not affect the principle that dismissal is always possible without observing the applicable notice period, in which case the notice period applicable in principle forms the basis for determining the severance pay. In other words, in many cases, the provisions relating to the notice period are thus in essence also the relevant provisions leading to the determination of the indemnity in lieu of notice. The employee's length of service with the same employer remains the decisive factor in determining the duration of the notice period (and thus the amount of the indemnity in lieu of notice).

(4) However, unlike before, it is provided that the fixed-term employment contract can also be terminated by notice. This is somewhat at odds with the systematics of Article 32, 3° of the Law on Employment Contracts, which states that the employment contract can be terminated 'at the will of one of the parties, if the contract was concluded for an indefinite period of time, or in case of urgent cause for termination'.

(5) In order to build up the new notice periods, the possibility of a trial clause (a clause in the employment contract providing for shorter notice periods for a limited period) is abolished.

(6) With respect to Article 63 of the Employment Contracts Act (arbitrary dismissal for blue-collar workers), Article 38 of the Unified Status Act provides that it will cease to apply as soon as an alternative arrangement (by collective agreement concluded in the NLC) is in place. This was not yet in place when the Act came into force, but that came into force (for the private sector) with a new national collective agreement, CA no. 109 on the motivation for dismissal, which came into force on 1 April 2014.

(7) The Unified Status Act introduced some measures to promote employability so that the employee's broader employment security (rather than job security) was also addressed.

527. Employability was addressed with the introduction of Article 39ter of the Employment Contracts Act by the Unified Status Act (Article 92, Unified Status Act) and obliges every sector (sector level joint committee) to conclude a collective agreement by 1 January 2019 that contains measures aimed at increasing the employability of employees on the labour market. This obligation only applies to employees whose employment contract is terminated with at least thirty weeks' notice or compensation (or a combination thereof). For them, a 'severance package' must be provided that consists of: one-third of measures that increase employability (such as outplacement, support for specific training courses), and two-thirds notice or compensation (with a minimum of twenty-six weeks) to be served or paid.

§3. NOTICE

I. Concept

528. Notice is a written form of unilaterally terminating the employment contract. It is the technique prescribed by the legislator to lawfully and unilaterally end an open-ended employment contract. If the contract is concluded for an indefinite period of time, each party has the right, according to Article 37, §1 of the Employment Contracts Act, to terminate it by giving notice to the other party. It should be noted that, since the introduction of the 'Unified Status', it is also possible, under certain conditions, to end a fixed-term employment contract prematurely by giving notice (Article 40, §2, Employment Contracts Act).

529. Termination with notice is a form of dismissal to which the legislator in principle attaches a term (a notice period) and formal requirements (a letter of termination). It is a format which contains the unilateral expression of will whereby one party informs the other that he no longer considers himself bound by the agreement existing between them as of a certain date.

II. Formal Requirements

530. The termination of the employment contract must be notified to the terminated party by means of a written (and signed) document, the notification letter. This is apparent from the provisions of section 37 of the Employment Contracts Act.

531. The possible ways of giving this notification letter, with notice of termination to the other party, are limited by law. If the notification letter is issued by the employee, it shall be made, on pain of nullity:

- by personal delivery of a copy to the employer (the signature of the employer on the duplicate of this document serves as an acknowledgement of receipt of the notification);
- or by registered postal mail;
- or by bailiff's writ (Article 37, §1 paragraph 3, Employment Contracts Act).

532. If the notification letter is issued by the employer, it can, on pain of nullity, only be made by the employer:

- either by registered letter;
- or by a bailiff's writ (Article 37, §1, paragraph 4, Employment Contracts Act).

533. Depending on the method of termination, the notification will take effect at a different time. If the notification letter is provided by registered postal mail, the notification will take effect on the third working day[248] after the date of sending. This principle applies regardless of the time at which the party giving notice actually receives or takes note of the letter of termination.[249] If the notification letter is carried out by handing over a document, or through a bailiff, it takes effect from the moment the notification letter is delivered or from the moment it is given or served to the other party.

534. It is expressly provided that, under penalty of nullity, the notification letter must state the beginning and the duration of the notice period (Article 37, §1, paragraph 2, Employment Contracts Act). This formal requirement requires diligence as it is subject to quite some discussions among parties as well as in case law.

535. An important remark should be noted. The nullity of the notification of termination resulting from a failure to comply with the formal requirements does not, according to the prevailing view, alter the fact that the underlying expression of the intention by the terminating party to unilaterally terminate the employment contract was valid.[250] In the absence of a valid notification, the termination of the employment contract therefore takes effect immediately from the moment the invalid notification was given. The sanction for this given unlawful notification will translate into the obligation to pay a severance payment.

536. The duration of the notice period to be mentioned is determined by law. When both the beginning and the duration of the notice period are included in the notice of termination, but the stipulated duration of the notice period is too short, the jurisprudence rules that there is a right to an additional indemnity in lieu of notice at the time of the notice of termination, and also that it is payable immediately.[251]

248. Working days are all days of the week except Sundays and public holidays.
249. Cass. 10 Jun. 1966, *TSR* 1966, 207.
250. See Cass. 26 Sep. 1973, *Arr.Cass.* 1974, 96 and *RW* 1973–74, 1556; Cass. 23 Mar. 1981, *Arr.Cass.* 1980-1981, no. 419, p. 817 and *JTT* 1981, 240, note M. Taquet and C. Wantiez; Cass. 11 Apr. 2005, *Arr.Cass.* 2005, no. 216, p. 846; Cass. 25 Apr. 2005, *Arr.Cass.* 2005, no. 241, p. 932; Cass. 30 May 2005, *Arr.Cass. 2005*, no. 304, p. 1155; Cass. 28 Jan. 2008, *Arr.Cass.* 2008, no. 67, p. 248.
251. Cass. 30 May 1968, *Arr.Cass.* 1968, 1191; Cass. 19 Sep. 1973, *Arr.Cass.* 1974, 60; Cass. 4 Jun. 1975, *Arr.Cass.* 1975, 1055; Cass. 17 Sep. 1975, *Arr.Cass.* 1976, 82; Cass. 3 May 1982, *Arr.Cass.* 1981–82, no. 515, p. 1071 and *JTT* 1984, 202, note; Cass. 6 Nov. 1989, *Arr.Cass.* 1989–90, no. 141, p. 318, concl. H. Lenaerts and *RW* 1989–90, 885, concl. H. Lenaerts; Cass. 6 Mar. 2000, *Arr-.Cass.* 2000, no. 155, p. 519; Cass. 14 April 2003, *Arr.Cass.* 2003, no. 253, p. 996 and *JTT* 2003, 357, note D. Votquenne; Cass. 26 Feb. 2007, *Arr.Cass.* 2007, no. 113, p. 470; Cass. 5 Jan. 2009, *Arr.Cass.* 2009, no. 3, p. 5, concl. R. Mortier and *RW* 2009–10, 152, concl. R. Mortier, note K. Mortier.

§4. NOTICE PERIOD

I. General

537. The term of notice, or the notice period, is the period which the terminating party must respect vis-à-vis the other party in order to enable the latter to prepare for the actual end of the employment contract.

538. Both the employer and the employee have, in principle, to respect a term of notice. No matter who gives notice, during the entire duration of the notice period, all mutual rights and obligations of the parties will continue to exist. This means that the employee will have to continue to perform his work, and the employer will have to provide the work and pay the wages.

539. Since the Unified Status Act, the law provides a general rule according to which all notice periods start on the Monday following the week in which the notice period was given (Article 37/1 and, as far as counter-notice is concerned, Article 37/2, §3, paragraph 4, Employment Contracts Act).

540. The day on which the notice of termination is notified is meant to be the day on which the notification of the termination 'takes effect'. As explained above, depending on the method of notification (registered postal mail, bailiff's writ, or, as far as the employee is concerned, possibly the handing over of the written document), the notice of termination may take effect at a different moment. Article 37 of the Employment Contracts Act, for example, stipulates that notice given by registered postal mail takes effect on the third working day following the date of sending.

541. The duration of the notice period depends on the seniority of the employee. Article 37/4 of the Employment Contracts Act provides that the notice period is calculated taking into account the seniority acquired at the time the notice period starts. The law defines what should be understood by seniority. It refers to the period during which the employee has remained continuously in the service of the same enterprise (Article 37/4, paragraph 2, Employment Contracts Act). It means that the seniority obtained by the employee with another (previous) employer does not normally count for dismissal rights with a new employer. It implies that an employee who changes employer will have to accrue a completely new length of service for the purposes of dismissal rights. Nevertheless, one can agree on a 'conventional seniority', which is a higher (or longer) seniority that parties agree about, for example, because the employee has past employment.

542. Since the Unified Status Act, the Employment Contracts Act also provides for the recognition of seniority which the employee built up as a temporary worker in the company, in other words the period of employment which an employee performed as a temporary worker for the employer in the capacity of a user. There are certain conditions. The temporary work period is recognised with a maximum of one year, provided that the recruitment follows the period of temporary work and that the function performed with the employer is identical to the one that was performed as a temporary worker (Article 37/4, paragraph 3, Employment Contracts Act).

543. The period of notice is automatically suspended in certain cases, at least in the event that the notice is given by the employer. If a situation arises in which the execution of the employment contract is suspended for reasons of holidays taken by the employee, because of incapacity for work or for maternity leave, the period of notice is suspended. When the employee gives notice, however, the notice period simply continues and is not suspended.[252]

544. In Belgian labour law, statutory notice periods are used. This means that they are determined by law. However, the legislator generally allows additional notice periods (or notice indemnities on top of notice terms) to be set by individual employment contract. In doing so, the hierarchy of legal sources and Article 6 of the Employment Contracts Act should be taken into account.

II. Statutory Notice Periods

545. Since the 2014 Unified Status Act, new statutory notice periods apply, built up according to the criterion of seniority and expressed in weeks. There is no longer a distinction between the notice periods of so-called blue-collar and white-collar workers. Nor is there any distinction made between 'lower' and 'higher' white-collar workers (more about this later). In other words, from 2014 on, one single system of notice periods applies. However, this only applies with a view to the future, as there is also a transitional regime for notice periods acquired under the old provisions of dismissal law (more about this later on).

546. Article 37/2(1) of the Employment Contracts Act lays down the period of notice to be given when the notice is given by the employer. Article 37/2(2) of the Employment Contracts Act lays down the notice period when the employee gives notice. In principle, the notice period to be observed by the employee corresponds to (no more than) half of the notice period that would have to be observed in the event of termination by the employer, rounded down to the nearest unit where necessary. However, a ceiling is provided. The maximum notice period that the employee must respect is thirteen weeks (which is reached with a seniority of eight years).

252. Art. 38 Employment Contracts Act.

547. The statutory notice periods are as follows:

Seniority	*Notice Period If the Employer Gives Notice*	*Notice Period If the Employee Gives Notice*
Less than 3 months	1 week	1 week
From 3 months	3 weeks	2 weeks
From 4 months	4 weeks	2 weeks
From 5 months	5 weeks	2 weeks
From 6 months onwards	6 weeks	3 weeks
From 9 months	7 weeks	3 weeks
From 12 months	8 weeks	4 weeks
From 15 months	9 weeks	4 weeks
From 18 months	10 weeks	5 weeks
From 21 months	11 weeks	5 weeks
From 2 years of age	12 weeks	6 weeks
From 3 years of age	13 weeks	6 weeks
From 4 years onwards	15 weeks	7 weeks
From 5 years of age	18 weeks	9 weeks
From 6 years onwards	21 weeks	10 weeks
From 7 years onwards	24 weeks	12 weeks
From 8 years onwards	27 weeks	13 weeks
From 9 years onwards	30 weeks	13 weeks
From 10 years of age	33 weeks	13 weeks
From 11 years onwards	36 weeks	13 weeks
From 12 years of age	39 weeks	13 weeks
From 13 years onwards	42 weeks	13 weeks
From 14 years onwards	45 weeks	13 weeks
From 15 years of age	48 weeks	13 weeks
From 16 years onwards	51 weeks	13 weeks
From 17 years of age	54 weeks	13 weeks
From 18 years of age	57 weeks	13 weeks
As from 19 years	60 weeks	13 weeks
From 20 years of age	62 weeks	13 weeks
From 21 years of age	63 weeks	13 weeks
From 22 years of age	64 weeks	13 weeks
From 23 years of age	65 weeks	13 weeks

Seniority	*Notice Period If the Employer Gives Notice*	*Notice Period If the Employee Gives Notice*
From 24 years of age	66 weeks	13 weeks
Etc. ...	...	...

548. There are shorter notice periods applicable in the case of so-called counter-notice. It refers to the situation in which the employee received notice of termination by the employer, but the employee wishes himself to give notice because he has found another employment and wishes to leave earlier. Article 37/2, §3 of the Employment Contracts Act stipulates that an employee who has been dismissed by his employer with a period of notice can terminate the contract with a reduced period of notice if he has found another employment. In that case, the notice period is reduced, depending on the employee's seniority going from one week to a maximum of four weeks.

549. Shorter notice periods also apply in the event of termination with a view to the legal retirement of the employee. The statutory retirement age is set at 65 years, but gradually increases to 66 (from 1 February 2025 onwards to 1 February 2030) and to 67 years (as from 1 February 2030). Section 37/6 of the Employment Contracts Act provides that if the employment contract concluded for an indefinite period is terminated with effect from the first day of the month following the month in which the employee reaches the statutory retirement age, the notice period is limited to a maximum of twenty-six weeks if the dismissal is initiated by the employer. If the normal notice period would be more than twenty-six weeks, the notice period in such a situation will therefore be capped at twenty-six weeks.

550. The Unified Status Act wanted to harmonise notice periods in reality. Therefore, the law provides that the statutory notice periods (set out in Article 37/2, Employment Contracts Act) cannot be derogated from by a collective agreement concluded in a joint committee or joint subcommittee (Article 37/3, Employment Contracts Act). Thus, the statutory notice periods cannot be derogated from by a sectoral collective agreement. It would therefore not affect agreements concluded at company level or individual agreements, provided of course that no discrimination is practised or that the provisions of Article 6 of the Employment Contracts Act are respected, namely that the employee's rights may not be curtailed or his obligations increased, which would make agreements with notice periods less favourable to the employee impossible.

III. Transitional Regime: Two Steps

551. The new regulation of the Unified Status Act, containing the new notice periods, entered into force on 1 January 2014 and provided for different statutory notice periods that were in force until then. In order to take into account the legitimate expectations of the parties whose employment contracts were entered into before 1 January 2014, the legislator provided for a transitional regime for contracts that were in place before the new Act entered into force in 2014. The transitional arrangement refers back to the distinction between blue-collar and white-collar workers (which paradoxically was meant to be abolished by the Act).

552. Article 67 of the Unified Status Act, which contains the principle of transitional arrangements, makes it clear that it refers to the situation of 'employees whose employment contract commenced before January 1, 2014'. The transitional rule relates to a dismissal served from (or after) 1 January 2014. It goes as follows. The notice period – or the notice indemnity based on it – is calculated in two separate steps (Article 67, Unified Status Act). The notice period will be the sum of two partial calculations.

- The first step concerns the determination of the first part of the notice period, in accordance with the provisions of the old dismissal law, based on the seniority of the employee acquired on (until) 31 December 2013.
- The second step concerns the determination of the second part of the notice period according to the provisions of the new dismissal law, based on the seniority of the employee acquired as from 1 January 2014.
- The result of the calculations made during the first and second steps will be added up and together constitute the complete notice period to be observed, or allow the determination of the amount of the possible severance pay.

553. The transitional rule also applies to the calculation of the notice period in the event of dismissal by the employee. In that case, too, the calculation will be made in two parts, subject to a cap.

554. Section 69(3) of the Unified Status Act provides for caps on the employee's notice of termination. In particular, in the event of dismissal by the employee, the second part of the notice period need not be taken into account if the ceilings provided for in Article 82(2)(3) of the Employment Contracts Act and Article 68(4) of the Unification Status were reached on 31 December 2013. If, on the other hand, the ceilings set out in Article 82(2)(3) of the Employment Contracts Act and Article 68(4) of the Unified Status Act had not been reached by 31 December 2013, the sum of the two parts may not exceed thirteen weeks (Article 69(3), Unification Statute Act).

IV. Complications in the Transitional Regime

555. The transitional regime looks like a simple adding up, with the determination of the notice period in two steps, as indicated above. However, it is remarkable that the Unified Status Act requires determining the first part of the notice period (first step) on the basis of legal provisions of the Employment Contract Act that were abolished by the 2014 Unified Status Act itself. Pursuant to Article 68 of the Unified Status Act, the first part of the notice period is calculated on the basis of the continuous service, as acquired by the employee on 31 December 2013. The Act states that the period shall be determined on the basis of 'the statutory, regulatory and contractual rules in force on 31 December 2013 and (which were) applicable in the event of termination notified on that date' (Article 68(2), Unified status Act).

556. It should be noted that, in the past, many notice periods for blue-collar workers were established by sectoral agreements, in deviation of the statutory terms. This of course complicates the application of the transition period.

557. For white-collar workers, a complexity is that the old provisions of dismissal law took into account the distinction between 'lower' and 'higher' white-collar employees (referred to in Article 68, paragraphs 3 and 4, Unified Status Act). The rules for determining the duration of the notice period for white-collar employees differed depending on whether the employee was a 'lower' or a 'higher' employee.

558. The distinction between lower and higher white-collar workers is not based on any function or hierarchy in the labour organisation, but on the level of the earned annual salary, as this was (previously) determined in (since 2014 abolished) Article 82, §2 and §3 of the Employment Contracts Act. The 'lower' employee was the employee with a salary that on 31 December 2013 did not exceed a gross amount of EUR 32,254[253] on an annual basis (Article 82, §2, Employment Contracts Act). The 'higher' employee was the employee with an annual wage higher than a gross amount of EUR 32,254[254] on 31 December 2013 (Article 82, §3, paragraph 1, Employment Contracts Act).

559. The terminology 'lower and higher employee' does not originate from the legislator, but from legal doctrine and practice. The distinction can partly be explained historically. The statutory notice periods were reserved for 'the least well-off, who cannot defend their interests themselves'.[255] Higher ranked employees were considered to be able to defend their interests themselves. Later on, the question arose whether the difference in treatment between 'lower' and 'higher' employees was in accordance with the Belgian Constitution, in the light of the constitutional principle of equality (Articles 10–11 Gw.). The Constitutional Court ruled that it was.[256]

560. The regulation regarding the determination of the notice period for 'lower' white-collar employees could be found in (the old) Article 82, §2 of the Employment Contracts Act. The Act fixed the minimum notice periods which the terminating party had to observe. When the notice was given by the employer, the notice period to be observed by the employer was at least three months per (begun) five years of seniority of the employee in the company (Article 82, §2, paragraphs 1 and 2, Employment Contracts Act – repealed). When the notice was given by the

253. Indexed amount for 2013 (*Belgian Official Gazette* 23 Oct. 2012).
254. *Ibid.*
255. Report of Committee on Labour and Social Welfare 25 Mar. 1953, *Parl.* Chamber 1952–53, No. 287, 10.
256. Constitutional Court 8 Jul. 1993, No. 56/93; Constitutional Court 3 Mar. 1994, No. 20/94.

employee, the notice period was reduced to half, without exceeding three months (Article 82, §2, last paragraph, Employment Contracts Act – repealed). This regime is thus still applied under the transitional regime's first step for 'lower' white-collar workers.

561. For 'higher' white-collar employees, the Employment Contracts Act provided that, in principle, the notice period to be observed was determined by agreement. As a result, this term had to be negotiated between the employee and the employer. The solution of the Unified Status Act to this is that employees who were white-collar workers on 31 December 2013 are subject to a specific arrangement. In the event of termination by the employer, the part of the notice period that is linked to the length of service on 31 December 2013 is statutorily determined in a fixed manner. Pursuant to Article 68, paragraph 3, for employees who were higher white-collar employees on 31 December 2013, (the first part of) the notice period is set at one month per started year of seniority in the event of termination by the employer, with a minimum of three months.

562. Another complexity concerns the 'highest' white-collar employees. This was actually a special category of white-collar employees who earned more than a gross amount of EUR 64,508 on an annual basis[257] (Article 82, §5 Employment Contracts Act – repealed). For 'higher' employees, the length of the notice period to be observed by the employer could be established by means of an agreement which had to be concluded at the latest when the employee started working. In 2018, the Constitutional Court ruled on the faith of validly agreed clauses in respect of those higher white-collar employees in the past.[258] According to the Court, Article 68(3) of the Unified Status Act should respect termination clauses that were validly in force for the highest white-collar employees in the past for the purpose of calculating the first part of the notice period linked to seniority acquired on 31 December 2013.

§5. Severance Pay

563. There is an immediate relationship between the notice periods and the indemnity to be paid in case of unlawful dismissal. A dismissal may be unlawful due to a lack of a proper term of notice and/or due to a violation of formalities related to the notification.

564. Such unlawful dismissal gives rise to the obligation, on the part of the dismissing party, to pay an 'indemnity in lieu of notice' pursuant *to* Article 39 or 40 of the Employment Contracts Act of 3 July 1978. It means that the damages are equal to the salary of the employee over the notice period that normally should have been respected.

257. Amount for 2013.
258. Constitutional Court 18 Oct. 2018, No. 140/2018.

565. In practice, notice periods are often translated to payment 'in lieu'. It may, for example, be the case that an employer does not wish to let the employee perform the term of notice, in which case the employer can decide to pay the damages (payment in lieu of notice) instead of giving the corresponding term of notice.

§6. DISMISSAL FOR SERIOUS CAUSE

I. Concept

566. The dismissal for a serious cause is a method of dismissal which forms an important exception to the principle that a period of notice must always be served in the event of the unilateral termination of an employment contract for an indefinite period, or that the term of the contract for a definite period must be observed.

567. Dismissal for serious cause is regulated by Article 35 of the Employment Contracts Act. This states that either party may terminate the contract without notice or before expiry of the term for a serious cause (section 35(1), Employment Contracts Act).

568. A serious cause is at hand in case of a serious shortcoming that makes any professional collaboration between the employer and the employee immediately and definitively impossible (Article 35, paragraph 2, Employment Contracts Act). There is much case law about the interpretation of this provision and on what does, or what does not, constitute a serious shortcoming that makes the professional collaboration immediately and definitively impossible.

569. This form of unilateral employment termination is open to both the employer and the employee: in practice, however, it is mainly the employer who uses this form of dismissal. It applies to all employment contracts, whether they are concluded for an indefinite or a definite period, for blue- or white-collar workers, for full- or part-time work. The dismissal for serious cause can be given at any time, thus also in cases of suspension of the employment contract.[259]

II. Two Terms

570. The law provides two important terms for a dismissal for serious cause. These are two periods of three working days:

- Three working days to react: dismissal for serious cause may no longer be given if the fact justifying it has been known to the party invoking it for at least three working days (Article 35, paragraph 3, Employment Contracts Act).

259. For example, during the employee's annual leave: Cass. 28 Nov. 1977, *Arr.Cass.* 1978, 349.

– Three working days to justify: only the serious cause justification notified within three working days after the dismissal to the other party can be invoked to justify the dismissal (Article 35, paragraph 4, Employment Contracts Act).

571. The terms are expressed in working days. Working days are all days of the week, except Sundays and statutory holidays.

572. The short-term results follow the logic of the nature of dismissal for an urgent reason. As it concerns a serious shortcoming, which makes any cooperation permanently and immediately impossible, the dismissing party is supposed to react rather fast and cannot take too much time to assess or doubt whether there is a serious cause for immediate termination.

573. The dismissing party must prove that he/she has respected the time limits (Article 35, paragraph 8, Employment Contracts Act).

III. First Term

574. The first period of three working days, indicated above, concerns the time frame in which dismissal for serious cause can be given. This period does not necessarily run from the moment at which the serious shortcoming occurs but starts from the moment at which the shortcoming became known to the party (e.g., the employer) wishing to invoke it.

575. The Court of Cassation is of the opinion that the period only starts to run when the employer has acquired actual knowledge of the facts.[260] The starting point of the 'three working day period' is the moment when the party wishing to dismiss has certainty about the failure which is sufficient for its own conviction allowing it to take a decision with full knowledge of the facts and the circumstances or nature making that fact an urgent reason.[261] This means, for example, that a party may wait for the dismissal until it has conducted the necessary investigation.[262] However, an investigation into the true facts does not imply an additional reflection period. After all, it can be deduced from too long a period of hesitation that the cooperation was not immediately and definitively impossible.[263]

576. The dismissal for a serious cause, thus given during the first term of three working days, is entirely without form. It is, for example, not necessary to follow the requirements of Article 37 of the Employment Contracts Act. Therefore, the dismissal must not be in official writing; it can also be given orally, by e-mail or by an electronic text message. Nevertheless, the dismissing party has the burden of proof to demonstrate that the dismissal was given in due time.

260. Cass. 15 Jun. 2015, AR S.13.0095.N.
261. Cass. 11 Jan. 1993, *JTT* 1993, 58.
262. Cass. 16 Jun. 1971, *JTT* 1972, 37.
263. Cass. 8 Apr. 1991, *Arr.Cass.* 1990–91, 811 and *Soc.Kron.* 1992, 36.

IV. Second Term

577. The second term of three working days relates to the notification of the reasons justifying the dismissal for a serious cause. From the date of dismissal, a new term of three working days is created in which the reasons for the dismissal must be communicated to the dismissed party.

578. It is, however, not prohibited from mentioning the reasons for dismissal already at the time of the dismissal for a serious cause itself, or in a letter of dismissal for serious cause if a written form of dismissal is chosen.

579. Unlike the dismissal itself, there are formality conditions. The notification of the reasons must be in writing. Under penalty of nullity, the serious cause must be notified either by registered letter or by bailiff's writ (Article 35, paragraph 5, Employment Contracts Act), or it may also be given by personal delivery to the other party (Article 35, paragraph 6, Employment Contracts Act), in which case the signature of the other party on the duplicate of this document serves as acknowledgement of receipt of the notification (Article 35, paragraph 7, Employment Contracts Act).

580. The Court of Cassation requires that the letter of notification of the reasons, justifying the dismissal for serious cause, must clearly set out the facts or shortcomings, in such a way that the person concerned is aware of the reasons why he is being dismissed and the Court has the opportunity to examine their seriousness.[264] A sufficiently comprehensive and detailed description of the facts is therefore required.[265] Facts not mentioned in this notification cannot normally be considered afterwards by the Court.

V. Effects

581. A dismissal for serious cause leads to the immediate termination of the employment contract. When the dismissal has been given lawfully, there is no compensation for the dismissed party.

Furthermore, the lawfully dismissed employee will not be entitled to unemployment benefits (at least temporarily) since he will be unemployed due to his own (wrong)doing. For the employee, dismissal for an urgent reason therefore has serious consequences.

582. If the dismissal is, however, considered lawfully by a court (the Court may intervene only afterwards, on the initiative of the dismissed party), the employment remains terminated but the dismissed party will be entitled to compensation. The

264. Cass. 12 Feb. 1959, *Arr.Cass.* 1959, 460; Cass. 29 Mar. 1963, *TSR* 1963, 176; Cass. 2 Apr. 1965, *TSR* 1965, 202; Cass. 16 May 1968, *TSR* 1968, 153.
265. Cass. 28 Oct. 1987, *JTT* 1987, 494 and *Arr.Cass.* 1987–88, 256.

Court therefore rules *post-factum*. In case of a violation of Article 35 of the Employment Contracts Act, either because of the absence of an urgent reason or because of the non-respect of the time limits or formalities, the Court can only establish that the dismissal was given without serious cause. The dismissal shall not be affected, but it shall be regarded as an irregular termination or breach of the employment contract, giving rise to the obligation on the part of the dismissing party to pay an indemnity in lieu of notice or compensation *in* lieu of notice *pursuant to* Article 39 or 40 of the Employment Contracts Law.

§7. Motivation of Dismissal

I. General

583. Until the introduction of the Unified Status for blue- and white-collar workers, Belgian labour law was based on the principle that dismissals were not subject to an explicit obligation to state the reasons. In other words, the employer did not have to communicate any reasons to the dismissed employee. The main document from which a dismissed worker could derive the reasons for his/her dismissal was the so-called C4 form, an unemployment certificate which the employer had to give to the worker when he/she left the company with a view to qualification of the employee for unemployment benefits (Article 137, §1 and §2, 2° Unemployment Decree). This certificate still exists and still includes a space to indicate the reason for the end of the employment contract. However, this is not considered to be an obligation to motivate the dismissal. The certificate is meant to indicate the cause of the unemployment with a view to checking the conditions in the unemployment regulations. Nevertheless, in practice, attestation sometimes plays a role in a discussion about dismissal between employer and employee.

584. The freedom to dismiss and the absence of a formal obligation to state reasons did not imply that the dismissal could be based on any grounds whatsoever. Apart from the cases in which the employer needs a valid reason to lawfully dismiss (e.g., the anti-discrimination legislation), the grounds for dismissal could be reviewed within the framework of the legal concepts of 'arbitrary dismissal' (for blue-collar workers) and 'abuse of rights' (for white-collar workers). Arbitrary dismissal was explicitly regulated by law for blue-collar workers (Article 63, Employment Contracts Act), but not for white-collar workers. It was therefore only natural that a harmonisation issue arose in this area in the light of the constitutional principle of equality. Indeed, the Constitutional Court also confirmed its jurisprudence concerning the unconstitutionality of the distinction between blue- and white-collar workers in a judgment of 21 June 2001, which concerned the arbitrary dismissal of blue-collar workers.[266] In a judgment dated 18 December 2014, the Constitutional Court was again called upon to rule on the matter and confirmed the unconstitutionality, but also ruled that the effects of the challenged legislation must be maintained

266. Constitutional Court 21 Jun. 2001, no. 84/2001.

until 1 April 2014.[267] It is no coincidence that the Constitutional Court mentioned 1 April 2014 as deadline to modify the legislation and bring it in line with the constitutional equality principle. This is the date of entry into force of the Unified Status Act.

585. It was, however, not until 12 February 2014 that the national social partners, represented in the NLC, concluded CA no. 109 on motivation for dismissal, which came into force on 1 April 2014 for dismissals given or served from that date (Article 12 CA no. 109). CA no. 109 thus came about somewhat later than expected. As far as employers (and their employees) who do not fall within the scope of this collective agreement are concerned, Article 63 of the Employment Contract Act will only disapply if a regulation similar to the one in the national collective agreement were to come into force. However, no such regulation exists yet, so that, in principle, Article 63 still applies to the relevant employers and employees, although this obviously gives rise to discussion in view of the case law of the Constitutional Court. In the private sector, however, most employers and employees are covered by CA no. 109.

586. CA no. 109 basically governs two related but different matters: the right of an employee to know the reasons for his dismissal, on the one hand, and the right to protection against unreasonable dismissal, on the other. This is also made clear in Article 1 of CA no. 109: 'The purpose of this collective agreement is, on the one hand, to establish the right of the employee to know the specific reasons which have led to his dismissal. On the other hand, this collective agreement introduces the right for the employee to receive compensation if his dismissal was manifestly unreasonable.'

II. Scope

587. In principle, CA no. 109 applies to all employees and employers who are linked by an employment contract and who fall within the scope of the Act of 5 December 1968 on collective agreements. Most employers in the private sector would qualify for this.

588. However, Article 2, §§2–5 of the collective agreement stipulates a number of exceptions. It is particularly important to note that during the first six months of employment of an employee, CA no. 109 is not applicable. In addition, CA no. 109 does not apply to temporary work, student work, for a dismissal with a view to obtain unemployment with company allowance, retirement, permanent cessation of activity, closure of the business and collective redundancy (Article 2, paragraph 2). The collective agreement also does not apply to workers for whom a special statutory dismissal procedure has been established, or in the case of multiple redundancies in the event of restructuring (Article 2, §3). Furthermore, dismissals for serious reasons (Article 2, §4) are also excluded from its scope.

---

267. Constitutional Court 18 Dec. 2014, no. 187/2014.

589. By regulating the grounds for dismissal by collective agreement, questions arise with respect to the employees employed in the public sector. CA no. 109 does not apply to contractual public sector employees. The Constitutional Court is of the view that the lack of a legal regulation for these employees does not prevent courts from safeguarding their rights in case of a manifestly unreasonable dismissal, guided by the principles of CA no. 109.[268]

III. Motivation of Dismissal

590. According to Article 3 of CA no. 109, the employee who is dismissed has the right to know from his employer the concrete reasons which led to his dismissal (Article 4, paragraph 1 CA no. 109).

591. The employer does not have to communicate the reasons automatically or spontaneously, but only when the employee requests it. The employee who wishes to know the specific reasons which led to his dismissal must address a written request to the employer, sent by registered postal mail within two months after the end of the employment contract. If the employment contract is terminated by the employer subject to a period of notice, the employee shall submit his request to the employer within a period of six months from the notification of the termination by the employer, without however being able to exceed two months from the end of the employment contract (Article 4, paragraph 2, CA no. 109).

592. The employer who receives such a request must, within two months after the employee's written request, communicate to this employee the concrete reasons or motives for the dismissal (Article 5 CA no. 109, paragraph 1). The employer's response is also given in writing by registered postal mail, and his letter must contain the elements that allow the employee to know the concrete reasons that led to his/her dismissal (Article 5 CA no. 109, paragraph 2).

593. The employer who would have, on his own initiative, communicated in writing to the employee the concrete reasons that led to his dismissal is not obliged to respond to the employee's request, insofar as this communication contains the elements that allow the worker to know the concrete reasons that led to his dismissal (Article 6 CA no. 109).

594. If the employer does not communicate the concrete reasons which have led to the dismissal to the employee who requested it, or communicates it without respecting Article 5 (the communication contains insufficient information, or is not made in due time), a fixed civil penalty corresponding to two weeks of salary is due to this employee (Article 7, §1 CA no. 109). The penalty is not applicable if the employer has voluntarily communicated the concrete reasons that led to the dismissal of the employee in accordance with Article 6 (Article 7, §2 CA no. 109).

268. Constitutional Court 5 Jul. 2018, no. 84/2018: Constitutional Court 30 June 2016, no. 101/2016.

IV. Manifestly Unreasonable Dismissal

595. CA nr. 109 also protects employees against 'manifestly unreasonable dismissal'. A 'manifestly unreasonable dismissal' is the dismissal of an employee who has been hired for an indefinite period of time, based on reasons that are not related to the employee's aptitude or behaviour, or that are not based on the necessities related to the functioning of the company, the institution or service and that would never have been decided by a normal and reasonable employer (Article 8 CA no. 109).

So there is a double test in order to establish a manifestly unreasonable dismissal. The test is whether the dismissal:

(a) is based on grounds other than the employee's fitness or behaviour, or the requirements of the functioning of the undertaking, institution or service; and
(b) which would never have been decided by a normal and reasonable employer (Article 8 CA no. 109).

596. The commentary under Article 8 gives a number of additional elements in relation to the standards that apply. The social partners mention that it concerns a marginal review: 'Only the manifest unreasonableness of the dismissal may be reviewed and not the feasibility of the employer's policy (to be understood as his choice from among the various reasonable policy alternatives he has). The addition of the word "manifestly" to the notion of "unreasonable" is intended to point precisely to the employer's policy freedom and to a review at the margin. The latter is also dictated by the practical impossibility of checking the employer's policy more than marginally.' According to the social partners, the review of the manifest unreasonableness of the dismissal is not related to the circumstances of the dismissal. The check is whether the reasons are related to the employee's aptitude or behaviour, whether they are based on the operational necessities of the undertaking, institution or service, and whether the decision would never have been taken by a normal and reasonable employer. The assessment of the exercise of the dismissal right by the employer against what would be its exercise by a normal and reasonable employer is, according to the social partners, a discretionary power at the margin as the employer is to a large extent free to decide what is reasonable. There should be respect for the different policy alternatives that a normal and reasonable employer would consider.

597. A manifestly unreasonable dismissal is sanctioned with damages to be paid by the employer, pursuant to Article 9, §1 of CA no. 109. The compensation awarded to the employee corresponds to a minimum of three weeks' pay and a maximum of seventeen weeks' pay (Article 9, §2). According to the social partners, the amount of the indemnity depends on the degree of manifest unreasonableness of the dismissal (commentary on Article 9).

598. Instead of the above sanction provided for in this article, the employee is free to claim compensation for his actual loss, in accordance with the provisions of the Civil Code (commentary on Article 9).

599. The indemnity may not be cumulated with any other indemnity due by the employer as a result of the termination of the employment contract, with the exception of a compensation in lieu of notice, a non-competition indemnity, an eviction indemnity (sales representatives) or an additional indemnity paid on top of social security benefits (Article 9, §3).

600. Article 10 CA no. 109 lays down the rules of evidence when contesting a manifestly unreasonable dismissal. If the employer has communicated the reasons for the dismissal, the party who submits the evidence bears the burden of proof. If the employer did not do so, then he must provide evidence for the dismissal reasons that he did not communicate to the employee, in order to prove that the dismissal was not manifestly unreasonable. If the employee did not request the reasons for dismissal, he bears the burden of proving the elements that indicate manifest unreasonableness.

§8. Arbitrary Dismissal and Abuse of Rights

601. Because of the introduction of CA no. 109, schemes relating to improper motivation of dismissals are increasingly losing their relevance. In fact, some old schemes are mainly relevant for employees who are not covered by CA no. 109.

602. As mentioned above, arbitrary dismissal applied in the past to blue-collar workers only. Nowadays, since the Unified Status Act, the provisions would still apply to employees employed in the public sector (to whom CA no. 109 does not apply), but subject to the ruling of the Constitutional Court in this respect. The concept of arbitrary dismissal is included in Article 63 of the Employment Contracts Act. For the application of this article, the term 'arbitrary dismissal' is understood to mean the dismissal of a blue-collar worker who has been hired for an indefinite period of time and dismissed for reasons that are not related to the ability or the behaviour of the employee or not based on the operational necessities of the company, the institution or the service. In the case of an arbitrary dismissal decided by a court, the employer has to pay an indemnity that corresponds to six months' wages.

603. In the past, the civil law doctrine of 'abuse of law' was, exceptionally, applied to dismissals of white-collar workers, for which there was no similar figure as the arbitrary dismissal for blue-collar workers. Theoretically, this doctrine is still applicable. However, an employee who is dismissed and who believes that his employer has abused his right to dismiss must provide proof of this himself. Furthermore, with CA no. 109 this civil law doctrine seems to have become less evident in employment termination cases.

§9. Implied Dismissal and Unilateral Modification

604. Above, dismissal has been defined as the legal act by which one party to the employment contract notifies the other of its intention to terminate the employment contract unilaterally. A characteristic of the notion of dismissal is that it terminates the employment contract immediately, without being subject to any formal conditions. This means that dismissal does not necessarily have to be given explicitly, but can also be implied from the circumstances. This leads to the notion of 'implicit dismissal'. An implicit dismissal concerns a contractual breach of contract that goes hand in hand with the implicit expression of the will of the party committing the breach to terminate the employment contract.

605. In principle, however, a breach of contract does not in itself cause the employment contract to end.[269] However, this is different in the case of a unilateral and significant modification of an essential element of the employment contract. Unilateral modification of contractual agreed terms can be an indication that the party in breach wishes to terminate the contract. At least, this is what the doctrine of implied dismissal contains. The cause of the termination lies not in the shortcoming as such, but in the (significant and unilateral) change of the contract which it reveals.[270]

606. The doctrine of unilateral change of employment conditions is largely governed by case law, with the Court of Cassation as the guiding authority. An important turnaround in the vision of this court occurred with a judgment of 20 December 1993.[271] Prior to the cassation judgment of 20 December 1993, it was assumed, *inter alia*, that an employer had a so-called ius variandi, i.e., a right to unilaterally change the employment conditions in certain circumstances. However, in its judgment dated 20 December 1993, the Court of Cassation stated that Article 1134 of the Old Civil Code implies that the employer cannot unilaterally change or revoke the conditions agreed upon, unless stipulated otherwise, and that the relationship of subordination that characterises the employment contract and the time over which the contract is executed do not alone provide a basis for this.[272] It may be inferred from the judgment that the employer does not have a right to unilaterally amend the employment contract. In a judgment dated 13 October 1997, the Court of Cassation specified that it is irrelevant whether the changes to the employment conditions stipulated are substantial or insignificant.[273]

---

269. Cass. 5 Jan. 1977, *Arr.Cass.* 1977, 487; Cass. 14 Apr. 1980, *RW* 1980–81, 979, concl. Adv. Gen. H. Lenaerts; Cass. 24 Nov. 1986, AR 5322, *Arr.Cass.* 1986, 403; Cass. 26 Mar. 1984, AR 4264, *RW* 1984–85, 1869; Cass. 13 Jan. 1986; Cass. 27 Oct. 1986; Cass. 12 Dec. 1988; Cass. 15 Dec. 1988; Cass. 4 Feb. 1991; Cass. 13 May 1991; Cass. 18 Nov. 1991; Cass. 22 Nov. 1993; Cass. 18 Dec. 2000, *RW* 2001–02, 842.
270. Cass. 7 Mar. 1994, AR S.930127.N; Cass. 26 Feb. 1990.
271. Cass. 20 Dec. 1993, *JTT* 1994, 443.
272. *Ibid.*
273. Cass. 13 Oct. 1997, *JTT* 1997, 481.

607. However, this does not mean that every unilateral change of the agreed terms of employment, which is prohibited in principle, becomes impossible and/or leads to dismissal. For example, a modification clause may be agreed upon, on the basis of Article 25 of the Employment Contracts Act.

608. Article 25 of the Employment Contracts Act provides that a clause by which the employer reserves the right to unilaterally change the terms of the contract is null and void. In a judgment dated 14 October 1991, the Court of Cassation stated that this Article 25 of the Employment Contracts Act only applies to terms which concern the modification of *essential elements* of the contract, but not to the modification of ancillary conditions agreed upon between the parties.[274] Thus, an employer is entitled to reserve the right to modify contractually *ancillary elements* of the employment conditions.

609. This leaves the doctrine that unilateral and significant change of an essential element of the employment contract is considered to be an 'implied dismissal' and equals an immediate and irregular termination of this contract.[275] As essential elements are considered aspects such as job description, working time, or place of work.

610. The substantial amendment of an essential element of the employment contract, amounting to an irregular termination,[276] gives rise to the obligation, on the part of the party unlawfully making the unilateral amendment, to pay an indemnity to the other party, equal to compensation in lieu of notice, as laid down by Articles 39 and 40 of the Employment Contracts Act. The employment contract will furthermore be considered to be terminated (on the initiative of the unilaterally modifying party).

274. Cass. 14 Oct. 1991, *RW* 1991–92, 809.
275. Cass. 15 Jan. 1979, *Arr.Cass.* 1978–79, 544; Cass. 1 Dec. 1980, *Arr.Cass.* 1980–81, 361; Cass. 7 Feb. 1983, *TSR* 1983, 208; Cass. 2 Feb. 2002, AR S.010103.N, *JTT* 2002, 121, note C. Wantiez.
276. Cass. 15 Jan. 1979, *Arr.Cass.* 1978–79, 544; Cass. 1 Dec. 1980, *Arr.Cass.* 1980–81, 361; Cass. 7 Feb. 1983, *TSR* 1983, 208; Cass. 2 Feb. 2002, AR S.010103.N, *JTT* 2002, 121, note C. Wantiez.

Chapter 8. Non-compete Obligations

§1. General

611. Arrangements restricting the employees' freedom on the labour market will, in principle, constitute an interference of the freedom of labour. Freedom of work is a well-established principle in Belgian law. It can be found in Article 23 of this Constitution providing for 'the right to work and to choose freely any kind of professional activity within the framework of a general employment policy, aimed among other things at ensuring the highest and stable possible level of employment'. This right to work, as freedom to work, can be seen to include both the negative freedom not to work (no one can be forced to work) and the positive freedom to choose one's occupation.

612. The Belgian Constitutional Court recognised the freedom of work as part of the guarantees of Article 23 of the Constitution, but it has also indicated that this right (or freedom) is not absolute. In its judgment (no. 84/2011) of 18 May 2011, the Constitutional Court examined the question of the compatibility of the regulations on the dismissal of professional sports persons with the right to the free choice of occupation or the freedom to work, as guaranteed by Article 23 of the Constitution.[277] Without deciding on the merits, the Constitutional Court stated that restrictions can be placed on the right to freely choose one's occupation, provided they are reasonably justified and not disproportionate to the objective pursued.[278]

613. The Court of Cassation referred to the *Decree d'Allarde Decree d'Allarde* of 2–17 March 1791 as the basis of the freedom of work, an old Decree from the French period (Belgium did not exist as a country until 1830). According to the Court, under the *Decree d'Allarde*, everyone is free to pursue any trade, profession, business or craft activity as he sees fit. This provision, which opposes an unjustified restriction on the freedom of trade and industry, the Court held, is considered to be part of the public policy order.[279] This means that this right is fundamental in the legal system.

614. Freedom of work would mean that regulations or agreements which are restrictive for the employee must be interpreted restrictively. This is in line with the provisions of Article 6 of the Employment Contracts Act, according to which any clauses contrary to the provisions of this law and of its implementing decrees shall be null and void, insofar as they are intended to reduce the rights of the employee or to increase his/her obligations.

---

277. Constitutional Court, no. 84/2011, considerans B.8.
278. *Ibid.*
279. Cass. 23 Jan. 2015, *NJW* 2015, 913, note C. Lebon, *Tijdschrift voor Rechtspersoon en Vennootschap* 2015, 460, note B. Bellen; *see also* Cass. (1st k.) (full court) AR C.14.0008.F, 25 Jun. 2015 (Maison Victor, L&T concept / L.M., B.S.), *Arr.Cass.* 2015, paras 6–8, 1757; *JTT* 2015, paras 1232, 483, note M. Wantiez; *NJW* 2015, paras 333, 914, note C. Lebon.

615. Nevertheless, specific statutory provisions apply. Under the Employment Contracts Act, an employee is obliged, both during and after the termination of the contract, to refrain from committing or aiding and abetting acts of unfair competition (Article 17, 3°, b), Employment Contracts Act). This should be read in conjunction with the statutory provisions on non-compete clauses (Articles 65 and 86, Employment Contracts Act).

616. A distinction must be made between (non-)compete obligations during the term of the employment contract and after its termination. A distinction must also be made between acts of fair competition and acts of unfair competition. Unfair competition is in principle always prohibited. But also, fair acts of competition by the employee (or former employee) can be restricted.

§2. Obligations During Employment

I. Acts of Competition

617. A traditional viewpoint is that fair competition by the employee (against his employer) is prohibited during the employment contract because of the (duty of) loyalty between the parties. This[280] is based, among other things, on the duty of good faith (Article 1134, paragraph 3 of the Old Civil Code) between the parties. This would prevent the employee from competing with the employer as long as he is bound by the employment contract. Of course, competitive activities are possible if the employee has permission from his employer.

618. However, loyalty must also be nuanced. As a general rule, one can say that preparing for the development of a competitive activity remains permitted. Thus, an employee cannot be prohibited from contacting a competing employer, even if his employment contract with his current employer has not yet been terminated,[281] nor can an employee be obliged to inform his employer of any steps that he might take to contract with a new employer (competitor).[282]

619. Finally, by analogy with what was said about the exclusivity clause, a non-compete clause during the term of the employment contract is not only at odds with the freedom of work in the case of part-time work. After all, in many cases, an employee with two part-time jobs will be able to work for competing employers. The question is therefore whether one should not assume for these employees that the non-competition obligation only relates to a double similarity (by analogy with the non-competition clause – *see* paragraph 624): both the activities of the second employer and the position with this second employer should be competitive.

---

280. Cass. 26 Feb. 2007, *JTT* 2007, 239, concl. J. Leclercq.
281. Labour Court Brussels 13 Apr. 1990, *JTT* 1990, 441; Labour Court Brussels 2 Feb. 1987, *TSR* 1988, 120; Labour Court Brussels 30 Mar. 1990, *JTT* 1990, 441.
282. Labour Court Brussels 2 Feb. 1987, *TSR* 1988, 120.

II. Exclusivity

620. The above raises the question of whether exclusivity can be required, or whether exclusivity clauses are possible, whereby the employee is contractually prohibited from carrying out any other (even non-competitive) activity outside the work (or working time) that is the subject of the employment contract.

621. Freedom of work, a fundamental and constitutionally protected right and value in the Belgian legal system, seems to preclude a full exclusivity clause, which would prohibit any secondary or side activity.[283] It is also a fact that the labour market is evolving and the number of employees working part-time – and combining part-time jobs – is increasing. In the Belgian legal system, the issue is, in this context, not fully clarified yet. Secondary jobs may probably be restricted, but, for example, a bricklayer who works part-time for two different construction companies is not seen as problematic.[284]

622. An important development has come from European law. The new European Directive on Transparent and Predictable Working Conditions (Directive (EU) 2019/1152 of 20 June 2019)[285] sheds a new light on the issue of secondary employment. This European legislation introduced a new principle with regard to employees who have multiple jobs. Article 9 of the European Directive provides that (Member States must ensure that) the employer cannot prohibit the employee from working for other employers outside the work schedule, with that employer. It is also stipulated that if the employee does so, he must not suffer any detrimental treatment as a result. It is still possible that conditions can be laid down regarding possible incompatibilities, but these restrictions then have to relate to objective reasons, such as health and safety, the protection of the confidentiality of company information, the integrity of public services or the avoidance of conflicts of interest.

§3. After the Employment Contract

623. After the end of the employment relationship, the freedom of employment is fully restored and, in principle, nothing prevents the employee from carrying out a competitive activity himself or from joining a competitor of his former employer. Nevertheless, even then, it remains forbidden to commit acts of 'unfair' competition. This follows from Article 17, 3°, b) of the Employment Contracts Act of 3 July 1978. Furthermore, as far as acts of 'fair' competition are concerned, the employee may be bound by a 'non-compete' clause (regulated by Articles 65 and 86, Employment Contracts Act).

283. Labour Court Liège 15 Jun. 1983, *JTT* 1984, 484; Labour Court Luik 19 Jun. 1985, *TSR* 1986, 221; Labour Court Bergen 21 Jan. 1988, *JTT* 1988, 160, noot; Labour Court Brussels 29 Jan. 2008, *JTT* 2008, 277.
284. Cf. Labour Court Ghent 10 Feb. 2006, AR 125/05.
285. *OJ* 11 Jul. 2019.

I. Non-compete Clause

624. A non-compete clause is defined as a clause whereby the employee undertakes not to carry on similar activities after leaving the company, either by running a business himself or by joining a competing employer, and whereby he has the possibility of damaging the company he has left by using the knowledge he has acquired in that company, whether in the industrial or commercial field, for himself or for a competing company (Article 65, §1, Employment Contracts Act).

II. Formal Conditions

625. The non-compete clause must be set out in a document that specifies the terms for applying the conditions listed above on pain of nullity. Joint committees may specify these terms in the light of the conditions specific to the sector (Article 65, §2, paragraph 8, Employment Contracts Act). The clause can in principle be entered into as long as the employee is employed.

III. Salary Conditions

626. Whether and to what extent a non-competition clause is legally possible depends on a number of conditions relating to the employee's earned annual salary. Non-compliance with this condition results in the nullity of the non-competition clause.[286] It is a 'relative' nullity in the sense that the employer himself cannot invoke it.

627. The provisions apply to both blue-collar workers (Article 65, §1, Employment Contracts Act) and white-collar employees (Article 86, §1, Employment Contracts Act). There are legal salary thresholds which are slightly modified (due to indexation) from year to year.

628. The non-competition clause is considered to be non-existent in employment contracts in which the annual salary does not exceed the first indexed salary threshold (Article 65, §2, paragraph 1, Employment Contracts Act). When the annual salary falls between the first and second indexed salary thresholds, the clause may only be applied to categories of functions or to functions determined by a collective agreement concluded within the sectoral joint committee. In the absence of such an agreement concluded, and after the failure of the conciliation procedure, the categories of jobs or jobs may be designated at the level of the undertaking and at the initiative of the most diligent party in an agreement between the employer and the representative employees' organisations (Article 65, §2, paragraph 2, Employment Contracts Act).

In the event of a persistent disagreement between the employer and the representative employees' organisations, the party most concerned may seek the advice of

286. Cass. 30 Jun. 2003, AR S.02.0098.F, *JTT* 2003, 398.

the Committee of Good Services set up by the NLC by virtue of CA no. 1bis of 21 December 1978 (Article 65, §2, paragraph 3, Employment Contracts Act).

629. When the annual salary exceeds the second indexed salary threshold, the non-competition clause may be validly included in the employment contracts, except for the categories of functions or functions which are excluded by a collective agreement concluded within the joint committee. In the absence of such an agreement, and following the failure of the conciliation procedure, these categories of posts or these posts may be determined at company level in accordance with the procedure set out above (Article 65, §2, paragraph 4, Employment Contracts Act).

630. The employee's annual salary should only exceed the specified limits *at the end of the contract.* For the application of the non-competition clause, the salary does not need to exceed the applicable statutory limit already *at the time the non-competition clause was concluded.*

IV. Material Conditions

631. For a non-competition clause to have any effect, it must meet three material conditions, which derive from its legal definition (Article 65, §1, Employment Contracts Act): it must prohibit the employee, after leaving the company, from engaging in similar activities (1) which might damage the company he is leaving (2), by exploiting knowledge which he has acquired in the industrial or commercial field of that company (3).

If the clause does not meet this description or if there is no special knowledge, e.g., because the employee has a supervisory position which provides him with only general knowledge,[287] both parties can claim its non-existence.[288]

V. Validity Conditions

632. The validity of any non-competition clause is subject to the following conditions (Article 65, §2, paragraph 5, Employment Contracts Act):

1° it must relate to similar activities; The clause may only prohibit the exercise of similar activities in similar undertakings. This is a requirement of 'double similarity': one looks at both the similarity of the employee's activities and the similarity of the employer's activities.[289]

2° it must be geographically limited to the places where the employee can effectively compete with the employer, given the nature of the business and

287. Labour Court Antwerp 3 Feb. 1997, *RW* 1996–97, 1444; Labour Court Brussels 5 Mar. 2004, AR 42.730; Labour Tribunal Brussels 10 Sep. 2010, AR 2600/09.

288. Labour Court Liège 8 Jan. 2004, *JTT* 2004, 331; Labour Court Ghent 27 Jun. 2008, *TGR-TWVR* 2009, 56.

289. Cf. for the first similarity: Cass. 25 Jun. 1970, *Pas.* 1970, I, 947.

its operating radius. However, it may not extend beyond the national territory. The clause must therefore be limited to the territory of Belgium. But it may be that it needs more limitations, as it must be limited to the place where the employee can *actually* compete with the employer.

3° it cannot exceed 12 months from the date of termination of the employment;

4° it must provide for the payment by the employer of a single lump-sum compensatory payment, unless he renounces the effective application of the non-competition clause within a period of 15 days from the date of termination of the contract. The employer must therefore compensate the employee's non-compete period. The minimum amount of this indemnity is equal to half of the gross salary of the employee which corresponds to the period of application of the clause. The basis of this amount is the gross salary that the employee received during the month prior to the day on which the employment ended (Article 65, § 2, paragraph 6 of the Employment Contracts Act). For employees whose salary varies in whole or in part, that amount shall be calculated, for the variable part, on the average gross salary of the twelve months preceding the date of termination of the contract (Article 65, §2 paragraph 7, Employment Contracts Act).

633. The law provides that the employer is not liable for the compensatory payment, mentioned above, when he renounces the application of the clause within a period of fifteen days from the date of termination of the contract. The employer can thus waive the non-competition clause.

634. The validity rules on non-competition clauses are supposed to protect only the employee, so that only the employee can invoke the nullity of the clause.[290]

VI. Effect

635. The non-competition clause is ineffective if the contract is terminated by the employer without serious cause or by the employee for serious cause (Article 65, §2, paragraph 9, Employment Contracts Act).

636. Although the *rationale* may be that the non-competition clause should be effective primarily if the employee leaves, the hypotheses of non-effectiveness are limited. For this reason, it is assumed that the non-competition clause will also be effective if the employment contract is terminated by mutual consent.[291]

290. Cass. 2 May 1988, *RW* 1988–89, 608; Labour Court Liege 12 Mar. 1992, *JTT* 1992, 359; *otherwise* Labour Court Ghent 9 Feb. 1987, *JTT* 1987, 355; Labour Cour Ghent 18 Nov. 1987, *JTT* 1988, 117 and *RW* 1987–88, 962.

291. Labour Court Ghent 17 Jan. 1975, *JTT* 1975, 203; Labour Court Brussels 1 Dec. 1987, *JTT* 1988, 235; Labour Court Ghent 22 Jun. 1998, *JTT* 1998, 428.

VII. Compensation to the Employer

637. The employee may be liable to pay damages to his former employer if, contrary to the provisions of a non-compete clause applicable to him, he nevertheless engages in competitive activities vis-à-vis the former employer. The law stipulates that if the employee violates the non-competition clause, he is obliged to pay the employer the compensatory sum, paid by the employer in the application of the non-competition clause, plus the same amount. However, at the request of the employee, the judge may reduce the amount of that fixed indemnity, taking into account in particular the damage caused and the actual duration of the period of compliance with the clause. The Court may also, at the request of the employer, award higher compensation, subject to the obligation to prove the existence and extent of the damage (Article 65, §2, paragraph 10, Employment Contracts Act).

VIII. Derogation Clause

638. For some white-collar workers, it is possible to deviate from the conditions of the normal non-competition clause (Article 86, Employment Contracts Act). This is referred to as a 'derogation clause'.

639. For a derogation clause to be applied in a company, the company must meet at least one of the two following conditions (Article 86, §2, paragraph 2, Employment Contracts Act):

(1) it must have an international field of activity or have important economic, technical or financial interests in the international markets; or
(2) it must have its own research department.

640. In such companies, the derogation clause can only be applied to employees who are engaged in tasks which enable them, directly or indirectly, to acquire knowledge of practices specific to the company, the exploitation of which, outside the company, could be detrimental to the company. For these employees, the non-compete clause can deviate from the general regulation on a number of points (Article 86, §2, paragraph 1, Employment Contracts Act). This means that the clause may extend beyond Belgian territory and may be valid for more than twelve months as from the day the employment relationship ended, or that it stipulates that the clause has effect even if the contract is terminated by the employer without serious cause.

641. The standards and conditions of these derogations are specified in CA no. 1bis of 21 December 1978.[292] Further modalities for the application of the derogation clause can be determined by a collective agreement at branch level or, failing that, by a collective agreement at company level or, failing that, by the individual employment contract.

292. Declared universally binding by Royal Decree 6 Mar. 1979, *Belgian Official Gazette* 7 Apr. 1979.

Chapter 9. Privacy and Data Protection

§1. General

642. The right to privacy is a fundamental right. It is recognised as such in the Belgian legal order and enshrined in Article 22 of the Belgian Constitution. Important international human rights treaties play a role in the Belgian legal order as well, certainly if they have direct effect, such as Article 8 of the ECHR. The Belgian case law increasingly makes reference to the ECHR in solving disputes related to privacy and the workplace.

643. At the heart of the law on personal data protection lies the GDPR. As it takes the form of a 'regulation' from the European Union, it is directly applicable in the Belgian legal order, without the need for further implementation. The obligations effectively took effect on 25 May 2018. In Belgium, the GDPR is complemented by the Act of 30 July 2018 on the protection of individuals with regard to the processing of personal data.[293]

644. For the employment context, there is no specific legislation relating to worker privacy. However, in the NLC, where the main national trade unions and employers' organisations are represented for the whole private sector in the country, some specific national collective agreements related to worker privacy have been adopted. Two of the national collective agreements relate specifically to electronic monitoring. On the one hand, there is National CA no. 68 of 16 June 1998 (CA 68), concerning camera surveillance in the workplace. It provides for the conditions and guarantees under which monitoring via video/camera is possible in the workplace. On the other hand, there is National CA no. 81 of 26 April 2002 (CA 81). This collective agreement concerns the monitoring of electronic communication in the workplace, regulating the guarantees in light of the monitoring of workplace-based communication, including internet and e-mail.

645. Two other collective agreements relate to issues that are rather sensitive for worker's privacy. It concerns CA no. 89 of 30 January 2007 on prevention of theft and exit control and CA no. 100 of 1 April 2009 on alcohol and drug policy in the workplace.

646. In 2012, the Belgian Data Protection Authority (DPA) issued a recommendation on electronic monitoring in the workplace,[294] in order to assist employers and workers in understanding and applying the relevant principles and legislation in this area. With regard to the employment relationship, the DPA has, however, also provided more guidance on its website, which is regularly updated.[295]

---

293. *Belgian Official Gazette* 5 Sep. 2018.
294. Belgian DPA, Recommendation no. 08/2012 of 2 May 2012.
295. www.gegevensbeschermingsautoriteit.be / www.autoriteprotectiondonnees.be.

§2. Informational Privacy and Data Protection

647. Informational privacy and data protection are, self-evidently, key issues in employment and HR practice. Many legal provisions may be a ground for justification for employers to collect personal data of workers. In many cases, employers will rely on the wide range of GDPR provisions. Employers (can) lawfully use personal data for a variety of reasons: recruitment and selection, personnel administration, wage administration, human resources and manpower planning, worker evaluation, monitoring and surveillance, social security and social insurance. These purposes have also been recognised by the Belgian Data Protection Authority (DPA).

648. With regard to individual consent, the Belgian DPA has strong reservations. It is of the opinion 'that the fact that the employee concerned must be able to give his consent 'freely' and always be able to withdraw it, it is difficult to regard consent as a legitimate basis in an employment relationship in which the employee is under the authority of the employer'.[296]

649. For the recruitment and selection phase, a well-known reference is national CA no. 38 from the NLC. It goes without saying that the employer may investigate whether a job applicant has the necessary qualities to properly perform the duties on the contract of employment. In doing so, the employer may encroach upon the applicant's private life. CA no. 38 stipulates, however, that the applicant's privacy must be respected during the selection procedure. This implies that questions regarding private life are only justified if they are relevant due to the nature and working conditions of the position (Article 11 CA no. 38). This applies not only to the employer but also to the persons who participate in the selection work on his behalf, such as psychologists and doctors (commentary on Article 11 CA no. 38). Nevertheless, in accordance with CA no. 38, the applicant is required to participate in good faith in the selection procedure, including providing all necessary information on professional and educational history, when this relates to the nature and working conditions of the job (Article 13 CA no. 38).

§3. Health-Related Data

I. Principles

650. With regard to health-related data, reference has to be made to the GDPR. Health data follow the regime of the GDPR. An employer has in principle no access to the health data of his employees. Although the employer is entitled to organise a health policy and even obliged to take all necessary measures for the health and well-being of his employees in the workplace, the legislator gives the occupational physician the responsibility for submitting (future and employed) workers to a health examination, in order to determine whether they are (still) fit for work.

296. https://www.gegevensbeschermingsautoriteit.be/gezondheidsgegevens.

II. Medical Examinations

651. Medical examinations of workers are allowed and based on the Wellbeing Act of 4 August 1996 and the Wellbeing Codex. These provisions give occupational medicine, as an organised system, and the occupational physician, as the medically trained expert, an important task. The physician will confine himself to informing the employer whether or not an employee is fit for work, without giving the employer any information about any illness or condition of that employee.

652. The health surveillance rules formulate the objectives of the health surveillance of workers and candidate-workers: to promote and maintain the health of workers by preventing risks; to promote employment opportunities for all, in particular by proposing working methods adapted to the employer, proposing adaptations of the work post and the search for suitable work, including for workers with limited work capacity; to prevent workers from being assigned to tasks of which they cannot normally bear the risks because of their state of health. It can therefore be said that the aim of health surveillance of workers is to include people rather than exclude them from the labour process. In principle, the employer can only subject workers (or prospective workers) to an occupational health examination if they occupy a safety function or a function that involves specific risks.

III. Specific Examinations (Including HIV/Genetic Tests)

653. With an Act of 28 January 2003 on medical examinations, the legislator interfered not only to secure the right to privacy of workers but also to avoid discrimination in health selection. The Act stipulates that biological tests, medical examinations or oral information gathering with a view to obtaining medical information on the health status or genetic information of a worker or prospective worker may not be carried out for reasons other than those related to the current suitability of the worker for and the specific characteristics of the vacant position (Article 3, §1, paragraph 1, Medical Examinations Act).

The main purpose of this Act is to regulate a number of specific medical examinations. In the first place, the law aims at a prohibition of predictive genetic research and HIV testing, in order to avoid that genetic or HIV tests would be used to determine the future risk profile of a worker, and thus to make a selection decision on that basis; or that the own appreciation in occupational medicine would too easily lead to the organisation of genetic and HIV testing.

IV. Alcohol and Drugs

654. Within the framework of alcohol and drug tests, national CA no. 100 of 1 April 2009 has been concluded, which makes a distinction between medical examinations within the meaning of the Act of 28 January 2003 and other tests. The latter refer to tests that are not calibrated and whereby the result only gives a positive or negative indication. They are permitted under certain circumstances. According to

CA no. 100, the employer must have a policy for all of its workers to collectively prevent and remedy dysfunctions at work due to alcohol or drug use. If testing for alcohol or drugs is part of the preventive alcohol and drug policy in the company, the employer must determine the further rules to be applied in this respect, including the nature of the tests that can be taken; the target group(s) of employees who can be subjected to the tests; the procedures to be followed in carrying out these tests; the persons authorised to carry out these tests; the time(s) at which testing may take place; and the possible consequences of a positive test result. The employer determines these elements and makes them known to the workers.

655. Testing for alcohol or drugs of workers is only permitted, according to CA no. 100, to the extent that the following conditions are met:

(1) The tests may only be used for purposes of prevention, in particular to determine whether or not an employee is suitable to carry out his or her work.
(2) The employer may not use the test result in a way that is incompatible with the law. In particular, the pursuit of this objective must not lead to any sanctioning decisions by the employer only based on data obtained through these tests.
(3) The alcohol or drug test must be adequate, relevant and not excessive.
(4) An alcohol or drug test may only be taken if the person concerned has agreed to this in accordance with the legal provisions in force.
(5) The possibility of taking alcohol or drug tests should not give rise to discrimination between workers. This does not preclude, subject to compliance with this requirement, that the possibility of being subjected to an alcohol or drug test may be restricted to part of the staff of the company concerned.
(6) The processing of personal data in a file with measurement results of alcohol or drug tests is prohibited.

V. Psychological Testing

656. With regard to psychological examinations, including information gathering or tests, the main relevant specific source concerns CA no. 38 which stipulates that questions regarding private life are only justified if they are relevant due to the nature and working conditions of the position (Article 11 CA no. 38). This applies not only to the employer but also to the persons who participate in the selection work on his behalf, including psychologists (commentary on Article 11 CA no. 38). Obviously, the provisions of the GDPR related to sensitive data remain fully relevant.

VI. Biometrics

657. There are no specific provisions in relation to biometrical data. However, according to the Belgian DPA, in the absence of other, more privacy-friendly ways to achieve the same objective, an employer may only instal a biometric verification system for serious reasons related to, for example, the fight against fraud, site security (dangerous activities) or seen the sensitivity of certain data processing.[297]

VII. COVID-19

658. With regard to personal data and privacy protection in light of COVID-19, the Belgian DPA has issued some guidance with regard to a number of questions.

659. The DPA has stated opinions holding that:[298]

- an employer cannot impose a COVID-test purely on the basis of his employer's authority. This is seen to affect the physical integrity of the employee. Without a legal basis, an employee may not be forced to undergo a test. However, the DPA emphasises that sometimes it can be very important for a staff member to be tested, for example, in the medical sector;
- an employer cannot ask workers to give information on infection, symptoms of infection, on having been in a risk area of having had risk contacts;
- an employer could apply a wearable bracelet for workers in order to monitor social distancing, when it sends out a signal in case a second bracelet is within a predetermined perimeter. The DPA does not see a problem if the two bracelets only measure the distance and if an alarm goes off to warn the people concerned, and, importantly, if there is no possible link with an identifiable person;
- if an employer wishes to use camera-detection, for example, to verify if workers wear a mask, the employer has to demonstrate that surveillance by camera images is the only efficient measure to supervise this, and that less privacy-intrusive solutions (such as visual inspection by supervisory staff) are insufficient. The DPA is nevertheless of the opinion that this method of detection is disproportionate in the majority of situations.

660. The most debated issue in Belgium in relation to COVID-19, besides the use of the 'covid safety app', is compulsory vaccination for workers. The dominant legal opinion is that employers cannot impose vaccination based on their own prerogatives, nor make a distinction between vaccinated and non-vaccinated workers. The government has been discussing the issue for a long time, but a countrywide obligation to vaccinate has never come into place. A bill of law is, however, in preparation by the government which would make vaccination compulsory for healthcare workers.

297. https://www.gegevensbeschermingsautoriteit.be/burger/thema-s/privacy-op-de-werkplek/gevoelige-gegevens/biometrie-op-de-werkplek.
298. https://www.gegevensbeschermingsautoriteit.be/burger/thema-s/covid-19/covid-19-op-de-werkvloer.

§4. ELECTRONIC MONITORING

I. General

661. With regard to electronic monitoring, there is much debate as well as case law about the monitoring of internet and e-mails, telephone communication, and the use of cameras in the workplace. The social partners, through national collective agreements, have tried to establish rules for the private sector. Those rules have to be seen and complemented in light of the GDPR, the fundamental right to privacy (Article 22 Constitution, Article 8 ECHR) and the broader case law of the European Court on Human Rights.

662. Belgian case law increasingly applies the notion of reasonable privacy expectations. The Court of Cassation confirmed the importance of the reasonable expectation of privacy in a judgment of 9 September 2008,[299] which did not relate to the workplace. It concerned the recording of a telephone conversation by the caller without the consent and knowledge of the other party to the phone call. The Court ruled that in assessing whether the use of the recording is lawful, a judge must also take into account the criterion of the reasonable expectation of privacy. Following the Court, this criterion relates, among other things, to the content and the circumstances under which the conversation took place. The Court of Cassation reiterated and further shaped this view in subsequent judgments.[300]

663. In respect of communications, specific telecommunication laws strongly limit the employer's monitoring competences. These laws are penal laws. The employer is not able to lawfully register or monitor a telephone conversation at which he does not actually participate, unless he has received the consent of all communicating parties. The law therefore requires the employer to ask third parties (like clients) for their consent. In practice, some solutions are found on a more pragmatic basis. For example, employers may ask their employees to register all telephone calls made with clients. This is probably not a criminal offence in the sense of the aforementioned telecommunication laws. However, it remains unclear what rights (e.g., under torts law or other legal provisions) third parties (e.g., clients) may invoke in such case.

II. Electronic Online Communication

664. National CA no. 81 with regard to electronic online-communication data has significantly influenced the employer's monitoring rights with regard to internet and e-mail at work. CA no. 81 has two main parts. The first part is concerned with

299. Cass. (2nd Chamber) 9 Sep. 2008, no. P.08.0276.N, ECLI:BE:CASS:2008:ARR.20080909.2 (juportal.be).

300. Cass. (2nd Chamber) 17 Nov. 2015, P.15.0880.N/1, ECLI:BE:CASS:2015:ARR.20151117.2; Cass. (2nd Chamber) 11 Feb. 2020, P.19.1028.N, ECLI:BE:CASS:2020:ARR.20200211.2N.1 (juportal.be).

the conditions in which monitoring of internet or e-mail may be considered to be lawful. The second part deals with procedures that need to be followed in case of individualisation of data regarding employee use of internet or e-mail.

665. With regard to the conditions of monitoring, the CA no. 81 provided that monitoring is only lawful for limited purposes. Summarised, these are: (1) the prevention of severe misbehaviour; (2) the protection of economic, commercial or financial interests; (3) the monitoring of safety and technical operation of IT-services; and (4) the monitoring of company policies with regard to internet or e-mail use. Apart from this, the employer also needs to take into account the principle of proportionality. For example, internet monitoring should concern general logging data and not an individualised employee's visited website.

666. Furthermore, CA no. 81 provides for procedural guarantees. Before introducing a monitoring system in the company, the employer needs to give information regarding all aspects of employee monitoring. This information is given to the works council if there is one. The employer also needs to inform the individual employees concerned of all aspects of monitoring activities, like company policy, the purposes of monitoring, whether or not data are kept, whether or not monitoring is permanent, rights and duties, disciplinary sanctions.

667. Another element of procedure concerns the rules for the individualisation of data (meaning establishing the identity of an employee behind one or more given data). The employer can only link general or global (logging) data with an individual employee if it relates to the purpose of: (1) prevention of severe misbehaviour; or (2) protection of economic, commercial or financial interests; or (3) monitoring of safety and technical operation of IT-services. If the employer's individualised control measures are concerned with the monitoring of company policies with regard to internet or e-mail use, an additional guarantee is put in place. In such case, the employer has to give a prior warning, and has to hold a hearing with the concerned employee before taking a decision that may influence the position of the employee. This additional guarantee may be left aside in the case of pure professional communications monitoring.

III. Camera Surveillance

668. Camera surveillance at the workplace is regulated by a specific collective agreement, namely CA no. 68 of 16 June 1998. It is applicable to the entire private sector and explicitly states that it must be seen as completing the data protection legislation on the issue of camera monitoring at work.

669. The lawful purposes of camera surveillance are enumerated in a limitative way in CA no. 68. Allowed are the following uses of cameras: 1°) the protection of health and safety, 2°) the protection of the employer's property, 3°) the monitoring of the production process and 4°) the monitoring of the work performance of the employees. Thus, in theory, CA no. 68 does not constitute an obstacle for electronic monitoring, as various uses of cameras may be justified on these grounds.

670. However, it must be noted that CA no. 68 also requires that specific procedures should be followed in case an employer would introduce cameras in the workplace. Indeed, CA no. 68 provides for information to be given to the employees concerned (such as the number of cameras, the position of the cameras, the purposes of the cameras). Furthermore, information and consultation (containing an exchange of views) is required with the workers' representatives, or in the absence thereof, with the workers concerned. Furthermore, if the camera surveillance would have an impact on the rights and duties of the supervising personnel or would be used for the determination of the workers' wages, an amendment of the work regulations is required.

IV. Theft Prevention

671. A national collective agreement has been concluded on 'exit controls'. It concerns national collective agreement n° 89 of 30 January 2007 concerning theft prevention and exit controls. The aim of this collective bargaining agreement is not only to ensure respect for the privacy of workers and the protection of their dignity but also to take into account the needs of the proper functioning of the company and its needs in relation to protection against theft.

672. For the purposes of this collective agreement, 'exit controls' shall mean checks on workers, which take place when they leave the company or workplace. According to Article 4 of CA no. 89, exit checks shall only be permitted if they are aimed at preventing or detecting the misappropriation of goods within the company or at the workplace. They should not aim to measure the workers' work performance or to check the workers' attendance.

673. According to Article 6 of CA no. 89, systematic controls shall, in principle, only be possible if they are carried out by electronic means and/or technical detection systems. When exit checks are carried out by persons, they may only be carried out by persons who are carrying out 'private security activities' within the meaning of the legislation on private security services. Exit checks carried out by private security officers, whether or not by electronic means, may only be carried out under certain conditions.

674. Before engaging in exit controls, information and consultation need to be held with the workplace representation institutions of the company.

V. Location Tracking

675. With regard to location data and GPS tracking, the main guidance comes from the Belgian Data Protection Authority (DPA). The DPA is of the opinion that geolocation tracking or GPS tracking is possible, but under strict conditions.

676. According to the DPA, the purpose of geolocation surveillance must be such that an intrusion into the private life of the employee can be justified. Purposes that may be considered legitimate include the following: the safety of the employee; the protection of the service vehicle; optimising the management of professional travel (salesmen, technicians, taxi drivers); the control of the worker's performance (but only if there is a specific justification for that).

677. In the view of the DPA, if the geolocation system is set up to monitor the performance of the tasks entrusted to the workers, such monitoring must be targeted and justified by indications of probable abuse by certain workers. Permanent monitoring with systematic reading of the data recorded by the location system should in principle be considered disproportionate. However, there the DPA can see certain situations where a more regular check may be justified if it is directly linked to the nature of the tasks to be performed by the employee or to optimise the management of company vehicle movements (e.g., in cases of salespersons, field service technicians, etc.). But even then, vehicles should not be tracked continuously. The DPA also finds that it must be possible to deactivate the system if the employee uses the vehicle outside working hours.

678. The DPA also requires sufficient transparency to the workers concerned. Therefore, it states that employer must provide the information to the workers in advance, such as the legal basis for the data processing; who will be surveilled; the extent of the monitoring; the objectives pursued by the monitoring; the nature of the wrongdoing that may lead to the monitoring; the duration of the monitoring; the data processed; whether the data is transferred outside the European Union; what the employee's rights are, such as the right to consult the data, the right to lodge a complaint with the DPA, the right to restrict the processing of the data, etc.; the procedure to be followed after the verification.

§5. Social Media

679. The impact of social media on the employment relationship is an issue that mainly comes up in the labour case law in Belgium. The general outlook is that the use of social media by workers may lead to negative consequences in the work sphere. Most of the known cases are dismissal cases. While most of the cases are dealt with through the lens of the right to privacy, also the freedom of expression angle is relevant, as it is related to the 'openness' and public character of social media. The reasonable expectations of privacy will play a role in these cases.

680. A well-known case appeared before the Labour Tribunal of Leuven and, subsequently, was dealt with in appeal by the Labour Court of Brussels. The case concerned an employee who was employed as a business development manager by a publicly listed technology company. In his position, the employee concerned belonged to the senior management and had frequent contacts with customers and partners of the company. The employer discovered that the manager concerned had posted a number of negative comments on the social networking site Facebook about the company's half-year results, a few hours after they had been announced. Upon further investigation, it was found that the manager concerned had for several months been systematically commenting on the company's state of affairs in a negative manner on the public section of his Facebook page. The employer decided to terminate the employment contract with the manager concerned on the grounds of serious cause.

The Leuven Labour Tribunal[301] dealt with the argument of the possible violation of the employee's privacy, but quickly turned it down. The Court pointed out that every Facebook user who logged on to the employee's profile was able to read the comments he vented about his employer via his public notice board. The Labour Court of Brussels dealt with the appeal of this case.[302] The Labour Court stated that a Facebook page can contain information that is accessible to everyone and further information that is only accessible to 'friends', whereby the owner of the Facebook page can set who has access to which information. According to the Labour Court, this division is important when assessing the legitimacy of the evidence obtained because in each of the two sections of the Facebook page a 'different reasonable expectation of privacy applies' on the part of the creator of the page. The Court stated that it is only when the employee makes comments on the private part of his page that he can expect that non-friends will not be able to know or make use of this information. According to the Court, this does not apply to the 'public' part of his page because the employee concerned knows that everyone has access to this public part and therefore cannot expect that non-friends will not be able to take note of or use this information.

§6. Artificial Intelligence

681. The rise of new technologies based on artificial intelligence (AI) and robotics bring new challenges for both labour law and privacy and data protection law. There is a lot of attention to the subject, also with policymakers and social partners. However, currently, few Belgian laws specifically address the issue of AI. The main reference will still be the GDPR, besides other European and international initiatives on AI.

301. Labour Tribunal Leuven 17 Nov. 2011, AR 10/2215; Link and summary in: *NB Arbeidsrecht*, 2011, no. 9.

302. Labour Court Brussels 3 Sep. 2013, AR 2012/AB/104, *JTT* 2013, 497, *RW* 2013–14, 1586 and *Or.* 2013 (I. Plets), 231.

Chapter 10. Settlement of Disputes

682. As far as the enforcement of labour law is concerned, there is an extensive arsenal of structures and legal rules of its own.

§1. Labour Courts

683. Belgium has specialised courts and tribunals for labour law as well as social security matters (cf. Article 578 of the Judicial Code). In principle, the competent court is the Labour Tribunal.[303] In appeal proceedings, it is the Labour Court.[304] In labour matters, the Labour Court consists of a professional magistrate and two judges in labour matters who are appointed as 'lay judges' on the proposal of the representative employers' and workers' organisations. The composition of the lay judges also applies to the labour courts. The highest court, the Court of Cassation, is composed of professional judges only. It has a dedicated 'social chamber' dealing with labour matters.

684. Most disputes in the labour courts relate to individual employment rights, including pay issues, modification of the contract, employment termination, non-compete clauses or a confidentiality clause, harassment or discrimination at work, as well as disputes concerning the applicability or non-applicability of labour law (so-called bogus self-employed status cases).

685. The existence of labour courts is not exceptional in Europe. In Belgium, however, it can be seen as a logical part of the broader system. The strong presence of representatives of trade unions and employers organisations in the Belgian system is reflected in the composition of the Labour Court through lay judges.

686. The origin of labour courts in Belgium can be traced back to the French period (seventeenth-eighteenth century), during which 'labour councils' (*Conseils de Prud'hommes*) were operative. Initially, they were councils of employers judging over labour disputes. The institutions became gradually bipartite (with the involvement of trade union representatives) and were professionalised (with a professional lawyer presiding the councils).[305]Furthermore, appeal bodies were installed.[306]

687. When, from 1954 until 1967, a new procedural code was drafted in the Parliament, the existence of separate judicial bodies for labour disputes was discussed. There were two visions: those who were in favour of keeping employment rights disputes in the hands of the labour councils and those who wanted to integrate employment rights disputes into the competences of the regular civil court system.

303. Arbeidsrechtbank / Tribunal du Travail.
304. Arbeidshof / Cour du Travail.
305. Acts of 31 Jul. 1889 and of 15 May 1910.
306. Act of 15 May 1910.

What followed was a compromise.[307] Employment rights disputes would be a matter for specialised labour courts.[308] However, these courts would be integrated into the regular court system and would operate under the final authority of the Supreme Court (*Cour de Cassation*). The composition of the labour courts was continued: one professional judge, assisted by two lay judges.[309]

688. The lay judges in the Labour Court are appointed by the government,[310] but on the basis of a list of candidates submitted by trade unions and employers organisations.[311] The lay judges, however, do not defend the interests of (the members of) their organisations. Once appointed, lay judges are impartial members of the Court.[312] Nevertheless, lay judges are seen as form of representation of the employee's and employer's interests in the Court.

689. The system of lay judges is explained with various arguments. Lay judges, who are often doing other work in their organisation, are supposed to be more familiar with the daily practice of labour law. Furthermore, the parity of lay judges, i.e., an equal number of judges from the employers' and employees' side, is seen as a factor increasing the trust in the judicial authorities as well as the legitimacy of labour court decisions.

690. In most rounds of modernisation and reform of the judicial system, the issue of labour courts is at the table. The existence of independent labour courts, including the system of lay judges, was, as indicated above, a compromise and the subject of high debate during the time of enactment of the procedural code. At that time, the Royal Commissioner and reporter for the legislative reform put it as follows: 'It is not difficult to imagine a judicial architecture in which all equal representation is excluded. One can even give reasons relating to logic, experience, harmony or easiness to suggest such solutions or justify them. The lay judges are not more aware of social law than a lawyer.'[313] Nevertheless, many professionals will see several important benefits from the use of lay judges in labour courts.

691. Another feature in the labour court system is the presence of a labour public prosecutor, called the 'labour auditor'.[314] The 'labour auditor' defends the public interest in an impartial way before the Court. He has a role to play with regard to labour provisions that are enforced through criminal sanctions, but he also intervenes in various labour law disputes, such as employment discrimination cases. In disputes with the social security administration, the 'labour auditor' has the task to

307. J. Petit, *Sociaal Procesrecht* 15 (die Keure 2007).
308. Arts 578–583 Judicial Code.
309. Art. 81 Judicial Code.
310. Arts 198 and 216 Judicial Code.
311. Arts 199 and 216 Judicial Code.
312. Art. 151 Constitution.
313. *Printed Documents* Senate 1963–64, 10 Dec. 1963, no. 60, 63.
314. Arts 152 and 145 Judicial Code; *auditeur du travail / arbeidsauditeur.*

make enquiries with the administration or public services, in order to complete the file of applicants.[315] This compensates the inferior position of citizens who are often in a weak position.

692. Another form of trade union and employer representation should be mentioned. In employment rights cases, special competences are attributed to the representative trade unions and employers' organisations, who can assume legal representation for their members before the Labour Court. In this way, the monopoly of attorneys is interfered with by trade unions. The trade unions can defend their members with regard to individual employment rights[316] as well as for their members' rights arising out of a collective agreement.[317] The possibility for trade unions to defend their members' interests before the labour courts can be seen as a factor connected with the high degree of unionisation in Belgium.

§2. Arbitration and Mediation

693. In the field of individual labour law (employment law), arbitration is almost non-existent. This is due to the fact that Article 13 of the Act on Employment Contracts of 3 July 1978 makes agreements on arbitration, *before* the dispute arises, legally impossible. Such clauses or agreements are considered null and void. Only after a dispute has arisen, arbitration may be legally possible. There is only a limited exception for higher managerial staff.

694. In addition to this, with the existence of well-functioning labour courts and with a strong presence of trade union assistance (with trade unions being able to represent their members before the Court), there is no big need, nor any real current practice, on employment law arbitration in Belgium.

695. A more recent development in Belgium is the introduction of 'mediation' as a form of dispute settlement, based on the Act of 18 June 2018, implemented in the Civil Procedural Code. It can be arranged within a court procedure, or outside the Court. In principle, it is a freely available option for the parties. All employment matters, including individual matters, can be subject of mediation. Meditation supposes the intervention of a trained expert-mediator, who facilitates the solution for a dispute between the parties involved. It is an increasingly important practice in employment relations, though not yet fully widespread.

315. Art. 138*ter* Judicial Code.
316. Art. 728, §3 Judicial Code.
317. Art. 4 Act of 5 Dec. 1968 regarding the collective agreements and joint committees, *Belgian Official Gazette* 15 Jan. 1969.

§3. Labour Inspection

696. The labour inspection is also referred to as the social inspection, but in principle there are several separate services. The variety of inspection services relate to labour and the broader social law in Belgium. In addition to the federal services, there are also regional inspection services based in the communities and regions.

697. The competences of the social inspectorate are strictly regulated by law. For example, the law determines the right of the inspectorate to enter the workplace or inhabited places, to gather information, to identify persons, to interrogate persons; contains provisions regarding the consultation or copy of data carriers; and so on.[318] The social inspectorate has a discretionary power to assess whether it will start an investigation, but it may be ordered to act by the Labour Court's public prosecutor, referred to above (the labour auditor).[319] The social inspectorate can make a *procès-verbal* in case a violation of employment rights is found.[320] The *procès-verbal* needs to be sent to the Labour Court's public prosecutor and to the labour administration of the Ministry of Work.[321] When it concerns a minor violation as determined by law, or when the public prosecutor decides not to instigate legal proceedings, the administrative department can impose a fine instead,[322] which can be appealed against before the labour courts.[323]

§4. Social Penal Code

698. Many statutory labour law provisions are subject to criminal sanctions. In the past, this concerned a confusing and inconsistent variety of provisions spread across different laws. In 2010, the Social Penal Code was introduced to provide a coherent set of criminal conduct and sanctions.[324]

699. The Social Penal Code is a uniform and coherent codification of social criminal law provisions. Uniformity and coherence were achieved in two ways. First, the separate sanctioning provisions in each individual employment act were removed, so that every behaviour subject to criminal sanctions can now be found in the code.[325] Second, only four different levels of sanctions have been created whereby every criminal behaviour conforms with a certain level of sanctions.[326] Only one issue has yet to be resolved, namely the criminal sanctioning of collective

318. Arts 23 until 28 and further social criminal code, *Belgian Official Gazette* 1 Jul. 2010.
319. Art. 21 social criminal code, *Belgian State Gazette* 1 Jul. 2010.
320. Art. 21 Act of 6 Jun. 2010 social criminal code, *Belgian Official Gazette* 1 Jul. 2010.
321. Art. 65 Act of 6 Jun. 2010 social criminal code, *Belgian Official Gazette* 1 Jul. 2010.
322. Art. 69 Act of 6 Jun. 2010 social criminal code, *Belgian Official Gazette* 1 Jul. 2010.
323. Art. 3 Act of 2 Jun. 2010 regarding provisions of social criminal law, *Belgian Official Gazette* 1 Jul. 2010.
324. Social Penal Code of 6 Jun. 2010, *Belgian Official Gazette* 1 June 2010.
325. Arts 116 until 237 social criminal code, *Belgian Official Gazette* 1 Jul. 2010.
326. Art. 101 Act of 6 June 2010 social criminal code, *Belgian Official Gazette* 1 Jul. 2010.

agreements which are declared generally binding. In principle, collective agreements declared generally binding are subject to criminal sanctions.[327]

§5. Limitation Period

700. In disputes concerning employment contracts, special rules of limitation apply. Pursuant to Article 15 of the Act on Employment Contracts of 3 July 1978, legal actions arising from the contract are subject to a limitation period of one year after the termination of the contract or five years after the event giving rise to the claim, without this period being able to exceed one year after the termination of the contract.

701. In practice, it is therefore important to know whether a legal claim arises from the employment contract or not. The Court of Cassation ruled that an employer's legal claim for reimbursement of a salary unduly paid to an employee is not a legal claim arising from the employment contract, and is therefore not subject to the limitation period of Article 15 of the Employment Contracts Act, but to the general limitation period of ten years under Article 2262bis, §1 of the Old Civil Code.[328]

327. Arts 56 until 57 Act of 5 Dec. 1968 regarding the collective agreements and joint committees, *Belgian Official Gazette* 15 Jan. 1969 juncto Art. 189 social criminal code, *Belgian Official Gazette* 1 Jul. 2010.
328. Cass. 10 Oct. 2016, AR S.14.0061.N.

Part II. Collective Labour Relations

Chapter 1. Introduction

702. Collective labour law in Belgium refers to the body of legal provisions governing the relations between a group of employees and their representatives on the one hand and employers and their representatives on the other, as well as, where appropriate, the role of the state in these relations. Collective labour law thus regulates collective labour relations, also pointed at as industrial relations.

703. Collective labour relations are an important part of the labour law system. The possibility for workers to unite in organisations, such as trade unions, enables them to redress the economic power imbalance vis-à-vis the employer to some extent. The imbalance of power can also be compensated by means of binding legal provisions, but a system of collectively made agreements is more in line with the contractual autonomy of employers and workers and their organisations, which allows them to determine employment conditions on their own initiative and in a more appropriate manner.

704. In the Belgian system, collective bargaining presupposes a trinity of fundamental rights: the freedom of association, the right to collective bargaining and the right to strike. These three rights are recognised as fundamental rights. The freedom of association implies that workers can group themselves as a trade union. This enables them to negotiate as a trade union with a view to concluding agreements, collective agreements. The right to strike ensures that, if necessary, one can use means of pressure to strengthen a negotiating position.

705. In addition to this collective formation of working conditions, collective labour law also provides for collective representation of workers, or worker involvement, in the company. Entrepreneurial life is based on the freedom to conduct a business, which is also a fundamental right that protects entrepreneurship, risk-taking and investment on the part of capital. However, the importance of the labour factor is also recognised. This factor represents people who also invest in the organisation and who try to acquire an income and build up their standard of living. In most cases, the ‘stakeholdership’ of workers is recognised and leads to the granting of representation rights in the company, whereby workers’ representatives can enter into dialogue with the employer and exercise the right to information and consultation. The right to information and consultation is also recognised in Article 23 of the Belgian Constitution.

706. Finally, it should be pointed out that the collective labour relations as a whole and the way in which they are designed, or have come about, are strongly influenced by historical developments and social choices. As mentioned above, the Social Pact of 1944[329] is an important reference for the design of collective labour relations in Belgium. It is still based on recognised, large, in principle national organisations of employers and employees, commonly called the 'social partners'.

707. Consultation or representation bodies have been created at various levels in the Belgian system. These are institutions in which collective consultation takes place between representatives of employees and employers. The recognised trade unions play a very important role in this. Consultative bodies exist at the national level (the NLC), at the regional level, at the sectoral level (the joint committees) and at the enterprise level (the works council, the CPPW and the trade union delegation). These institutions will be discussed further below.

329. Draft agreement on social solidarity, *Arbbl.* January–March 1945, 9–19.

Chapter 2. Freedom of Association

§1. Constitutional Freedom

708. The freedom of association in labour law is based on the constitutionally recognised right to freedom of association. This freedom of association is constitutionally guaranteed in Belgium (Article 27 Constitution). However, the Act of 24 May 1921 is considered to be at least as important. In 1921, not only was Article 310 of the Penal Code abolished, which prohibited the hindrance of the freedom of trade. The Act of 24 May 1921 also came into being, guaranteeing the freedom of association.[330] This legislative impulse was therefore of great importance for the trade union movement.

§2. International Recognition

709. Freedom of association is also based on internationally recognised fundamental rights. Belgium recognises and ratified the relevant conventions of the International Labour Organisation, such as ILO Convention no. 87 (9 July 1948) and ILO Convention no. 98 (1 July 1949). Within the framework of the Council of Europe, the freedom of association is recognised both under Article 11 of the ECHR (ECHR, 1950) and in Articles 5 and 6 of the ESC (ESH, 1961, Revised ESH, 1996[331]).

§3. Positive and Negative Freedom

710. The freedom to establish a trade union is recognised both positively and negatively. Positively speaking, everyone has the right to form a trade union and to become a member of a trade union. Negatively, everyone also has the right not to belong to a trade union.

711. The positive aspect of trade union freedom is recognised not only in the Act of 24 May 1921 but also in the national CA no. 5 of 24 May 1971 concerning the status of the trade union delegation (cf. Article 3 CA no. 5). As to negative trade union freedom, the Act of 24 May 1921 states that 'no one can be forced to belong to a union' (Article 1 Act of 24 May 1921). This negative freedom is also recognised internationally.

330. Act of 24 May 1921 guaranteeing freedom of association, *Belgian Official Gazette* 28 May 1921; Act of 24 May 1921 abolishing Art. 310 of the Penal Code, *Belgian Official Gazette* 28 May 1921.
331. Act of 15 Mar. 2002 on assent to the revised European Social Charter and its Annex, done at Strasbourg on 3 May 1996, *Belgian Official Gazette* 10 May 2004.

Chapter 3. Trade Unions and Employers' Associations

§1. Trade Union Organisations

I. Representativeness

712. The Belgian system knows a number of representative organisations of employers and employees. With the notion of 'most representative organisations', a number of organisations are given a privileged status in collective labour law. Only these organisations have a seat in the NLC, and only these organisations can conclude a collective agreement as referred to in the Collective Agreements Act of 5 December 1968.

713. In the past, Belgium has been criticised by the International Labour Organisation's Committee on Freedom of Association for the absence in the National Labour Council Act of objective, clear and pre-established criteria for assessing the representativeness of the workers' organisations eligible for representation. With the Act of 30 December 2009 containing various provisions,[332] the legislator wanted to put an end to this situation by formulating a number of criteria that would provide more objective elements to assess the representativeness of the eligible employees' organisations. With regard to the organisation of collective bargaining, the legislator aimed at introducing new objective representativeness criteria that the most representative employees' organisations must fulfil in order to take a seat in the NLC.

714. In order to belong to the most representative workers' organisations, an organisation must meet four cumulative conditions that can be found in the renewed Article 2 of the Act of 29 May 1952 establishing the NLC.

The most representative workers' organisations must (Article 2, §4, paragraph 2, Act 29 May 1952):

(1) be established for the whole country and have an interprofessional character;
(2) represent the absolute majority of sectors and staff categories in the private and public sectors, insofar as the majority of employees are also represented;
(3) have at least 125,000 dues-paying members on average over a four-year period, including members of its affiliated or associated organisations;
(4) have the defence of employees' interests as their statutory objective.

715. The mandates for the most representative workers' organisations are distributed among these organisations by a Royal Decree deliberated in the Council of Ministers.

716. The seat in the NLC is also important within the framework of collective agreements law. The Collective Labour Act of 5 December 1968 stipulates that only

332. Cf. Arts 91–106 Act of 30 Dec. 2009 containing various provisions, Belgian Official Gazette 31 Dec. 2009.

representative employees' organisations can conclude collective agreements within the meaning of this Act. Here again, reference is made to the interprofessional organisations of employees and employers, which have been established for the whole country and are represented in the Central Council for Industry and in the NLC (cf. Article 3, Collective Agreements Act).

717. The main criterion for representativeness therefore remains whether or not it is represented in the NLC. A trade union that is not represented there cannot possibly be 'representative' in the sense of the law, unless it would join a trade union that is represented in the NLC. De facto, it implies a monopoly of three large trade unions. There are, in fact, three trade unions recognised as representative that have a seat on the NLC; these are the General Christian Trade Union and the socialist General Belgian Trade Union, which each have more than 1,000,000 members, as well as the General Confederation of Liberal Trade Unions of Belgium, which has over 200,000 members.

II. Unionisation

718. The existence of large and main trade union organisations is also connected with the degree of unionisation in Belgium. Although it is not easy to exactly determine, on average around 55% of workers are unionised. Among white-collar workers, it is somewhat lower and among blue-collar workers it is higher (in some sectors, it goes up to 80% or 90%). The average figure also takes into account that also many unemployed workers are unionised. This is, in its turn, connected to the fact that trade unions are the main administrators of unemployment benefits in Belgium.

III. Legal Status of Trade Union Organisations

719. A specific feature of the Belgian industrial relations system is that trade unions have managed to acquire a rather unique legal status. Although it is perfectly possible as a trade union to legally adopt a form of legal personality, trade unions have not done so. Legally speaking, therefore, the trade unions are 'de facto associations'.

720. Trade unions fear that accepting legal personality would make them subject to too many restrictions and vulnerable to legal actions.[333]

721. This does not take away that the legislator, including to a large extent the Collective Agreements Act of 5 December 1968, grants a number of prerogatives to the most representative trade unions, allowing them to take part in legal transactions, although they formally do not have legal personality:

333. *Parl.* Senate 1967–68, no. 78, 42; a union cannot be sued even by an employee of that union who believes he has been unfairly dismissed by his union, Cass. 3 Apr. 2017, S.15.0009.N.

- they can conclude collective agreements within the meaning of the Collective Agreements Act (Article 3, Collective Agreements Act);
- they may take legal action in all the disputes that may arise from the application of the Collective Agreements Act and to defend the rights that their members derive from the agreements they have concluded; they may also take legal action in the cases expressly provided for by law (e.g., disputes concerning works councils, committees for prevention and protection at work, bullying, etc.) (Article 4, paragraph 1, Collective Agreements Act);
- compensation may only be claimed from them for non-compliance with the obligations of a collective agreement to the extent that this is expressly provided for in the agreement (Article 4, paragraph 2, Collective Agreements Act).

§2. Employers' Organisations

722. The freedom of association does not only apply in the light of the establishment of employees' representative organisation. It also applies to the benefit of employers who want to organise themselves.

723. Employers have also grouped together in the form of employers' organisations. In this capacity, they participate in negotiations and social dialogue with the trade unions. The most important national employers' organisations are the Federation of Belgian Enterprises (FEB), UNIZO, which focuses on SMEs, and its Walloon counterpart UCM (Union des Classes Moyennes). In addition, there are employers' organisations that defend regional interests, such as VOKA and *l'Union Wallonne des Entreprises*.

724. Employers' organisations also need to be representative. The notion of representativeness applies, among other things, with a view to the conclusion of collective agreements within the meaning of the Collective Agreements Act of 5 December 1968 and to participation in the NLC. However, no minimum number of members is required for employers' organisations (cf. Article 3 Act of 29 May 1952). The government may, furthermore, recognise certain employers' organisations as representative of a certain sector (Article 3, paragraph 1, 3 Collective Agreements Act). This means that sectoral employers' organisations, which have no connection with an interprofessional organisation, can be recognised as representative employers' organisation.

Chapter 4. Institutionalised Relations Between Employers and Employees

§1. National Labour Council

725. The NLC was established by the Act of 29 May 1952 establishing the NLC. It is a public-law body, established for the private sector at national and interprofessional level.

I. Composition

726. The NLC has a joint composition. This means that it consists of an equal number of representatives of the representative employees' organisations on the one hand and of the employers' organisations on the other (Article 2, §2, NLC Act). The NLC is composed of twenty-six members with equal representation (Article 2, §1, NLC Act). The ordinary and the substitute members of the social partners are appointed for four years. Their mandate is renewable (Article 5, NLC Act).

727. The NLC is chaired by a person who is independent with regard to the interests of the social partners and is appointed by the King, i.e., de facto the government (Article 2, §1 and §6, NLC Act).

728. The King appoints as many substitute members as the Council has working members (Article 2, §7, NLC Act). Four vice presidents are also elected from among the members themselves (Article 2, §8, NLC Act).

729. The NLC is run by a secretariat, which works under the direction of a secretary appointed by the King and whose other staff is appointed by the Council itself (Article 7, NLC Act).

II. Tasks

730. The NLC has three main tasks:

(1) conclude collective agreements (Article 6 *j°* Article 1, 3, Collective Agreements Act).
(2) issue opinions or proposals on general social issues of concern to employers and employees, to a minister or to the legislative chambers, either on their own initiative or upon request (Article 1 NLC Act);
(3) deliver an opinion on disputes of competence that could arise between joint committees (Article 1, NLC Act);

731. As far as the NLC's advisory power is concerned, it should be noted that this can be done either on the NLC's own initiative or at the request of the Minister or the Parliament. However, the Minster, the government or the Parliament do not have the obligation to ask the advice of the NLC in social matters on which they want to take measures, nor have to follow the opinion of the NLC. The opinion of the NLC is not binding. Nevertheless, these opinions are important in practice and in practice, it is (politically) difficult for a government or Parliament to deviate from a unanimous opinion of the NLC. After all, it reflects the consensus of the representatives of employers and employees.

732. As regards the authority to conclude collective agreements, reference should be made to the Collective Agreements Act of 5 December 1968, which provides for this possibility (Article 6 *j*° Article 1, 3, Collective Agreements Act). The scope of a collective agreement concluded in the NLC extends, in principle, to the various branches of industry and to the whole country (Article 7, Collective Agreements Act). NLC-collective agreements are numbered, as a rule declared universally applicable, and rank high in the hierarchy of legal sources (Article 51, Collective Agreements Act).

§2. Joint Committees

733. There is a lot of sectoral consultation between trade unions and employers' organisations. The joint committees provide the formal framework for this consultation. It should come as no surprise that joint committees are regulated by the same law as the result of the consultation that takes place within them, the collective agreement. The Collective Agreements Act of 5 December 1968 is, in full, the Act on Collective Agreements and Joint Committees.

I. Establishment

734. Joint committees are set up by the King (de facto, on the initiative of the Minister of Employment, through a Royal Decree). He can do so on his own initiative or at the request of one or more representative organisations of workers or employers. The King then determines the persons, the branch of activity or undertakings and the territory to which the joint committee applies (Article 35, Collective Agreements Act). At the request of a joint committee, the King can also set up one or more joint subcommittees (Article 37, Collective Agreements Act). Some 180 joint committees and subcommittees are active.

II. Composition

735. Joint committees (and joint subcommittees) are also composed of equal numbers of representatives of employers' organisations and of employees' organisations (Article 39, 2, Collective Agreements Act).

736. As far as the representatives of employers' organisations and of employees' organisations are concerned, the law does not stipulate a precise number, but requires parity. The exact number is thus determined by the King (Article 41, Collective Agreements Act). In principle, the competent minister decides which organisations are eligible for representation. Only representative organisations qualify for representation. In addition to the traditional organisations, these can also be employers' organisations that the King recognises as representative for the sector concerned.

737. The term of office of the members of the joint committee is four years. It can be renewed (Article 43, paragraph 1, Collective Agreements Act).

738. The joint committees are chaired by an independent chairperson (Article 39, 1, Collective Agreements Act). The chair is an important function. The chairperson is independent and, in practice, is a 'social mediator' competent for the concerned sector. Social mediators intervene in case of collective conflicts in the sector and are attached to the Ministry of Employment, Labour and Social Dialogue.

739. The secretaries are appointed by the Minister of Employment (Article 39, 3 CLA).

III. Scope

740. Each joint committee has a specific scope, which usually coincides with a certain sphere of activity, or sector in the economy, such as metal, textile, construction, transport, and food. This is referred to as a branch of activity or sector.

741. It is the main activity of the undertaking that determines which joint committee is responsible for this undertaking. It implies that only the collective agreements of that concerned joint committee then apply to this undertaking. It is generally assumed that a company can only fall under one joint committee.

742. The Court of Cassation has qualified this principle. According to the Court, there is no general principle of labour law according to which an undertaking is subject to one joint committee, namely that of its main activity.[334] However, in most cases, the Royal Decree, which determines the competence of the joint committee, does not specify whether the activities that fall within its scope relate to the main, secondary or ordinary activity of an undertaking. In that case, the main activity of the enterprise may be taken as the starting point.[335] In the event of difficulties in this matter, an appeal can be made to the General Direction of Collective Labour Relations from the Ministry of Employment, Labour and Social Dialogue. His service

334. Cass. 17 Feb. 1992, AR 7688, *JTT* 1992, 223.
335. Cass. 24 Dec. 1990, *JTT* 1991, 176 and *RW* 1990–91, 1373; Cass. 9 Sep. 1991, *RW* 1991–92, 881.

will conduct an investigation, possibly through the intervention of the Labour Inspectorate, and will issue an opinion. In the last instance, of course, a judge will decide.

IV. Tasks

743. The joint committees have the following tasks (Article 38, paragraph 1, Collective Agreements Act):

(1) concluding collective bargaining agreements by the represented organisations;
(2) preventing or settling disputes between employers and employees;
(3) advise the government, the NLC, the works councils, at their request or on their own initiative, on matters within their competence;
(4) perform any other duty assigned to them by or under the law.

744. The conclusion of collective agreements can be seen as the most important task of the joint committees. As a rule, collective agreements reached by this body are declared universally applicable so that they become binding throughout the sector.

745. However, joint committees also play an important role as conciliation bodies in the event of disputes in the sector. Especially the chairperson of the joint committee, who is also a social mediator, leads this conciliation and mediation. Often, this is done by means of a conciliation 'bureau' established within the joint committee, composed of a delegation of the social partners of the sector.

§3. Regional Consultations

746. Because of the various state reforms and the defederalisation of competences for work, education and labour market policy, collective consultation is increasingly taking place at the level of the country's sub-entities/regions.

747. For instance, in the Flemish Region, the Flemish social partners consult with the Flemish Government within the framework of the Flemish Economic and Social Consultation Committee. The socio-economic themes that affect the region are discussed there. Moreover, there is a practice whereby the Flemish Government undertakes to respect and implement in its policy the consensus that arises from that consultation.

748. The main national trade unions, with their Dutch-speaking divisions, are represented on the workers' side. On the employers' side, there is the involvement of the Union of Self-Employed Entrepreneurs (UNIZO), also represented nationally, and a Flemish organisation, the VOKA-Flemish Network of Enterprises as well as the Farmers' Union (BB).

§4. Works Council

I. General

749. A works council is a body set up at the level of the enterprise in which the staff of this enterprise is represented vis-à-vis the employer in order to exercise participation rights with regard to the social and economic policy of the enterprise.

750. Works councils are regulated by various sources of law. The most important are:

- Act of 20 September 1948 on the organisation of the enterprise community (we will abbreviate this as Works Councils Act);
- CA no. 9 of 9 March 1972 organising the national agreements and collective agreements concluded in the NLC concerning works councils;
- Royal Decree of 27 November 1973 regulating the economic and financial information to be provided to the works councils;
- Act of 23 April 2008 supplementing the transposition of Directive 2002/14/EC of the European Parliament and of the Council of 11 March 2002 establishing a general framework for informing and consulting employees.

II. Establishment

751. Works councils do not just come into being. Their establishment requires the organisation of social elections. This refers to elections held among the company's employees whereby they elect the representatives who will sit on the works council. In principle, social elections are held every four years, during a limited period of the year (usually in the month of May), for all undertakings in the country that reach the thresholds (section 21, §1, Works Councils Act).

752. The legislator sets a threshold for the establishment of a works council (and organising the social elections for it). The Act literally provides that works councils must be established in all undertakings that usually employ an average of at least fifty employees (section 14, §1, subsection 1, Works Councils Act). However, it should be mentioned that the number fifty in the Act is only considered to be a target number. In other words, it is meant to be reached in time. The actual threshold is determined by a Royal Decree (section 28, Works Councils Act). On the basis of this, currently, the actual threshold is hundred employees.

753. Influenced by the European Directive 2002/14/EC of 11 March 2002 on information and consultation of employees, which speaks of companies with fifty or more employees (or, optionally, in establishments with twenty or more employees), the Act of 23 April 2008 came into being. This Act did not change the threshold for the establishment of a works council. However, a chapter was added to the Act of 4 August 1996 on the well-being of workers in the performance of their work, in order to empower the CPPW, which in principle is set up in undertakings with fifty or more employees, with the information and consultation rights that arise from the Directive for undertakings with fifty or more employees.

754. The threshold is determined on the basis of the number of employees of the company, i.e., the number of employees that are usually employed on average (section 14, §1, paragraph 1, Works Councils Act). These are employees who are employed under a contract of employment for an indefinite period of time, for a definite period of time or for clearly defined work.[336] In principle, personnel strength is calculated on the basis of full-time equivalents. Part-time employees are also counted, but only pro rata. Temporary workers employed within the framework of the regulations on temporary work and agency work must be included with the user to whom they are assigned, unless they replace an employee whose employment contract has been suspended (Article 25 Act of 24 July 1987).[337] In the latter case, the replaced employee whose employment contract has been suspended must be counted.

755. The workforce is determined for each undertaking. The notion of 'undertaking' is referred to in the law as a 'technical business unit' (abbreviated as TBU), determined on the basis of economic and social criteria (section 14, §1, paragraph 2, 1°, Works Councils Act). The 'technical business unit' does not necessarily coincide with the 'legal entity' of the company. The legal entity refers to the legal form of the company. The notion of technical business unit rather corresponds to the more factual socio-economic reality of a company. The law states that the technical business unit is determined on the basis of economic and social criteria. In case of doubt, the social criteria will prevail (section 14, §1, paragraph 2, 1°, Works Councils Act).

756. The law provides that an undertaking is obliged to establish a works council if, as a legal entity, it employs at least hundred employees, which is also the number of employees employed in each of its registered offices (section 14, §2, subsection a, paragraph 1, Works Councils Act). Therefore, if it concerns a legal entity with hundred employees that is divided into several smaller, separate TBUs that do not employ hundred employees, a works council must still be established at the level of the legal entity.

757. The principle of staffing at the level of the TBUE also means that several legal entities, which individually employ less than hundred employees, can together form a TBU, so that the establishment of a works council becomes mandatory.

758. It is a situation that regularly gives rise to discussion with also a certain fear of law evasion, for example, by artificially dividing a large company into several smaller legal entities in order to escape the legal threshold.

---

336. Cass. 3 Apr. 1984, *JTT* 1985, 327, *Pas.* 1984, I, 917 and *RW* 1984–85, 1981.
337. According to the Court of Cassation, temporary workers should not be taken into account when dividing the mandates between the different categories of workers, Cass. 15 Apr. 2013, AR S.12.0071.N.

For this situation, the legislator has introduced a presumption (section 14, §2, b°, Works Councils Act). Several legal entities shall be presumed, until proven otherwise, to constitute a technical business unit when:

(1) either these legal entities are part of the same economic group or are managed by the same person or by persons having an economic link between them, or these legal entities have the same activity or activities which are coordinated with one another; and
(2) there are elements indicating social cohesion between these legal entities, such as, in particular, a community of people gathered in the same premises or in nearby premises, a common personnel management, work regulations or collective agreements which are common or contain similar provisions.

Where evidence is provided of one of the conditions referred to in (1) and evidence of certain elements referred to in (2), the legal entities concerned shall be regarded as forming a single technical business unit, unless the employer(s) provides evidence that the personnel management and policy do not reveal social criteria characteristic of the existence of a technical business unit. The legal presumption is therefore rebuttable.

Following the social elections, according to a procedure established by the King, the notion of technical business unit is further defined.

III. Composition

759. The works council is composed of representatives of the employer and representatives of the staff in the enterprise.

760. However, the legislation does not provide for full parity. It is provided that the employer representatives, including the head of the undertaking, may not be more numerous than the employee representatives (section 16, a), Works Councils Act). The number of employee representatives in the works council can therefore be larger than the number of employer representatives. In practice, this is often the case.

761. On the employer's side, the works council consists of the head of the company and one or more deputy delegates appointed by him, in accordance with the provisions laid down by the King, who are authorised to represent him and to bind him on the basis of the managerial position they hold in the company (Article 16, a) Works Councils Act).

The head of the company is the person who runs the company. The other members are appointed from among the company's managerial staff. These are persons who are authorised to represent and bind the employer. They are appointed for the entire (four-year) term of office of the works council, on the condition that they do not lose the mentioned managerial functions (section 16, a), Works Councils Act).

The list of managerial positions is determined at the beginning of the election procedure. These persons are very often employees of the company and can therefore not be elected as employee representatives or serve on the works council.

762. The employees' representatives are appointed based on election by all employees of the company. These so-called social elections are in principle held every four years.

The elections are held on the basis of lists of candidates. There are separate mandates for blue- and white-collar workers. In addition, a separate category of personnel was introduced through the Social Rehabilitation Act of 22 January 1985,[338] namely a representation of 'cadre personnel'.[339] This only happens in companies where at least fifteen 'cadre' employees are employed. It refers to employees, excluding managerial staff, who occupy a higher function in the company, which is generally reserved to the holder of a diploma of a certain level or to those who have an equivalent professional experience.

763. There is a special provision for the submission of lists of candidates for employee representation. For blue-collar workers and white-collar workers, such candidate lists can only be submitted by the representative employees' organisations. This means that only the three main trade union organisations can do so. For managerial staff, the possibility of nomination has been extended to the representative organisations of managerial staff, or even to independent candidates who have sufficient support from the managers of the company (Article 20ter, Works Councils Act).

764. The number of effective delegates may not be lower than two and may not be higher than twenty-five. The exact number is determined on the basis of the size of the company. There are as many substitute delegates as effective delegates (section 16, paragraph 1, a), Works Councils Act).

765. The works council is chaired by the head of the enterprise or by someone authorised by the head of the enterprise as chairperson. In any case, it must be someone who can represent and bind the employer. He must be able to speak on behalf of the employer. A vice president is also appointed to replace an absent chairman (section 22, §1, subsection 1, Works Councils Act). The secretariat of the Works Council, on the other hand, is run by an employee representative. A deputy secretary is also appointed to replace the secretary when he is unable to act (section 22, §1, paragraph 2, Works Councils Act).

IV. Competence

766. The competences of the works council are of a social, economic and financial nature. They are numerous and can be found in various sources, such as the

338. *BS* 24 Jan. 1985.
339. 'Personnel de cadre' / 'Kaderpersoneel'.

Works Councils Act of 20 September 1948 itself, as well as in CA no. 9 of 9 March 1972 and the Royal Decree of 27 November 1973.

Numerous other laws, royal decrees and collective agreements grant powers to the works council. One example is the Act of 8 April 1965 on work regulations, which provides that the works council has the power to draw up and amend the work regulations of the company.

767. The power of the works council is in principle limited to a right of information and consultation. There is no co-decision (with a few exceptions, such as what is said above in relation to the drafting of the work regulations).

V. Operation

768. The works council meets at the seat of the company (section 22, §1, subsection 1, Works Councils Act). It is convened at least once a month at the request of the head of the company or at least (one-third) of the members of the council representing the personnel (section 22, §1, subsection 3, Works Councils Act).

769. Works councils also draw up internal rules (section 22, §2, Works Councils Act).

770. Meetings of the works council, even outside working hours, are considered actual working time and are remunerated as such. The premises and equipment required for the meetings are made available to the works council by the head of the enterprise (section 23, subsection 1, Works Councils Act).

§5. Committee for Prevention and Protection at Work

I. General

771. Another consultative body at the enterprise level concerns the CPPW (or Committee). It was established by the Act of 4 August 1996 on the well-being of workers in the performance of their work (abbreviated to Wellbeing Act).

II. Establishment

772. The Act of 4 August 1996 on Wellbeing at Work repeats what is provided in the Works Council Act and stipulates that committees are installed in all companies that normally employ at least fifty people on average (Article 49, Wellbeing Act). Contrary to what applies to works councils, the number fifty here is the real personnel threshold. The notion of employees, the calculation of the usual average and especially the notion of undertaking is regulated in the same way as for the works council, also with regard to the notion of TBU.

III. Composition

773. The principles regarding the formation and composition of the CPPW are very similar to those of the works council. The employee representatives in these committees are elected at the same social elections as for the works councils.

774. In the framework of health and safety law (with the principles established in the Wellbeing Act and the detailed regulations in the Wellbeing Codex), a company must refer (or hire) prevention advisers, specialised in general or specific health and safety issues. A company must in principle also have an 'internal prevention service'. As a rule, several prevention advisers are involved in the functioning of well-being in an enterprise, including the prevention adviser occupational physician, or the prevention adviser specialising in the psychosocial aspects of work and of violence, harassment and sexual harassment at work.

775. The prevention adviser in charge of the internal prevention service attends the meetings of the CPPW. The prevention adviser is an important figure in the functioning of the committee, as he is the independent expert on well-being at work. In principle, the employer shall appoint, replace or remove the prevention advisers, but only with the prior agreement of the CPPW or, in its absence, the trade union delegation or the employees. The protection against dismissal of the prevention advisor is organised through the intervention of the committee.

IV. Competence

776. Pursuant to Article 65 of the Wellbeing Act, the committee has the task of identifying and proposing all means of improving the well-being of workers in the performance of their work and actively contributing to that improvement. The powers of the Prevention Committee are further detailed in the aforementioned Wellbeing Codex.

777. As mentioned above, the competence of the committee was extended by the Act of 23 April 2008 transposing European Directive 2002/14/EC of 11 March 2002 on informing and consulting employees. Reference can be made to Articles 65bis to 65undecies of the Wellbeing Act.

778. In an enterprise without a prevention committee but with a trade union delegation, all the tasks and powers of this committee are transferred by law to the trade union delegation, with the exception of the powers pursuant to the Act of 23 April 2008 (Article 52 Wellbeing Law). In the enterprises where neither a committee nor a trade union delegation exists, the workers themselves participate directly in the treatment of questions related to the well-being of the workers in the performance of their work (Article 53, Wellbeing Act). How this is done in practice is laid down in the Wellbeing Codex.

V. Operation

779. In the Wellbeing Codex, in the provisions on the tasks and functioning of the committees for prevention and protection at work, further rules can be found on the functioning of the committee.

780. The employer shall ensure that the committee meets at least once a month, as well as when at least one-third of the employee representatives in the committee request it. The employer chairs the committee, but the secretariat of the committee is provided by the internal service if the employer must set up a single committee (Wellbeing Codex).

§6. The Trade Union Delegation

I. General

781. The third body at company level is the trade union delegation, also called the union delegation. This is a representation, at company level, of the personnel of the company who are members of a trade union.

The trade union delegation is not regulated by law, but by (national) CA no. 5 of 24 May 1971. This framework agreement lays down the general principles concerning the status of trade union delegation. The further elaboration of these principles is done by collective agreements concluded in the joint committees.

In principle, the trade union delegation is a body that represents the staff members affiliated to a trade union to the employer in the undertaking. However, the collective agreements concluded in the joint committees may provide that the representation is extended to non-organised workers (Article 6 CA no. 5). Until now, this option has been used on occasion.

The trade union delegation represents the staff in the company and not the trade union itself. Because of the distinction that exists in practice between blue-collar and white-collar workers, it happens that there is a trade union delegation competent for each of these categories separately.

II. Establishment

782. Contrary to what applies to the works council or the CPPW, there is no fixed staff threshold for the establishment of a trade union delegation. The threshold varies from sector to sector, depending on the agreement made in a collective labour agreement (cf. Article 8, 1° CA no. 5). In most cases, the personnel threshold is lower than for setting up a CPPW.

The establishment of a trade union delegation takes place via a request from the representative trade union(s) to the head of the company (Article 7, paragraph 1 CA no. 5). These representative trade unions have the right to propose candidates for the designation or election of the trade union delegation (Article 7, paragraph 2, CA no. 5). CA no. 5 thus leaves the choice between an appellation and an election of the trade union delegation.

III. Composition

783. CA no. 5 remains silent on the effective composition of the trade union delegation. This is left to the various sectors. However, it is stipulated that the maximum term of office is four years and is renewable (Article 16 CA no. 5).

IV. Competence

784. The competences of the trade union delegation include (Article 11 CA no. 5):

(1) labour relations;
(2) the negotiations with a view to concluding collective agreements or settlements within the company, without prejudice to collective agreements or settlements concluded at other levels;
(3) the application in the company of social legislation (labour and social security law), collective agreements, work regulations and individual employment contracts;
(4) compliance with the general principles laid down in Articles 2 to 5 of CA no. 5.

785. Thus, the trade union delegation has a fairly broad power in labour relations in the company. It should be noted that the trade union delegation has the power to negotiate with a view to concluding collective agreements. However, the conclusion of a collective agreement within the meaning of the Collective Agreements Act of 5 December 1968 remains the competence of a representative trade union itself. Furthermore, CA no. 5 states that the trade union delegation is competent for the application in the company of social legislation and agreements made. In that sense, it therefore has a 'watchdog' function in the enforcement of labour law.

786. With regard to individual labour disputes, CA no. 5 states that each individual complaint shall be submitted by the employee concerned in the usual hierarchical way. However, this employee may, at his request, be assisted by his trade union delegate. The trade union delegation shall have the right to be heard with regard to any individual dispute or any dispute that could not be solved in this way (Article 13 CA no. 5).

787. The trade union delegation may also intervene in collective labour disputes. The trade union delegation has the right to be heard by the head of the company or his representative in any dispute or disagreement of a collective nature that arises in the company. It also has that right when such disputes or disagreements threaten to arise (Article 12 CA no. 5).

788. If there is no works council in the company, the trade union delegation can exercise the tasks, a number of rights and duties that, in principle, are assigned to the works council by CA no. 9 of 9 March 1972 (Article 24 CA no. 5). The trade union delegation exercises the tasks of the CPPW when this committee does not exist (Article 52, Wellbeing Act).

Chapter 5. Collective Bargaining

§1. General

789. As becomes clear from the above, the Belgian system of industrial relations is well developed with different institutions and a lot of practice.

790. There are three main levels of collective bargaining: the national level, the sector level, and the level of the company.

791. The Belgian social model promotes cooperation and consensus between trade unions and employers' organisations, called the 'social partners'. Due to a Belgian tradition, social and economic policies initiated or desired by the government also rely on the views and consensus of the social partners. It has led to a practice of social consultation, not only between the representative organisations of employers and employees themselves but also between these organisations and the government. At the national level, and increasingly at the regional level, government social policy is influenced and guided by the consensus of these representative organisations.

792. This Belgian practice also gives rise, on an informal basis, to rounds of negotiations every two years between the social partners with a view to concluding a national 'Interprofessional Agreement' (IPA), which serves as a reference basis for wage developments, government policy and sectoral collective bargaining for the following two years. These discussions and negotiations take place within an informal body of top negotiators of major trade union and employers associations in Belgium (who also play a role in the NLC), named the 'Group of 10', since it concerns ten persons in addition to a presiding representative of the major Belgian employers' association.

§2. Collective Agreements

I. Concept

793. The collective agreement is a typical labour law instrument of industrial relations and a source of rights and obligations. This source of law is regulated by the Collective Agreements Act of 5 December 1968.

794. A collective agreement is defined in the Collective Agreements Act as the agreement concluded between one or more employees' organisations on the one hand, and one or more employers' organisations or one or more employers' on the other hand, establishing individual and collective relations between employers and employees in undertakings or in a branch of activity and regulating the rights and obligations of the contracting parties (Article 5, Collective Agreements Act).

795. Being an agreement in essence, a collective agreement is a contract and therefore also governed by civil law.

II. Parties

796. A feature of the collective agreement concept is that the agreement is concluded by one or more trade unions on the one hand and one or more employers or employers' organisations on the other. Individual workers are therefore not parties to a collective agreement, although they are subject to it, as regards both the rights and obligations it contains.

797. On the employee side, a collective agreement can only be signed by one or more employee organisations (cf. Article 5, Collective Agreements Act). Thus, the signature of one employee organisation is sufficient to be able to speak of a collective agreement, at least as far as the employees' side is concerned (the employers' side must, of course, also sign).

798. The Collective Agreements Act limits the concept of a collective agreement to that which is concluded by representative organisations that meet the criteria laid down by law (Article 3, Collective Agreements Act). On the workers' side, only the three major national trade unions, or their affiliated trade union federations, are therefore eligible to conclude a collective agreement on the workers' side.

799. Unlike individual employees, employers can be individual signatories to collective agreements. This will usually be the case when it comes to a collective agreement concluded at the level of a company.

800. However, if it concerns employers' organisations, the restriction that they must be 'representative organisations' within the meaning of Article 3 of the Collective Agreements Act also applies here. In addition, the King may, on the advice of the NLC, recognise an organisation as representative of a certain branch of industry (Article 3, paragraph 1, 3 Collective Agreements Act). This is, of course, relevant for the conclusion of sectoral collective agreements.

801. The former implies that a collective agreement concluded by another than a representative organisation, which therefore falls outside the scope of the Collective Agreements Act, cannot be regarded as a real collective agreement under Belgian labour law.

III. Levels

802. A collective agreement can be concluded at different levels: national, sectoral or company level.

803. The collective agreements concluded at national interprofessional level apply in principle to the entire private sector in the country, including the non-profit sector. In principle, these collective agreements are concluded in the NLC. These collective agreements all have a serial number.

804. Collective agreements concluded at sectoral level relate to a particular sector or branch of the economy, such as metal, textile, and food. These, too, often have a national scope of application, but only for the undertakings of the sector concerned. They are often concluded within a joint body, i.e., the joint committee that covers the sector in question. If the collective agreement is concluded within the competent joint committee, it must be signed by all the organisations represented on that body (Article 24, Collective Agreements Act). Each organisation represented in that joint committee therefore has a right of veto. This does not mean, however, that it is not possible to conclude a valid collective agreement outside the joint committee.

805. There are also regional collective agreements, which apply, for example, in a specific province.

806. Finally, collective agreements can be concluded at company level. The collective agreement then only applies to the employer concerned and its employees. At the enterprise level, the trade union delegation has a role. Indeed, it is authorised to conduct negotiations with a view to concluding a collective labour agreement (Article 11, 2° CA no. 5). However, the trade union delegation cannot validly sign the collective agreement itself because it is not a trade union organisation within the meaning of the legislation. The legally valid signing of the collective agreement itself will have to be done by a representative of one or more employees' organisations.

IV. Contents

807. Collective agreements regulate wages and working conditions of employers and employees. The legal definition of a collective agreement shows that it is about establishing 'individual and collective relations between employers and employees' on the one hand and regulating 'the rights and obligations of the contracting parties' on the other hand (Article 5, Collective Agreements Act).

808. This shows that, in principle, a collective agreement consists of two main types of provisions. On the one hand, there are the provisions that relate to the individual employers and employees to whom the collective agreement applies, called the 'normative' provisions. On the other hand, there are the provisions that regulate the relationship between the contracting parties, called the 'obligatory' provisions.

In principle, the possible content of a collective agreement can be interpreted broadly, so that parties can agree on all matters related to work and labour relations.[340]

809. The pay and working conditions included in a collective agreement are normative provisions as they set standards that will govern the employment relationships of employer(s) and their employees that are covered by the collective agreement. Thus, the collective agreement's provisions create rights and obligations on the part of employers and employees who fall within the scope of the collective agreement in a particular company or sector.

These provisions may have an impact on both the individual and collective relations between these employers and their employees. Hence, a distinction is made between individually normative provisions on the one hand and collectively normative provisions on the other. The individually normative provisions of a collective agreement contain employment conditions that influence the individual relationship between an employer and an employee. These are provisions of a collective agreement which could just as well have been included in an individual employment contract. In fact, they are automatically incorporated into the individual employment contract. On may think about wages, salary increases, indexing of wages, payment of premiums, professional classifications, working time regulations, additional holidays, etc.

The collectively normative provisions of a collective agreement regulate the collective relations between employers and employees in an enterprise or industry. They have no direct influence on the individual employment relationship between an employer and employee. They are provisions that concern the employer and the collectivity of his staff. For example, the establishment of a trade union delegation, the organisation of a conciliation procedure in the event of social disputes, the establishment and functioning of social security funds, the obligation to draw up employment contracts in writing, health and safety arrangements in the undertaking, the ban on subcontracting or temporary work, etc.

810. A collective agreement also creates rights and obligations between the parties who sign it. These are called the 'obligatory provisions' of the collective agreement. These provisions may be expressly stipulated in the contract. However, it is considered that a number of obligatory provisions are always implicitly included in the conclusion of a collective agreement. They flow, as it were, from the very essence of a collective agreement. These are the peace obligation, the duty to inform and the duty to influence.

811. The peace obligation means that the parties must keep the social peace, from the conclusion of a collective agreement and during its duration, which means that they may not use any means of conflict, such as strikes, lockouts and the like, in order to change the content of the agreement. The obligation of peace is in principle relative, i.e., unless otherwise agreed, and it only relates to what has been agreed in the collective agreement and thus does not relate to what has not been

340. Constitutional Court 8 May 2019, no. 59/2019.

agreed therein. However, it should be assumed that the duty of peace also applies to matters that were negotiated but not agreed to, or to matters 'related' to collective agreement provisions. A strike by a trade union that has not signed the collective agreement is also not a breach of the peace obligations.

812. The duty to inform is the obligation of the trade unions and, as the case may be, the employers' organisations, which have concluded the collective agreement, to inform their members of the scope and content of the collective agreement. This obligation is linked to the duty to influence. Indeed, each signatory party is obliged to influence its members to cooperate in the implementation of and compliance with the normative provisions of the collective agreement. This also ensures that, in principle, no individual agreements are made that would be contrary to the provisions of the collective agreement, which, by the way, is not possible in principle according to Article 51 of the Collective Agreements Act.

V. Duration

813. A collective agreement can be concluded for a fixed term or for an indefinite term. If the collective agreement has been concluded for a fixed term, it is possible to insert a renewal clause (Article 15, paragraph 1, Collective Agreements Act). The collective agreement for an indefinite period or for a definite period with an extension clause can, in principle, be terminated by either party (Article 15, paragraph 2, Collective Agreements Act). Termination must be in writing, on pain of nullity (Article 15, paragraph 3, Collective Agreements Act).

VI. Formal Requirements

814. A collective agreement must be concluded in writing, on pain of nullity (section 13(1) of the Collective Agreements Act). It must be signed by the persons who enter into it on behalf of their organisation or in their own name (Article 14, Collective Agreements Act). The Collective Agreements Act lists a number of statements that must be included (Article 16, Collective Agreements Act).

815. Organisations and employers who have not entered into the agreement may always accede to it with the consent of all parties that have entered into it, unless the agreement provides otherwise (Article 17, paragraph 1, Collective Agreements Act). Accession is made in writing, on penalty of nullity (Article 17, paragraph 2, Collective Agreements Act).

VII. Deposit and Registration

816. Every collective agreement must be deposited with the Ministry of Employment, Labour and Social Dialogue (Article 18, Collective Agreements Act).

This deposit is made at the Collective Labour Relations Department of the Ministry, which then registers the collective agreement.

817. The law does not explicitly provide for a sanction in the event of failure to deposit a collective agreement. It is assumed that the failure to deposit it does not affect the validity of the collective agreement as such, but that the collective agreement does not have all the legal consequences that collective agreements law, in principle, grants.

818. Anyone can obtain a copy of a deposited collective agreement against payment (Article 18, paragraph 3, Collective Agreements Act).

VIII. Binding

819. The collective agreement binds not only the parties who have entered into it but also the employers and employees who fall within its scope. However, the obligatory provisions only bind the signatory parties.

820. The normative provisions of the collective agreement are, according to the law, binding for (Article 19, Collective Agreements Act):

(1) the organisations which have entered into them and the employers who are members of those organisations or have entered into the agreement, from the date of entry into force;
(2) the organisations and employers which accede to the agreement and the employers which are members of those organisations as from accession;
(3) the employers who become members of a bound organisation, from the date of their membership;
(4) all employees of a bound employer.

The binding of employees to the provisions of a collective agreement is therefore determined by the employer to whom the collective agreement is binding. It makes no difference whether an employee is a member of a trade union or not, or whether that organisation was a party to the collective agreement or not.

821. In the case of a collective agreement concluded within a joint body, such as a joint committee, the individually normative provisions are *additionally* binding for non-organised employers who belong to the resort of the joint body within which the collective agreement was concluded and insofar as they fall within the scope defined in the agreement. The same binding effect applies to the employees of these employers (Article 26, paragraph 1, Collective Agreements Act). It is of a supplementary binding nature. This means that the provisions apply unless the individual employment contract contains a clause providing otherwise (Article 26, paragraph 1, Collective Agreements Act).

822. By concluding a collective agreement, the individually normative provisions of the collective agreement automatically become part of the individual employment contract that exists between a bound employer and his employee. This is called 'incorporation'. The individually normative provisions are automatically incorporated in the individual employment contract, and as such get the same legal status as individually agreed employment conditions. This also means that, after the end of the collective agreement, these provisions do not automatically disappear from the individual employment contract, but continue to form part of it until the parties agree otherwise or until they are amended again by a new collective agreement.

These principles are confirmed in the Collective Agreements Act: the individual employment agreement, which was tacitly amended by a collective agreement, remains unaltered when the collective agreement ceases to have effect, unless otherwise stipulated in the agreement itself (Article 23, Collective Agreements Act).

823. When a company is wholly or partially transferred, the new employer must respect the agreement concluded by the former employer until it ceases to have effect (Article 20, Collective Agreements Act). This regulation is in line with the issue of transfer of undertaking as governed by CA no. 32bis. It concerns, for example, a sale of the company, a merger, etc.

The purpose of the Collective Agreements Act is to ensure that employees whose employer is legally succeeded by another employer retain the benefits agreed upon in an existing collective agreement. The new employer is therefore bound by these collective agreement provisions on the basis of Article 20 of the Collective Agreements Act. However, this does not exclude that the new employer would have to apply more favourable employment conditions on the basis of a collective agreement which would apply to his own company.[341]

824. The legislator has also taken into account the possibility of the employer terminating his membership from an employers' organisation. Such an employer, whose membership expires from an organisation that is bound by an agreement, shall remain bound by that agreement until an amendment is made to it which results in a significant change in the obligations arising therefrom (Article 21, Collective Agreements Act). A similar arrangement has been made in case of dissolution of an employers' organisation. The collective agreement will then also continue to apply to the members of that organisation until an amendment is made to the contract which significantly alters the regulated relations (Article 22, Collective Agreements Act).

IX. Declaration of Universal Applicability

825. The collective agreement concluded within a joint body may be declared universally binding by the King at the request of the body or of an organisation represented therein (Article 28, Collective Agreements Act). The enacting terms of the

341. Cass. 31 Mar. 2003, *JTT* 2003, 321, note.

agreement declared universally binding shall be published in the *Official State Gazette*, the *Moniteur Belge,* as an annex to the Royal Decree declaring the agreement universally binding (Article 30, Collective Agreements Act).

826. The declaration of universal applicability makes the collective agreement binding on all employers and employees who belong to the resort of the joint committee and in so far as they fall within the scope as defined by the agreement (Article 31, Collective Agreements Act). This binding obligation applies to all normative provisions.

827. The declaration of universal applicability can therefore be described as the King's act of making a collective agreement concluded within a joint body, generally binding in respect of all employers and employees who fall under the area of responsibility of the joint body in which the collective agreement was concluded.

Chapter 6. Strike, Lockout and Other Industrial Action

§1. General

828. In case of a collective conflict in the field of labour relations, means of pressure are regularly used. The ultimate means of pressure on the part of workers is the strike weapon. The right to strike, or more broadly the right to collective action, is an essential part of the protection of workers. It is also an essential part of collective labour law and recognised as a fundamental right.

829. The various forms of industrial action should be seen in light of the Belgian social model, in which social peace and social partnership between trade union and employers' organisations are found to be important. The industrial relations culture of preferring dialogue over collective action does not exclude the recognition of strikes or other action, but it assumes that parties respect collective agreements that have been made (peace obligation) and that recourse to collective action would be used in last resort, i.e., when peaceful means such as conciliation has been exhausted.

§2. Strike and Collective Action

I. Recognition

830. The right to strike, or the right to collective action, is not laid down in the Belgian Constitution. Nor is it explicitly recognised in Belgian legislation. There is no general legislation establishing or regulating the right to strike. The right to strike is recognised in Belgian case law and developed by legal doctrine.

831. In this context, the international recognition and effect of the right to strike are important for the Belgian legal order. In Belgium, the right to strike has been recognised on the basis of the direct effect of Article 6, 4 of the ESC.[342]

832. Furthermore, the right to strike is recognised in Belgium on the basis of the case law of the Court of Cassation. The case law of the Court of Cassation was initially established with regard to the question of the impact of a strike on the individual employment contract. In the absence of legislation, this was not clear. In 1967, the Court of Cassation stated that the participation in a strike does not in itself imply the will of the employee to terminate the employment contract, so that the strike does not entail the termination but the suspension of the execution of the employment contract.[343] It would therefore be a lawful ground for suspension. On a subsequent occasion, the Court of Cassation clarified that a strike, in itself, would not cause the employment contract to end.[344]

342. Council of State 3 Dec. 2002, *NJW* 2003, 779.
343. Cass. 23 Nov. 1967, *Arr.Cass.* 1968, 421.
344. Cass. 14 Apr. 1980, *Arr.Cass.* 1979–80, 1002, 11376.

However, the indication of a legal basis for the right to strike had to wait until the judgment of 21 December 1981.[345] The Court of Cassation implicitly derived the recognition of the right to strike from the Act of 19 August 1948 on services of general interest in peacetime. This Act regulates how and which measures, benefits and services must be ensured and determined in the event of collective and voluntary suspension of work (thus in case of a strike). The Court of Cassation stated that it follows from this legislation that striking employees are therefore only obliged to perform the work imposed by the law and that the Act of 19 August 1948 thus entails the recognition of the employee's right not to perform the contractually stipulated work on account of a strike, and therefore, in derogation from Article 1134 of the Old Civil Code, not to fulfil the obligation included in the employment contract. All this applies, according to the Court, even if the right to strike as such is not expressly recognised by law. This judgment is thus seen as a recognition of the right to strike by the Court of Cassation based on an implicit inclusion in the Act of 19 August 1948.

833. The International Labour Organisation (ILO), which has no explicit instruments in this field, is also brought up in strike discussions. In the context of the organs of the International Labour Organisation, the Committee on Freedom of Association is of importance, at least as a source of interpretation of the right to strike.

834. Other attention must be paid to the instruments of the Council of Europe. Both the ESC (ESC, 1961, Revised ESC, 1996) and Article 11 of the ECHR (ECHR, 1950) are relevant. In 1996, the ESC, established on 18 October 1961 within the framework of the Council of Europe, was revised. The Revised ESC of 3 May 1996 was signed by Belgium on the same date and ratified on 2 March 2004.[346] In this Revised ESC, the right to collective action is laid down in Article 6, §4 ESC. There is a monitoring procedure which leads to assessments by the 'European Committee of Social Rights'. The cases assessed by the European Committee of Social Rights are not legally enforceable in themselves, but Belgian strike law has been the subject of various cases in the past.

II. Interpretation and Limits

835. Due to the lack of specific legislation on the right to strike, the scope and confines of that right remain much debated in Belgium. While the right to strike is an individual right of workers (not an exclusive right of a trade union), it remains a collective right. But it implies that a strike not recognised or supported by a trade union is not per se unlawful.

---

345. Cass. 21 Dec. 1981, *Arr.Cass.* 1981–82, 541.
346. Act of 15 Mar. 2002 on assent to the revised European Social Charter and its Annex, done at Strasbourg on 3 May 1996, *Belgian Official Gazette* 10 May 2004.

836. In Belgium, the role of the judge in the implementation of the right to strike is, furthermore, limited. It is often assumed that in the Belgian model of social consultation and industrial relations, the parties themselves should settle their conflicts of interest. If they cannot reach a solution themselves, a system of conciliation and mediation, under the responsibility of the government, is available. Social mediators are civil servants that operate under the authority of the Minister responsible for labour or employment. They preside joint committees and can set up a conciliation bureau and chair it within the applicable joint committee. In this context, it is assumed that the labour courts do not have any jurisdiction over disputes involving the right to strike according to the provisions of the Judicial Code. On the other hand, civil courts find themselves regularly to be competent.

837. The availability of a dispute settlement mechanism, therefore, does not prevent the judiciary (civil courts) from ruling on legal disputes arising in the context of collective or strike action. This may be the case if subjective rights are at stake. This is how case law on 'factualities'[347] came into being. A 'factuality' can be understood as an act done without any title or right, which disturbs the legal order and harms the rights of others. Violent behaviour during a strike action will be qualified as a factuality and, therefore, prohibited. To the extent that this determines limits to the right to strike, it is almost inevitable that an opinion will be formed about the (lawful) exercise of the right to strike.

838. Important in this context is the judgment of the Court of Cassation of 31 January 1997 in which, in the context of the setting up of strike posts, the Court ruled that it is not unreasonable to hold that employees have a societally qualified right to strike.[348] According to this judgment, one may therefore test the legitimacy of a collective action according to criteria of what constitutes normal exercise according to societal standards.

839. A highly contested topic in Belgium is whether road blockades are lawful as a form of collective action. In a judgment of 7 January 2020, the Court of Cassation clarified this issue and held that deliberately obstructing traffic during a trade union action can amount to malicious obstruction of the public roads, criminally sanctioned by Article 406 of the Criminal Code. With reference to the European sources of law, the Court of Cassation states that the exercise of the right to strike, or the right to demonstrate, can be subject to restrictions provided that these restrictions actually correspond to objectives of general interest and are not to be regarded as a disproportionate and intolerable interference impairing the very substance of the protected rights.[349]

---

347. Factualités / Feitelijkheden.
348. Cass. 31 Jan. 1997, *Arr. Cass.* 1997, 140.
349. Cass. 7 Jan. 2020, AR P.19.0804.N.

III. Essential and Minimum Services

840. In some cases, the government limits the right to strike in order to provide an essential or minimum service.

841. In Belgium, the right to strike is already restricted in some public services, such as for military personnel or police officers. A special arrangement is, furthermore, provided by the Act of 19 August 1948 on services of general interest in peacetime.[350] Pursuant to Article 1 of this Act, the joint committees must, for the companies that fall under their respective competence, determine and lay down the measures, benefits or services that must be ensured in the event of collective and voluntary suspension of work or lockout, in order to meet certain vital needs or to carry urgent works or tasks. It is therefore up to the joint committees to determine the 'minimum services' for the sector concerned.

842. With the Act of 29 November 2017, the legislator[351] introduced a procedure that tries to guarantee the continuity of the (public) national railway services during a strike. This is not done by denying workers (many of them are civil servants) the right to strike or by imposing a minimum service, but by making the best possible use of staff members who voluntarily do not want to participate in the strike. The management committees of the national railway operators must determine which occupational categories they consider essential in order to provide an adapted transport offer to users in the event of a strike. They also have to determine (and regularly review) the transport plans on the basis of which an adapted transport offer can be provided to users in case of strike. If trade unions or staff wish to strike, they must respect a minimum notice period and, before the start of the strike day, the staff members of the selected essential categories of workers have to declare their intention to participate or not in the strike day. If on the strike day, a sufficient number of staff members are available in each of the essential categories, the railways' managing director can give the order to implement the adjusted transport plan.

843. Some railway unions went to the Constitutional Court as they argued that the Act of 29 November 2017 was in violation of the freedom of association, the right to collective bargaining and the right to collective action, as guaranteed by the Belgian Constitution read in conjunction with international standards. However, the Constitutional Court did not follow this view and upheld the constitutionality of the legislation.[352]

350. *Belgian Official Gazette* 21 Aug. 1948.
351. Act of 29 Nov. 2017 on the continuity of passenger rail transport services in the event of strike, *Belgian Official Gazette* 17 Jan. 2018.
352. Constitutional Court 14 May 2020, no. 67/2020.

IV. Effect of a Strike on the Individual Employment Contract

844. A strike is a legal situation of suspension of the execution of the employment contract. The strike does not terminate the employment contract as such.

845. The most important issue relates to how the employee's salary is determined. The principle of 'no work, no pay' should be applied. It means that there is, in principle, no right to remuneration of an employee who does not work because of strike action in the company. A distinction must, however, be made between a striking worker and the worker who is willing to work. A striker is not entitled to wages as he does not fulfil his obligations to work. With regard to a worker, who cannot work due to a strike but who is willing to work, a difficulty arises. Since the willing employee does not work, in principle, no right to remuneration arises. Also, Article 27 of the Employment Contracts Act, which provides for guaranteed daily wages, does not apply in the case of a strike. However, it is usually assumed that only in case of force majeure the employer, in principle, can be relieved of his obligation to pay the wages. Therefore, it can be assumed that an employee who is available to work is still entitled to wages, even if he cannot work due to a strike, unless the employer can prove that the strike constitutes a case of force majeure for him. The Court of Cassation states that the employer, wishing to be released from his obligation to provide work for those who are willing to work, must prove that the strike was a case of force majeure for him that prevented him from fulfilling his obligations. He must prove, as a debtor, that it was impossible for him to fulfil his obligations.[353]

§3. Lockout

846. On the part of the employer, the right to apply a *lockout* is recognised. It concerns the temporary non-execution of the obligation to provide work to the employee, i.e., not to allow him to perform his work. The Court of Cassation recognised the right to *lock out*. Like a strike, a lockout suspends the execution of the employment contract. However, it must be examined whether the employer has sufficient justification to suspend the execution of the employment contract.[354]

847. Lockouts, however, rarely occur in Belgian industrial relations. If an employer would make use of a lockout, it would rather be used as a response to industrial action and the fear of violent or other problematic situations and/or to bring rest or a cooling-off situation within an industrial conflict.

---

353. Cass. 14 Sep. 2015, AR S.13.0030.N.
354. Cass. 7 May 1984, *Arr.Cass.* 1983–84, 1161.

Chapter 7. Settlement of Industrial Disputes

§1. General

848. The Belgian social model relies strongly on social partnership of large and representative trade unions and employers' organisations. A feature is also a strong autonomy and a degree of voluntarism of these social partners, which implies that they have room to take own initiative. This can also be seen with regard to dispute settlement. In the first place, in a case of a collective labour conflict, the social partners will need to make attempts themselves to reconcile their difference. The approach is that this needs to be done in a peaceful manner, through negotiations. If those attempts fail, collective action may be reverted to. In case of an arising or occurring conflict, certainly if collective action is announced or undertaken, the government may interfere through social conciliation services. In the Belgian model it can be assumed that social partners respect this idea and have recourse to collective action only in last resort, i.e., when peaceful means such as conciliation have been exhausted.

849. The general perception of Belgium is rather specific. On the one hand, Belgium knows an industrial relations system where social peace and partnership stands central. On the other hand, there is a fair degree of conflictual interest in industrial relations and the parties use their bargaining power in a rather unregulated context.

850. According to information based on ETUI data, Belgium ranks rather high in the European strike overview if measured according to days not worked due to industrial action.

Figure 1 Average Days Not Worked Due to Industrial Action in Europe, 2000–2018

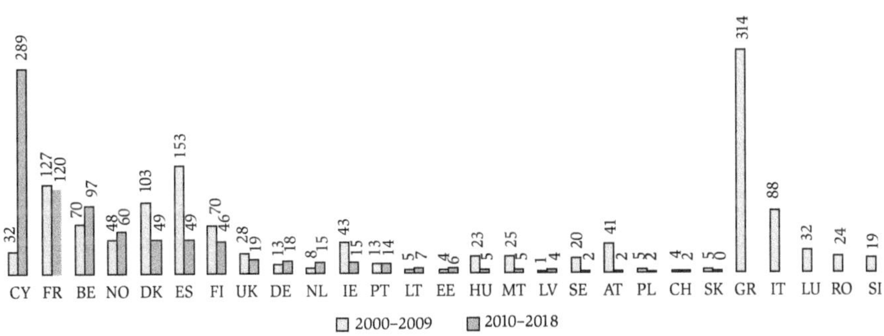

Note: Insufficient or no data for Bulgaria, Croatia, Czechia, Greece, Italy, Luxembourg, Romania and Slovenia. Excluding strikes in the public administration in Portugal (all years) and some general and public strikes in 2010, 2012 and 2013 in Spain.

Source: ETUI, own calculation.[355]

355. https://www.etui.org/sites/default/files/2020-06/Strikesmap_20200407_1.pdf.

851. In this Belgian picture (Figure 1), an important remark is related to the fact that the trade unions regularly call for a 'national' strike day, mobilising large groups of workers throughout the country, going along with public demonstrations.

§2. SOCIAL CONCILIATION

852. A feature of the Belgian dispute settlement system is that the institutionalisation of collective bargaining and dispute settlement is strongly interwoven. Joint committees are responsible for collective bargaining at sector level.[356]

853. Within the Federal Public Service Employment, Labour and Social Dialogue (Federal Ministry of Labour), the Directorate-General for Collective Labour Relations is staffed by a number of civil servants that are specialised in collective labour relations. They are qualified, and appointed, to function both as presidents of the various joint committees which exist in the country and in which sector bargaining takes place and which may lead to collective bargaining and sector agreements. The joint committees have, however, also the task of dealing with collective labour conflicts that occur in their sector. The joint committee's president is, as a rule, also the social conciliator for all employers falling within the resort of that sector.

854. Article 1 of the Royal Decree of 27 October 2009 regarding the selection of holders of the position of social conciliator[357] provides that at the Federal Public Service Employment, Labour and Social Dialogue (Ministry of Labour), the Directorate-General for Collective Labour Relations is in charge of social mediation. Social conciliation comprises the following tasks: preventing social disputes and monitoring their outbreak, progress and termination; fulfilling all social conciliation tasks; maintaining permanent contact with the professional organisations of employers and employees and with the social inspectors and auditors of the Federal Public Service Employment, Labour and Social Dialogue; drawing up all reports concerning social relations in an industrial sector or in a particular company; where appropriate, chairing or vice-chairing joint committees and subcommittees.

855. From this, it can be read that prevention of industrial disputes is an important task of the social conciliator (who thus also presides one or more joint committees).

856. If a collective conflict occurs in the enterprise of one of the employers in the concerned sector, the social conciliator can take initiative and will assist the conflicting parties to find a solution. The social conciliator cannot impose a solution,

356. Jan Rombouts, 'De rol van de sociaal bemiddelaar bij arbeidsconflicten', *Oriëntatie* 1993, 242.
357. *Belgian Official Gazette*, 19 Nov. 2009.

but will give his best effort to restore social peace and stable industrial relations. In practice, most joint committees have established a so-called reconciliation bureau, under the presidency of the social conciliator, in which also a representation of the sector trade union and employers' organisations is present. They can share their insights and expertise to assist in finding a solution in case of collective conflict. They also can make a joint recommendation to the conflicting parties. In practice, this often leads to a consensus followed by the concerned parties. If the social conciliation would fail, then collective action may be the only path left for the parties, although new attempts could be made.

§3. Court Intervention

857. It has been mentioned above that the labour courts do not have any jurisdiction over disputes involving the right to strike according to the provisions of the Judicial Code. Furthermore, do the fact that Belgium has a system of social conciliation, organised by the government, for collective labour conflicts, it is often assumed that courts have no role to play in industrial disputes. This has, nevertheless, not taken away that civil courts find themselves regularly to be competent, for example, to judge over 'factualities'. This leads to much debate.

858. A major discussion point in the Belgium system led to a complaint by the Belgian trade unions in 2009 before the European Committee of Social Rights of the Council of Europe. The unions claimed that judicial intervention in social conflicts in Belgium, in particular concerning restrictions imposed on the action of picketing, violates Article 6§4 (right to strike) of the Revised ESC. The issue is related to court cases that are introduced (on the initiative of employers) under a procedure of emergency relief, through the 'unilateral applications procedure', governed by the Belgian Judicial Code. Under such procedure, the judge has to verify the facts as presented by the applicant, usually the employer, and for that purpose 'may' summon the applicant and the intervening parties, usually trade unions. On pain of paying damages, collective actions, such as (planned) picketing activities, have often been declared illegal by courts, even before the action occurs. The committee concluded (by eight votes against four) that these are restrictions on the right to strike that indeed constitute a violation of Article 6§4 of the Revised Charter.[358] It has, however, not ended the discussion in Belgium. Employers have still reverted to unilateral procedures before courts in summary proceedings.[359]

358. No. 59/2009 *European Trade Union Confederation (ETUC)/ Centrale Générale des Syndicats Libéraux de Belgique (CGSLB)/ Confédération des Syndicats chrétiens de Belgique (CSC)/ Fédération Générale du Travail de Belgique (FGTB) v. Belgium* (Decision on the merits, adopted on 13 September 2011).

359. Cf. P. Pecinovsky, 'Collectieve actie', in F. Hendrickx & C. Engels (eds), Arbeidsrecht, III, die Keure, Bruges, 2020, 652–657.

Chapter 8. Business Restructuring

§1. Restructuring

859. Corporate restructuration or reorganisation concerns an issue where collective and individual rights come together. It is related to the transfer of undertakings, collective dismissals (or collective redundancies) and the closure of the undertaking. In principle, labour law will not prevent an employer from restructuring or reorganising the company, but will guarantee rights of employees, and workers' representatives, in such situations.

860. The field is strongly influenced by European legislation. There are important cases in the field of collective redundancies. Also, the issue of transfer of undertaking is the subject of a large amount of case law of the Court of Justice of the European Union. Hereinafter, the analysis is limited to the provisions of Belgian labour law.

§2. Transfer of Undertakings

861. In Belgium, the issue of transfer of undertakings is regulated by a national collective agreement. The European legislation on the transfer of undertakings was transposed in Belgium by national Collective Agreement no. 32bis of 7 June 1985 (which, however, does not regulate the situation in the public sector).[360] However, also Article 20 of the Collective Agreements Act of 5 December 1968 is relevant here, according to which the employees' acquired rights in collective agreements have to be respected in case of a transfer.

862. Article 1 of CA no. 32bis makes it clear what situations it wishes to regulate:

- ensuring the preservation of employees' rights in all cases of change of employer following the transfer of an undertaking or part of an undertaking by agreement;
- arranging for the information of employees affected by a transfer if there are no representatives of the employees in the undertaking.

863. CA no. 32bis also regulates the rights of employees in the event of a transfer of undertaking within the framework of a judicial agreement and in the event of the takeover of assets after bankruptcy.

864. Pursuant to Article 6 of CA no. 32bis, the transfer of undertaking regulations applies in principle to any change of employer resulting from any transfer of

360. Collective Labour Agreement no. 32bis, NAR, 7 Jun. 1985 concerning the safeguarding of employees' rights in the event of a change of employer following the transfer of undertakings by agreement, and regulating the rights of employees who are taken over in the event of the takeover of assets following bankruptcy or receivership, amended by later collective agreements.

an undertaking or part of an undertaking by virtue of a contract (with the exception of a takeover in the event of bankruptcy). A transfer is considered to be a transfer of an economic entity which retains its identity, meaning an organised grouping of resources, with a view to pursuing an economic activity, whether or not that activity is central or ancillary.

865. The application of the transfer of undertaking regulations is the subject of much debate. It is therefore the subject of much case law, not least by the Court of Justice of the European Union. One can say that the following conditions must be present:

- a change of employer;
- transfer under agreement;
- transfer of a *going concern.*

866. The change of employer condition assumes that the 'legal' employer changes. Therefore, there must be a new natural or legal person on the part of the employer. The comments of the social partners under Article 6 in CA no. 32bis speak of 'the change of the legal status of an enterprise'. Here, it is important to distinguish between a so-called *asset deal* (where tangible or intangible assets of a company are transferred) and a *share deal* (where shares are transferred). In a share deal, there is no change of legal employer and therefore no transfer of undertaking.

867. The transfer by agreement condition means that a transfer of undertaking must be based on an agreement. The commentary of the social partners under Article 6 in CA no. 32bis itself mentions 'the incorporation, the assignment, the merger and the absorption'. However, this condition is interpreted broadly by case law, so that transfers of a concession or outsourcing operations are also covered. For example, there can be a transfer of undertaking when a company outsources a contract or service to a company other than the one that previously performed the contract or service,[361] or when a client terminates the contract with a service provider of a catering activity and subsequently concludes a new contract for this service with another service provider.[362]

868. The transfer of a *going concern* is also a condition. For there to be a transfer of undertaking, the undertaking (or the part thereof) must retain its economic identity. It must be an economic entity that retains its identity, which is understood to mean a set of organised resources.[363]

869. Article 7 of CA no. 32bis provides for protection of employees in the event of a transfer of undertaking. The rights and obligations arising for the transferor from the employment contracts existing at the time of the transfer are, by virtue of

361. ECJ 14 Apr. 1994, no. C-392/92C, *Schmidt v. Spar- und Leihkasse der früheren Ämster Bordesholm, Kiel und Cronshagen. See also* Arbh. Brussels 7 Jan. 2008, AR 45.284.
362. ECJ 24 Jan. 2002, no. C-51/00, *Termo Services Industries NV.*
363. Cf. Art. 1.1 of Directive 2001/23.

the transfer, transferred to the transferee. So the transferee must take over the obligations arising from the employment contracts existing at the time of the transfer. The transferor and the transferee are, by virtue of Article 8 of CA no. 32bis, bound *in solidum* to pay the debts existing at the time of the transfer arising from the employment contracts existing at that time, with the exception of the debts arising from supplementary social security schemes.

870. Furthermore, pursuant to Article 9 of CA no. 32bis, a change of employer may not in itself constitute grounds for dismissal by the transferor or transferee. However, employees who change employer may be dismissed for an urgent reason or for economic, technical or organisational reasons entailing changes in employment. Moreover, CA no. 32bis itself does not provide for any sanctions against this prohibition of dismissal. It means that, de facto, a dismissal cannot always be avoided.

§3. Collective Redundancies and Closure

871. In the case of collective redundancies, there is a redundancy of several workers at the same time or within a well-defined period. Thresholds (number of redundancies) apply for the application of collective redundancy schemes.

872. This issue is also regulated by European legislation. In Belgium, it is regulated by CA no. 10 of 8 May 1973, CA no. 24 of 2 October 1975 and a Royal Decree of 24 May 1976 on collective redundancies. The regulation was supplemented by the so-called Renault Law,[364] which was adopted after the closure of the Renault company in Belgium, and which made the information obligation more precise and introduced more effective sanctions in the event that the obligations in this respect were not respected. Another addition concerns the Royal Decree of 9 March 2006 on the activating policy for restructuring, which regulates the establishment by the company of an 'employment unit' in the event of restructuring, in which support measures are implemented for workers who are dismissed.[365]

873. The scope of collective redundancy regulations is related to the number of redundancies within a given period. In Belgian labour law, it concerns any dismissal for one or more reasons not related to the individual worker, affecting at least the following number of workers, over a period of sixty days:

– ten employees: in undertakings which, during the calendar year preceding that in which the redundancy occurred, employ on average more than twenty and less than hundred workers;

364. Act 13 Feb. 1998 containing provisions to promote employment, *Belgian Official Gazette* 19 Feb. 1998.

365. *Belgian Official Gazette* 31 Mar. 2006.

- 10% of the number of employees: in enterprises which, during the calendar year preceding the redundancies, employ on average at least hundred and less than three hundred workers;
- thirty employees: in enterprises which employ, on average, at least three hundred workers during the calendar year preceding that in which the redundancy occurred.

874. The reference to reasons not related to the employee's person corresponds to the reasons for dismissal inherent in the undertaking and is seen as equivalent to broadly defined 'economic or technical reasons'.[366]

875. In the event of collective redundancies, the employer is obliged to follow a prescribed procedure in order to inform and consult the workers' representatives and, where applicable, to pay additional compensation to the redundant workers. The procedure of information and consultation which is provided for in the legislation states that the employer shall first communicate his 'intention' to make collective redundancies and consult with the workers' representatives (Article 6 CA no. 24). The consultations shall cover ways and means of avoiding or reducing the collective redundancies as well as of mitigating the consequences (Article 6 CA no. 24).

876. The employer also needs to notify the government via the responsible employment services and the federal public service for Employment, Labour and Social Dialogue.

877. During the information and consultation procedure, it is often typical that the involved employer and workers' representatives discuss and agree on a 'social plan'. This is not provided by the law, but it follows from a broadly shared practice. A social plan contains the arrangements that have been concluded upon by the parties with regard to the social (and the financial) consequences for the dismissed workers who are dismissed or for whom an intention of dismissal exists.

878. A typical feature in the Belgian system is the existence of a regime called the 'system of unemployment with company allowance'. It is a system in which workers of a certain age, who are dismissed, are entitled to an unemployment benefit and, in addition, to a supplementary allowance (a company allowance) payable by the employer who dismisses the workers.[367] The regime is based on a national collective agreement concluded in the NLC, CA no. 17 of 19 December 1974, which was later repetitively revised as well as complemented by additional collective agreements. It is only available for workers who have reached a certain age, in principle the age of 62, but this can be lowered to the age of 60 in some cases, or even to the age of 55 in the case of a collective dismissal. It is therefore an 'early retirement' scheme. The system was called 'bridge-pension' in the past. However, the new terminology ('unemployment with company allowance') introduced in 2012 is

366. Cf. Commentary under Art. 2, CA no. 24.
367. Cf. Royal Decree of 3 May 2007, *Belgian Official Gazette* 8 Jun. 2007.

basically the continuation of the old scheme with some modifications. In general, the dismissed worker will fall under the unemployment insurance scheme and will receive a payment every month until his official retirement age. The payment will be made by the (former) employer, although it is possible that this obligation will be taken over by a sectoral fund.

879. The closure of a business involves the cessation of all or part of a business. Additional obligations that apply in this case are listed in the Act of 26 June 2002 on the closure of companies.[368] A guarantee fund has also been set up, i.e., the 'Fund for compensation of workers made redundant in the event of closure of undertakings' ('Closure Fund'), which pays the closure allowance and any outstanding pay or severance payments to redundant workers in the event of the employer's defaulting.

368. *Belgian Official Gazette* 9 Aug. 2002, *err. Belgian Official Gazette* 4 Dec. 2002.

Selected Bibliography

For a general overview of Belgian labour law, the following essential works can be consulted:

J. Clesse & F. Kéfer, Manuel de droit du travail, published by Larcier. Last version of 2018.

D. Cuypers & P. Foubert, Schets van het Belgische arbeidsrecht, Intersentia, 2011.

F. Hendrickx, Inleiding tot het Belgische arbeidsrecht, published by die Keure. Regularly updated. Last version of 2021.

F. Hendrickx & C. Engels (eds), Arbeidsrecht (3 volumes), published by die Keure. Regularly updated. Last version of 2020.

P. Humblet, W. Rauws & R. Janvier (eds), Synopsis van het Belgische arbeidsrecht, published by Intersentia. Regularly updated. Last version of 2020.

W. Van Eeckhoutte, Sociaal Compendium: Arbeidsrecht met fiscale notities (3 volumes), published by Kluwer, yearly updated.

F. Lambinet & S. Gilson, Découvrir le droit du travail, published by Anthemis. Last edition 2021.

Selected Bibliography

Index

The numbers here refer to paragraph numbers

Index

Index

www.ingramcontent.com/pod-product-compliance
Ingram Content Group UK Ltd.
Pitfield, Milton Keynes, MK11 3LW, UK
UKHW020140290926
15471UKWH00003B/613

9 789403 548517